ALSO BY RICHARD HOWARD

Paper Trail: Selected Prose, 1965–2003

Talking Cures

Trappings

Like Most Revelations

No Traveller

Lining Up

Misgivings

Fellow Feelings

Two-Part Inventions

Findings

Untitled Subjects

*Alone with America: Essays on the Art of Poetry
in the United States Since 1950*

Damages

Quantities

INNER VOICES

INNER VOICES

SELECTED POEMS

1963–2003

RICHARD HOWARD

FARRAR, STRAUS AND GIROUX

NEW YORK

Farrar, Straus and Giroux
19 Union Square West, New York 10003

Copyright © 2004 by Richard Howard
All rights reserved
Distributed in Canada by Douglas & McIntyre Ltd.
Printed in the United States
First edition, 2004

Library of Congress Cataloging-in-Publication Data
Howard, Richard, 1929–
Inner voices : selected poems, 1963–2003 / Richard Howard.— 1st ed.
    p.   cm.
ISBN-13: 978-0-374-25862-7
ISBN-10: 0-374-25862-7 (alk. paper)
    I. Title.

PS3558.O8826A6 2004
811'.54 — dc22

Designed by Jonathan D. Lippincott

www.fsgbooks.com

1   3   5   7   9   10   8   6   4   2

For
Sanford Friedman
and
David Alexander

CONTENTS

QUANTITIES

L'Invitation au Voyage

Wandering with you the shore
That parallels our river
    Like a second thought,
Singular and sad I wore
The habit of a lover
    Almost inside out.

Night in its black behaving
Muffled every lamp and dyed
    The wooly season,
Pig-iron boats were leaving
For the lake, slowly the loud
    Bridges had risen:

A landscape for the lonely
Or the lewd, as you observed,
    When of a sudden
Something steep and with only
Momentary warning moved
    Out of the hidden

Harbor. It was a dark boat
And *Cytherea* it said
    Low on the long bow.
"A cabin for two," cried out
A voice, and I saw a head
    That I thought I knew—

"Fifteen days to the Island:
We sail tonight with the tide!"
    I remember now,
Turning, how your face went blind.

The river sighed in its bed
    And although a few

Gulls were loud in their abuse
You did not once look up. When
    To their obloquy
No protest was made, I chose
To learn what I've always known:
    We shall never go.

Sandusky—New York

Ohio from a train
Looked always other; half his way across
    The unimportant chain
Of Alleghenies that intended east.
    An early morning rain
Made dubious the sky and in its stead,
    As if all hope were gone
Of reckoning climate by his calendar,
    Ran April like a stain
Across the glass—unfinished, unfulfilled
    And frankly alien.

As in the past, today
Landscape and weather were his enemies;
    It seemed unlikely they
Would yield. But if in answer to their terms
    Of terror he could say
For sure how mountains fell from monstrous size
    To minor lumps of clay
Behind his eyes, how every season turned
    Within his heart to gray:
This once, perhaps, the darkness too would fall
    In less pronounced a way.

He thought how many times
He had construed the weather like a verb,
    Declined the rain, that comes
As water will—unasked, but a forgiven guest—
    And even in his dreams
Had pressed a grammar on the land. Somehow
    They were important themes,
Such wet beginnings as he knew, this earth

That April never seems
To satisfy, the sullen passage of
His unprotesting homes.

Distance made the weather
Disappear. The clouds that filled the sky
Conformed until they were
Illustrious with being. Time was before
Him, no need to hurry
Understanding. Where the towns had loomed
Dark with incoherence
Of houses, the primary colors, after rain,
Startled him to praise. Here
The land grew lovely in the stillness of
Accumulated air,

As one would have it first,
Not later hope occasionally; here
The sun, that had abused
His eyes a moment by the distances
Of moving mountains, placed
Perspectively the shoulders of the earth,
Discovered as he passed
The consequentialities of weed
And water moving west
Against his progress, while his purpose grew
Within him like an East.

Such travelling was true
In parallel. Along the simple tracks
Which accurately flew
Beneath, he followed himself away, away
From weather came into
That unconditional country of his blood
Where even landscape grew
Dim as he had never dared to hope,
And when he breathed he knew
The air as sick men breathe and know the spring:
Cold still, but coming to.

Now, the train running on,
He clambered up the enterprising bones
      His body reached him down
So carefully for the ascent, he climbed
      The scaffold skeleton
Up shoulders to the summit of his skull
      (Past marshes overgrown
And hollows filled by sudden rubbishes)
      Until he stared upon
The shore of all his history, as it
      Would look when it was done.

      The clumsy body, where
He had before been always caught, imposed
      An image of its care
Upon the country's custom, made him feel
      (Generous in passing for
Pausing in passing): *only when you leave*
      Will you know where you are.
He travelled, putting distance into sense.
      The mountains fell, and far
Ahead he thought he saw the sea. What if
      It was, if it was there?

      Then that was where, tonight,
He wanted to arrive. Thus he would leave
      The suburbs of his heart,
Would come to the capital city where it was.
      The sun became as bright
Above him as the sight could bear. He knew
      It then, that he would find
The fabulous city and the fact of seas
      Already in his mind,
And only there: the landscape lived in him
      As he might live in it.

DAMAGES

A Far Cry After a Close Call

For if they do these things in a green tree what
shall be done in the dry?   —Luke 23:31

Nuns, his nieces, bring the priest in the next
Bed pralines, not prayers for the next world,
    But I've had one look myself
      At *that* one (looking

Back now, crammed in the convalescent ward,
With the Invisible Man opposite
    Sloshing most of the Black Sea
      Around in his lungs,

While the third patient coughs and borrows *Time*).
No one turned over when I was wheeled in;
    The efficient British nurse
      Snipped off my soggy

Trousers and put me right, "sure as Bob's your
Uncle." The water roared and ran away,
    Leaving only words to stock
      My mind like capsules

Crowding a bottle. Then the lights blew up,
Went out, someone was going through My Things
    While I rowed—rowed for my life
      Down the rubber floor—

But the waves failed me. The hallway heaved where I
Foundered and turned in my doctor's dry hands
    To sovereign selflessness:
      Meaning had melted.

"*Mon corps est moi*," Molière said. They're more than that,
This monster the body, this miracle

Its pain—when was I ever
    Them, when were they me?

At thirty-three, what else is there to do
But wait for yet another great white moth
    With eager, enlarging eyes
        To land on my chest,

Slowly, innocently choking me off?
The feelers stir while I lie still, lie here
    (Where on earth does it come from,
        That wind, that wounding

Breath?), remembering the future now,
Foreseeing a past I shall never know,
    Until the little crisis
        Breaks, and I wake.

For as Saint Paul sought deliverance from
The body of this death, I seek to stay—
    Man is mad as the body
        Is sick, by nature.

Seeing Cousin Phyllis Off

The SS *France*, Second Class, Cabin U–20

Few sights were lovelier
Than my watch laved in the *brut* champagne
Exploding from a jiggled magnum.
Your foreign cabin-mates' *Schadenfreude*
    Helped them help each other
    To more caviar, and your handsome
    Husband brushed me off, as handsome does;
Wizened by a decade of adultery,
    You whispered some final
    Instructions under the din, patted
    Your graying bun: for a dozen years
The Sacred Fount had been flowing in his
    Favor, and you knew it.
    In Paris, a daughter was pregnant,
    Unmarried, impatient for your next
Round of meddling to begin. The cycle
    Of all our messy lives
    Alters so little from war to war
    I wonder how any of us
Dares to hope for a private happiness.
    Wilde said what we want is
    Pleasure, not happiness—it has more
    Tragic possibilities. Your caviar
Must be second-class too: I miss the old
    Normandie, Narrenschiff
    Of our fashionable thirties. Now
    The diesels suddenly start to throb
In a sickening vibrato that drives
    The implacable screw

Up through even the *Pont Supérieur.*
My stomach turns, but all the champagne
Is gone, except for the foam in my watch.
I nod at the nightmare
Of a class that we both belong to:
Repetition, and hurry away
To give your worried lover messages.
My poor mad Cousin Phyl,
No use trying to drown time on these
Harridan voyages of ours—once
They called them maiden—not by wet watches
Or even dry champagne.

Bonnard: A Novel

The tea party at Le Cannet. Just as we arrived it began,
    a downpour, and kept on.
    This might have been the time
before: Charles-Xavier playing Scriabin études, all the others
    at the open window.
    A landscape—lawn, garden,
strawberry patch, Japanese footbridge, barges moving on the river
    beyond—as in Verlaine,
    behind a mist of rain,
and the regular noise of the rain on tens of thousands of leaves:
    such is the prose that wears
    the poem's guise at last.
White cats, one in almost every chair, pretend not to be watching
    young Jean worry the dog.
    Sophie, damp, dashes in
dishevelled from the forest, dumping out a great bag of morels
    on the table: the white
    cloth will surely be spoiled,
but the mushrooms look iridescent, like newly opened oysters
    in the raindark air, blue
    by this light. Calling it
accidental is only declaring that it exists. Then tea
    downstairs, Jean opening
    the round pantry window:
the smell of wet soil and strawberries with our cinnamon toast: all
    perception is a kind
    of sorting out, one green
from another, parting leaf from leaf, but in the afternoon rain
    signs and shadows only,
    the separate life renounced,
until that resignation comes, in which all selfhood surrenders . . .
    Upstairs, more Scriabin

and the perfect gestures
of Sophie and Jean playing ball with the dog. All the cats are deaf.
Steady rain. The music
continues, Charles-Xavier
shouting over the notes, ignoring them: "Beatitude teaches
nothing. To live without
happiness and not wither—
there is an occupation, almost a profession." Take the trees:
we could "contrive to do
without trees," but not leaves,
Charles-Xavier explains from the piano, still playing, "we require
their decorum that is
one of congestion, till
like Shelley we become lewd vegetarians." Apprehensive
about the rain, I ask
Jean to order a closed
carriage for Simone. The doctor frowns—a regular visitor
these days?—and frightens her,
eyeing Sophie's mushrooms;
his diagnosis: toadstools. Scriabin diminishes. Is the dog
lost? Jean rushes outside.
Punishment of the dog:
he is forbidden the strawberry patch. Darker now. One candle
is found for the piano,
and the music resumes
with Debussy, a little sphere of yellow in the sopping dusk.
The river's surface looks—
is it the rain?—like the sea
in shallows: this moment is an instance of the world becoming
a mere convenience,
more or less credible,
and the old questions rise to our lips—but have we spoken a word?—
before we remember,
prompted by the weather
probably, or the time of day, that we already know something:
we are not newborn, then.
What is it that we know?
The carriage comes at last, but it is an open carriage, merely
hooded. We crowd under,

   fending off the last drops
with a violet golf umbrella Charles-Xavier has somehow
   managed for us. A slow
   cold drive under the trees,
Simone balancing the suspect mushrooms in her lap. I tell her
   it is not dangerous:
   we cannot die, but are
in this light or lack of it—trees dripping, the sky fraudulent—
   much less individuals
   than we hope or fear to be.
Once home, we shall have a little supper of Sophie's fresh-picked
   morels.

The Author of *Christine*

for Sanford Friedman

Often waking
before the sun decreed the kind of day
           this one would be
      or by its absence left
      the verdict up to him,
he gazed in doubt
at the blank slate and wondered, blue or gray,
          what *he* might leave
      scribbled against the time
      the darkness came for good;
that was his text
The trouble was, he realized, to choose.
             He roused the rooms,
      walking around the house
      that had to share the day
with his despair,
raising each blind as if it were the dead,
          the morning light
      a record of his progress
      in sudden shafts of dust.
The trouble was
in trying so: imagining Christine
          to be this way
      or that. Reality
      had to be happened on,
one had to *find*,
not create it. There is always life itself
          beyond the prose
      that declares it to us,
      life being an absolute
we aspire to,
bliss, but surely cannot reach. Today

                         he would write more,
              creating in Christine
              his hopes of what was real,
knowing 'the real'
by what becomes of it and of ourselves.
                         Dust was his proof:
              the life we know we live
              is simply not enough:
the work dissolves,
leaches into the medium and is lost
                         there like water;
              the words sink into sand,
              dust dances in the sun.
Christine was chaos,
parcels of his own childhood where the past
                         appeared to be
              no more than behavior,
              merely authority.
Take the big scene
when Giorgio, leaving the attic, hobbles down
                         and asks Christine
              about the box, she pales
              and follows him back—why?
"The novelist
seldom penetrates character, the mystery
                         remains intact."
              Thank you, Thomas Hardy,
              sighing over the mess
you made for her
yet asking, "Where was Tess's guardian angel *then*?"
                         He much preferred
              Hardy the poet now,
              that doubting Thomas who
when Swinburne died
declared him "the sweet rival of the waves
                         and once their peer
              in sad improvisations."
              That was character.
To make Christine

out of what was not his choice, participate
in what would change
her, like the waves, and him . . .
Shoving his desk outside
into the sun,
he decided *Christine* could not be written from
his waking hopes:
by will to set himself
or the reader apart
from what the world
might be without the waves, bereft of wet
and wilderness.
No, he would have to let
the weeds of wavering
flourish, rehearse
to both of them, the reader and himself,
not ways that help
us on but that will help
acknowledge our defeat
in getting on—
that would be *Christine*, his novel, and
Christine be him.

An Old Dancer

Because there is only one of you in all of time . . . the world will not have it . . .
— Martha Graham

Your props had always been important:
Preposterous poniards, rings and thorns,
Things without a name you fell upon
Or through. Now they are your props indeed.
Take that iron prong you dangle from,
Strung up, slung like a sick animal
Who used to rise as straight as any tree
Without such corporal irony.

Propped then, you make no bones, or only
Bones, of husbanding your strength. For strength
Was your husband, and you're widowed now.
The face that was a mask of wonder
Wizens into the meaninglessness
Of some Osaka marionette,
And there is properly little more
That you can do for us than think.

What thoughts are yours, or were yours when
Half-visionary and half-voyeur
You tore the veils from Remembered Women,
Rarely lovely, except as the space
That took them into its hugest mouth
Makes any movement lovely: at first
It was enough for you to be them,
Violent, often vague as they come,

Until the years and the work of years
Led you beyond being into more
Than self supplied: now you must review
What you have been and let the others
Do. What you were a whole theater

Has become. What have you lost by that
Exchange, save as the tree loses by
Giving up its leaves and standing bare?

O Dancer, you have lost everything,
Shuddering on your iron gallows-tree.
Bane, bone and violence, you answer
Yeats in kind, unkindest witch of all:
"We know the dancer from the dance" by age,
By growing old. The dance goes on,
The dancers go, and you hang here
Like stale meat on your dead steel branch.

UNTITLED
SUBJECTS

1801
Among the Papers of the Envoy to Constantinople

The writer had settled in England in 1771 on Garrick's invitation to superintend scene-painting at Drury Lane. The Envoy to Constantinople was the seventh Earl of Elgin, who arranged for the Parthenon frieze to be conveyed to England in 1803.

May it please Lord Elgin, Earl of Kincardine,
to consider the undersign'd, sole author
and inventor of the Eidophusikon,

for the position so lately rejected
by Mr. Turner. On giving the measure
of its Effects—calm & storm both, sunset

or moonlight, the accurate imitation
of Nature's sounds: approaching thunder, the dash
of waves on a pebbly beach, the distant gun—

my Device was pronounc'd by no less a judge
than Richard Wilson, R.A.—the same who cried out
at the sight of Terni Cascade, "O well done,

water, by God!"—was pronounc'd, I say, by him
"highly successful in agitated seas,"
by reason of the high finish carrying

severally their satellites of color
into the very center of the Pictures.
As it happens, your Lordship, I visited

the same Joseph Turner known to your Lordship
(I believe) only this week, and found a man
pacing to and fro before his pale muslin

on which the sick and wan Sun, in all the doubt
of darkness, was not allow'd to shed one ray,
but tears. Even as he work'd, pouring wet paint

onto paper till it was saturated,
then tore, then scratch'd, then scrubb'd in a frenzy
at the sheet, the Whole being chaos, until

as if by enchantment, the Scene appear'd then,
great ships gone to pieces in order to fling
magical oranges on the waves — but I

digress: even as he shew'd me two books fill'd
with studies from Nature, several tinted
on the spot — which he found, he said, much the most

valuable to him — this Turner discuss'd
the present urgency of your Lordship's need
for an artist who might draw Antiquities,

with suitable finish, before Removal,
by your Lordship's design, from Athens. He said
he could not, himself, endure the Ideal,

but enjoy'd and look'd for only *litter* — why
even his richest vegetation is confus'd,
he delights in shingle, debris and mere heaps

of fallen stone. Upon communicating
the intelligence that your Lordship's stipend
must include assistance to Lady Elgin

in decorating fire-screens and the like,
the man turn'd back in some heat to his labor
upon what I took to be that mysterious

forest below London Bridge, where great ships ride,
sails filling or falling, disorder'd too
by the stress of anchorage, all beautiful

though wild beneath the Daemonic pressure
of his inquiry (with so much of the trowel,
surely a touch more *finishing* might be borne!).

Enough of Turner, I have not to speak here
of him, though what I saw was but the *scribbling*
of Painting, surely. What I would say is this:

I venture to suggest in myself a man
your Lordship, and my Lady, most certainly,
might rely upon for accurate Service,

work of a conclusive polish, not a sketch.
There is, may I make so bold, a point at which
in Turner's Picturesque, as Fuseli says,

two spiders, caressing or killing each other,
must have greatly the advantage, in roughness
of surface and intricacy of motion,

over every athletic or am'rous
Symplegma left by the Ancients. I do not
wish to speak further of the man who renounc'd

your Lordship's commission to copy marbles,
muttering (though plain to hear), "Antiquities
be damn'd, by Thames' shore we will die," and went on

raking at the sea with his untidy thumb;
but only to call your Lordship's kind notice
and gracious favor, for the appointed task,

to the creator of the Eidophusikon,
these many years a loyal British subject,
Yours, &c.
          PHILIPPE-JACQUES DE LOUTHERBOURG

1851
A Message to Denmark Hill

The writer is John Ruskin, on his wedding journey in Venice.

My dearest father, it is the year's First Day,
　　Yet so like the Last, in Venice, no one
　　　　Could tell this birth from the lees.
　　　　　　I know it is some while
Since you received a word of mine: there has been
　　The shabbiest sort of interruption
　　　　To our exchanges (to mine
　　　　　　At least) in the shape
Of a fever—nights of those imaginings,
　　Strange but shameful too, of the Infinite
　　　　By way of bedcovers and
　　　　　　Boa constrictors,
With cold wedges of ice, as I thought, laid down
　　At the corners of the bed, making me
　　　　Slip to its coiling center
　　　　　　Where I could not breathe.
You knew from my last, I think, I had again
　　Gone to the Zoological Gardens
　　　　And seen the great boa take
　　　　　　Rabbits, which gave me
An idea or two, and a headache. Then
　　I had too much wine that same night, & dreamed
　　　　Of a walk with Nurse, to whom
　　　　　　I showed a lovely
Snake I promised her was an innocent one:
　　It had a slender neck with a green ring
　　　　Round it, and I made her feel
　　　　　　The scales. When she bade

Me feel them too, it turned to a fat thing, like
        A leech, and adhered to my hand, so that
            I could scarcely pull it off—
                And I awakened
(So much, father, for my serpentine fancies)
        To a vermillion dawn, fever fallen,
            And the sea horizon dark,
                Sharp and blue, and far
Beyond it, faint with trebled distance, came on
        The red vertical cliffs in a tremor
            Of light I could not see without
                Recalling Turner
Who had taught me so to see it, yet the whole
        Subdued to one soft gray. And that morning
            I had your letter, father,
                Telling of the death
Of my earthly master. How much more I feel
        This now (perhaps it is worth noting here
            The appearance of my first
                Gray hair, this morning)
—More than I thought I should: everything
        In the sun, in the sky so speaks of him,
            So mourns their Great Witness lost.
                Today, the weather
Is wretched, cold and rainy, dark like England
        At this season. I do begin to lose
            All faith in these provinces.
                Even the people
Look to me ugly, except children from eight
        To fourteen, who here as in Italy
            Anywhere are glorious:
                So playful and bright
In expression, so beautiful in feature,
        So dark in eye and soft in hair—creatures
            Quite unrivalled. At fifteen
                They degenerate
Into malignant vagabonds, or sensual
        Lumps of lounging fat. And this latter-day

Venice, father! where by night
The black gondolas
Are just traceable beside one, as if Cadmus
Had sown the wrong teeth and grown dragons, not
Men. The Grand Canal, this month,
Is all hung, from end
To end, with carpets and tapestries like a street
Of old-clothes warehouses. And now there is
Even talk of taking down,
Soon, Tintoretto's
Paradise to "restore" it. Father, without
The Turner Gallery, I do believe
I should go today and live
In a cave on some
Cliffside — among crows. Oh what fools they are, this
Restoring pack, yet smoothing all manner
Of rottenness up with words.
My Turner would not
Phrase like these, and only once in all the years
I knew him said, "Thank you, Mr. Ruskin."
My own power, if it be that,
Would be lost by mere
Fine Writing. You know I promised no Romance —
I promised them Stones. Not even bread.
Father, I do not feel any
Romance in Venice!
Here is no "abiding city," here is but
A heap of ruins trodden underfoot
By such men as Ezekiel
Angrily describes,
Here are lonely and stagnant canals, bordered
For the most part by blank walls of gardens
(Now waste ground) or by patches
Of mud, with decayed
Black gondolas lying keel-upmost, sinking
Gradually into the putrid soil.
To give Turner's joy of this
Place would not take ten

Days of study, father, or of residence:
    It is more than joy that must be the great
        Fact I would teach. I am not sure,
            Even, that joy is
A fact. I am certainly only of the strong
    Instinct in me (I cannot reason this)
        To draw, delimit the things
            I love—oh not for
Reputation or the good of others or
    My own advantage, but a sort of need,
        Like that for water and food.
            I should like to draw
All Saint Mark's, stone by stone, and all this city,
    Oppressive and choked with slime as it is
        (Effie of course declares, each
            Day, that we must leave:
A woman cannot help having no heart, but
    That is hardly a reason she should have
        No manners), yes, to eat it
            All into my mind—
Touch by touch. I have been reading *Paradise
Regained* lately, father. It seems to me
        A parallel to Turner's
            Last pictures—the mind
Failing altogether, yet with intervals
    And such returns of power! "Thereupon
        Satan, bowing low his gray
            Dissimulation,
Disappeared." Now he is gone, *my* dark angel,
    And I never had such a conception
        Of the way I must mourn—not
            What I lose, now, but
What I *have* lost, until now. Yet there is more
    Pain knowing that I must forget it all,
        That in a year I shall have
            No more *awareness*
Of his loss than of that fair landscape I saw,
    Waking, the morning your letter arrived,

No more left about me than
A fading pigment.
All the present glory, like the present pain,
Is no use to me; it hurts me rather
From my fear of leaving it,
Of losing it, yet
I know that were I to stay here, it would soon
Cease being glory to me—that it *has*
Ceased, already, to produce
The impression and
The delight. I can bear only the first days
At a place, when all the dread of losing
Is lost in the delirium
Of its possession.
I daresay love is very well when it does not
Mean *leaving behind*, as it does always,
Somehow, with me. I have not
The heart for more now,
Father, though I thank you and Mother for all
The comfort of your words. They bring me,
With *his* loss, to what I said
Once, the lines on this
Place you will know: "The shore lies naked under
The night, pathless, comfortless and infirm
In dark languor, still except
Where salt runlets plash
Into tideless pools, or seabirds flit from their
Margins with a questioning cry." The light
Is gone from the waters with
My fallen angel,
Gone now as all must go. *Your loving son*,
JOHN

1881

A Beatification

Began with A Moral Tale Though Gay, as bold
as brass, as good as gold, or gilt along
the edges, entitled (*sic*) *The Young Duke*
—"though what," old Isaac d'Israeli wailed,
"does Ben know of dukes?"

Closed on the golden molars of the Earl
of Beaconsfield waving *The Woman in White* away:
"When I want to read a novel, damme, I write one!"
The interval beguiled to great effect
by a Jew *d'esprit*,

or so he claimed: "I am the empty page
between the Testaments"—proving thereby
that only the road of appearances may lead
to the palace of essence. And indeed his least
superficial trait

was his frivolity, which from the first
sank to a considerable depth. Consider then
Chapter Seven of Book Two, which the old fox
could never be persuaded that he wrote:
"I never deny,

I never contradict. But I sometimes
forget." The scene forgotten is the one
where George Augustus Frederick, the young duke,
dresses for a party ("persons of great
consideration:

some were noble, most were rich, all had
ancestors") in something of a rush—

"no time was to be unnecessarily lost
in his preparations (and those of both valets)
for his appearance . . ."

Or for the apparition of a god:
the teakwood dressing-box has been unpacked,
and the shrine for his devotions soon arrayed
with rich-cut flagons of every size and shape
adroitly mingled

with china vases, golden instruments
and the ivory and rosewood brushes, sable-tipped,
worthy even of Reynolds' exquisite device . . .
His Grace was master of the art of dress,
and consequently

consummated that paramount enterprise
with the categorical rapidity of one
whose principles are settled. He then gave
orders with the decision of a Wellington
—the battle was pitched

upon a sparkling plain: ". . . Now let me have
the rose-water—before it dries, you fool!
Light over here, I must have evidence
of how the pores will take another dose
of strychnine. There. Stop!"

The young man's taste was for magnificence;
but he was handsome, and a duke. Pardon him.
Possessed of skin whose pellucid ivory
had never yielded to the Season's strain,
his Grace did not fear

the want of relief ostensibly produced
by a white face, white waistcoat, white cravat.
A hair-chain set in diamonds was annexed
to a glass reposing in the waistcoat seam—
this the only weight

the young duke ever bore. It *was* a bore,
but indispensable. Now it is done.
He stops one moment at the tall pier-glass
and shoots a glance that might have read the mind
of a Talleyrand:

it will do! He assumes an air that best befits
the occasion—sublime but cordial—and descends
like a deity from Olympus to dinner below,
the banquet of fortunate mortals who await
an undivulged god.

Had young Disraeli learned the discipline
of being shallow enough for a polite audience?
And Beaconsfield, old, discovered after all
that he loathed the vainglory he lived for,
dyed for, rouged for still?

Good to read the dreadful pages, warmed
by these two words together: *much admired.*
Upon him was bestowed that rarest gift,
the Grace of self-delighting fantasy.
Beatified? Yes,

who shows we must hallow *ourselves* if we are
to enter paradise. No good wishing to be
saints like Joan of Arc or John of the Cross—
"der alte Jude, ja, das ist der Mann,"
as Bismarck observed,

an Image of the Truth, if but the truth
of vanity on the grandest possible scale:
illusion without deceit, solitude without
loneliness. The Young Duke's dressing-table,
a map of Eden.

1889
Alassio

Dear Ross, your letter arrived in the same mail
    with more drivel from Havelock Ellis
who evidently has sought from you, as well,
    the penetralia of a life he knows
to be out of the common, by admission
        if not by practice.
Can you conceive—he has also sent his quiz
    or inquiry to Swinburne. Swinburne!
Faugh! I can listen to a fellow talking
    pederasty: we understand that,
but the Lesbian!—little beast, I am
        resolved to abstain,
without appeal, from any undertaking
    in which that Pygmy has any part,
squatting in his cesspool and adding to it;
    further, I shall now endeavor
to warn you off likewise, though I have no doubt
        (as the great author
of *Justine* says of Parricide combined with
    Sodomy) these things *are* a matter
of taste. But I never in my life, besides,
    have kept a journal such as he asks
for *extracts* from: all that memory should save
        is with me best left
to the brain's own process, if there is a brain
    surviving the vexations I am
put to, and have been suffering all the while
    I tried to live in *France*. Your letter
addressed to Cannes has found me here (Hell, my dear,
        is preferable
to Cannes, Purgatory to Menton, French boys
    being far too keen in their native

perception of material advantage) . . .
   Yet what shall I say in favor of
this place in which I have, at last, *gone to ground?*
      It is a landscape
out of "Childe Roland," more like Browning's barren
   than anything you have ever seen:
bare, scored, broiled, scraped, blotched, scalped, flayed, flogged &
                                          ruined,
   a country calcined, grimy, powdered,
parboiled, without trees, water, grass—*with* blank
      beastly orange-groves
and senseless olive-clumps like mad cabbages
   gone indigestible. My two rooms
here in the town have seven doors in them, which
   as you open or shut them offer
a choice of sounds and sensations varying
      between the apex
of a windmill, the works of a paddle-box
   steamer and the eye of a maelstrom.
Not only Earth is brass, but also Heaven
   iron: in this accursed climate
life oozes from me, destructions by night and
      diarrhea by day.
I live an odd fungoid life on some dead branch
   of my soul, an odoriferous
decay, eyes smarting and inflamed under blue
   spectacles and a green silk eyeshade:
the blank prose of such debility is all
      I dare write *or* read . . .
Meanwhile, my books, my blue paper, my quill pens,
   my cough, my yawnings at dawn, at dusk
my solitary pacings on the gray beach,
   my languors, my martyrdoms, dear Ross,
my sickness unto death—woe to those who waste
      the best years of their
virginity in vain, *yearning* . . . O my sins
   of omission! including perhaps
some omitted sins, for these too strike me as
   mistakes, life wearing on. This morning

as I came up from the sea, Pippo rode past:
        he comes here later.
A naked boy on a naked horse, that is
        a very fine sight. I had no sense
how well the two animals suited each other.
        Yet it is only one more vision,
a vanity: I was not made to live, Ross,
        in the realm of Time.
Under this sun, at noon, when all the hot world
        which is not hugely brilliant is blue,
Priapus withers to a mere fig-tree stump,
        and I reel from one droll devotion
to another misshapen passion. Pardon
        this enthusiasm,
for that is what it is. I never narrate
        my exile without putting on strong
the Hautboys and Trumpets of my Organ, for
        it is an oppression to live here
under which I hope you may never lament,
        a deep into which
no angel can descend . . .
                        This room overhangs
        the water murmuring and lapping
just beneath the window, gently at all hours;
        Pippo has left me for the last time.
Again. The point is, he has left me again:
        white flesh with green eyes,
frog-green, shining like his hair in the white air
        of afternoon, trembling in white light
reflected in the white flat sea. *La bella
        noia!* You see, the consolations
of tragedy are gone out of my life here.
        Farce is all I have;
and a few poems to write, calculated
        to make even some not over-nice
hairs stand on end, to say nothing of other
        erections equally obvious.
I tremble for the result of *your* reading,
        and cannot expect

a British public to drink out of my pond,
        even if I bring it up to their
very noses. As for an audience *here*,
        their patter has no claim to be called
articulate: it is like a man clearing
                his throat. Moreover,
there is little to be gained by pandering
        to their affected fashion (they *all*
do it so) of pronouncing their own language.
        And how I loathe their society!
Why, at one great dinner here—you know the style
                of their days: morning,
a little Mass; noon, a little dice; midnight,
        a little woman (I quite dislike
the shape of women, can scarcely bring myself
        to sketch it in a landscape study,
though it stays in the mind unconscionably)
                —I wander. At one
such party as they are forever giving
        to one another, it was the most
I could do to withhold myself from falling
        flat upon the floor and crying out:
"Behold one who is a scarecrow, I am not
                what I look to be,
tear off the clothes and flesh, find the death
        inside—you who have a God, let Him
search me, let Him scatter me to the four winds
        and scour my emptiness!" Yet I said
nothing. Why speak so? One discovers the dead
                wall in each of us,
and the great fact of my life (I know it, here)
        is that the spiritual cannot
emerge from the matter of me. Still I feel,
        within, the rebellious, unspoken
word: I will not be old. And I fall upon
                the wicked Pippo
and his kind like a man athirst. One puts them
        in good humor by offering each
a white linen suit with a red sash, telling

them they are wanted two at a time
(always, it is safer, with these Italians,
        to arrange a choice:
one or the other is nearly sure to fail
    at the crucial moment). I confess,
myself, to a Chinese sort of love for red—
    the very names, vermillion, scarlet,
warm me, and to dress in floating crimson silk
        I half understand
being a Cardinal, a woman wholly . . .
    Enough of that life you are so good
to ask after, Ross. I leave off in order
    to belabor Ellis a bit now,
as I trust you shall do . . . You may tell people,
        if they ask you still,
I am not dead, but by no means encourage
    the notion of so much life as might
suggest human intercourse. I move as yet—
    eppur si muove!—an assiduous
mummy, from tea to dinner, making myself
        the wretched mouthpiece
of these unapprehended feelings. I have
    the contortions of the Sibyl, but
the inspiration? But the utterance?
    A mystery. My nature must be
at the root male and passionate—I want no
        affection given
which I may not return: kindness but suggests
    to the beast in me unspeakable
desires. Do not inquire too deeply of this,
    my words like my nature are obscure,
uncertain, wide of the mark that is on them.
        You know not the whole
of me, Ross, as I know not the whole of you.
    We are all and everlastingly
alone; which leads me to expect I shall make
    a good death, whereof the essence is
loneliness, and I have had sufficiency
        of practice at that.

Tell yourself, rather, the glare of contentious
 eagerness is not for me. I shall
end in the state described by the Laureate:
 "Dozing in the vale of Avalon,
and watched by weeping queens." My dear Ross, good-night.
 (Remember, Ellis
must be *stopped*. I trust you as I do myself.)

1824–1889

The virtues which distinguish the present generation were not invented in my time.
—Wilkie Collins

The reek of a "moral hospital," something wrong
    in the nursery, the sickroom, the old men's home:
that England of your bearded friends who lay blasted
    as it might be like Ruskin and shy Dodgson
by a passion for girls under twelve, like Carlyle
    by the desperate rant of wisdom that kept him
from passion at all, like Lear by the "terrible demon"
    he dared not admit—England was your Native Strain.

Whatsoever things are snug, whatsoever things
    are influential, if there be any money: think
on these things. You mocked them all (it was the season
    of cant and Christmas) riding around the City
in an omnibus, looking for the Actual—
    no, not looking, *glaring* was your word for Truth,
a woman in white glaring out to sea across
    the dimpled meander of the Shivering Sands.

Then later, prowling Italy with great Dickens
    and your new friends Lemon and Egg—Augustus Egg!—
visiting a school for the deaf and blind, quibbling,
    while each installment kept a nation up till dawn,
over Method: *suspense* vs. *surprise*, until
    the schoolroom echoed with your shout: "Inquire of *them*,
Charles," stabbing with your stick at the empty faces,
    "there lies your answer, there in the silent dark!"

Even amid the "festive diableries of France"
    (as Dickens winked over the Burgundy) you were
victimized by the Victorian disaster
    of your initials: all cisterns emptied behind
a door marked W.C.—here too, Household Words.

Of all their entertainers, only you relied
not on "the white flower of a blameless life" but
    on the testimony of servants, invalids,

paupers, lunatics and foreigners. It kept you
    from being a gentleman, your *first* addiction
to an ignominy the police had known so long:
    the worst crimes of all are committed in the home,
that sanctuary out of the law's reach. *We belong,*
    you insisted—richer now than Dickens, ruder
than even Thackeray in a world of slights, and,
    after each day's Battley's Drops, your eyes bags of blood—

to one great inescapable community
    of suffering. Life, you added, and kept us hanging
on every word, *was at best a hopeless disease.*
    Never marrying either mistress—not Martha
who gave you three daughters, not bourgeois Caroline
    who took up with a plumber for spite (but came back)—
your only troth was plighted to Lady Laudanum,
    to whom nor gout nor Paris could make you untrue.

By the end, at bedtime, you would meet at the turn
    of the stairs, beside the bust of William Collins,
R.A. on the landing, a green woman with tusks
    and a trick of biting a piece out of your neck—
her way of saying good-night. Was it, I wonder,
    surprise, by then, or suspense? It turns out you were
Actual all along, and Meredith's snide regret
    that "Wilkie was not literature" redeems you:

him we forget, who found only the real to be
    imaginable, but you remain. We need you.
"I was not only pleased and astonished," you said
    when *The Moonstone* was finished in a laudanum jag,
"but did not recognize it as my own." After
    Caroline the titular but unvisitable
mistress died, Martha Rudd, to whom you left your watch,
    your girls, and £200, tended both your graves.

November, 1889

for Harold Bloom

Well met, children! yet *I* am not well.
In their corruption, dear Fanny, all things are
   possible, none without. I thought so
today, riding on the water here to you,
      ill as I am, but not
      so ill as not to think,
   and with my burden besides —
   as blessings are a burden.
Has your man brought in
a bolted box, safe
   from the gondola? The burden
   I must give into your hands . . .
      Do I express myself,
      or but exploit myself?
Astonishing, Pen, what you have done,
and managed yet to leave undone! Ruin at bay,
   procrastinated, nay proannuated!
Ca' Rezzonico and its eternal glooms,
      but not eternal now.
      We use the word amiss,
   as if it meant no more than
   "everlasting." Well! each bird
Sings to itself, so
then shall I, and make
   no more of your palace than
   that you have not made it less:
      here is a pile at last
      enabled to assume
the full aspect of the past, which is
in Venice the period taken, or given,
   for crystallization. I had thought
these walls beyond repair, like all such

castles of misconduct,
  victims of villainous
  improvements else, reduced
  or even enlarged to being
one further orifice
in the peep-show here,
  lurid, livid, but always
  burnt out. It is easier,
  Venice and I have learnt,
  to endure than to change—
hardest of all to endure what you
have not changed into. The bolted box is . . . but
I shall explain. I am not very well.
Last week at Mrs. Bronson's, it was no more
  than a migraine, or so
  the doctor in Asolo
  pronounced it—splendid fellow,
  what I liked most in him was,
he did not leave me
verses of his own.
  Curious symptoms withal
  for migraine: patterns moving
  over surfaces, faint
  most often, fine designs
that would come as a kind of cobweb
cast iridescent upon others, a net
intervening between me and them.
Lord! the things one sees when a fever-lit mind
  grants no middle distance.
  Prolixity of the real!
  And just when we are grateful
  for the dark, when night resumes us,
comes prolixity
of what is unreal,
  the melting waxworks of our sleep
  called dreams. I am against dreams,
  not being one to trust
  memory to itself.
In my delirium, then, I had

conviction of divided identity,
    never ceasing to be two persons who
ever thwarted and opposed one another.
        Then wakened to the faint
        smell of drugs and nostrums
    from the bedside—like a new-made
    mummy. And as if in answer,
the post at Padua
(last month's, to be sure)
    announcing Collins is gone.
    Collins, Pen—Wilkie Collins,
        the *Moonstone* man, although
        fits and starts are the best
    of what he left us: perhaps their length
is his measure. Well, we are all stewing-pans,
    and can cook only what we can hold.
Some more than others. Collins had, poor fellow,
        finicking manners but
        a luxurious gut,
    and he took his way sadly,
    certain he had fallen among
grocers. A kind of
indispensable
        liability to life,
        that man's power of suspense;
        and his tenacity!
        One only does not call
    a labor like *The Woman in White*
Herculean because Hercules could not
    have done it! Whereas your father runs
after interruptions, leading or led by
        the intransitive life
        of a fool who foments
        his poems whilst he dines out
        and disappoints. Consider:
the torment of starch
in my new shirts, Fan,
        has made me physically
        irritable, morally

46

impotent, and *for days*!
Who could write, with a sense
of chalky grit rubbed into each pore,
clogging all perspiration, chafing every
inch of cuticle, desiccating
the blood itself! I share Gautier's opinion
that Christianity
and laundry cannot sort
together. Perhaps it was
Christianity and sculpture.
In either case, for
laundry *and* sculpture,
we should have one leg firm on
the Acropolis, and one
in Florence, for God's sake!
what organ have we then,
my boy, in Venice? If Asolo
be my *pied-à-terre*, here you keep, I suppose,
your *ventre-à-l'eau*. Monstrous levity,
to mask a lack. Shelley calls the great god Pan
a want, you know, and all
this Italian earth seems
now to me the sense of what
can never be. It burgeons
without us, and lives
the lewd life of things
that look for no existence
but in themselves. The canal
I came by—leave it and
it comprehends you not.
Worse, the admiration of mountains,
surely a Calvinist plot: strange confusion,
among minds defiant of meaning,
between the mere lofty and the beautiful.
If mountains turn a tree
into a fir, fancy
what they can do with a man!
Italy lets us know it:
the life of April

sunlight has to die;
　　　　it is now quite dead, and I
　　　　have another kind of life.
　　　　　　　Beauties there, of course, but
　　　　　　　coming only in bursts,
　　　　coming to a mind long crumpled (till
the creases stay), coming only in escapes
　　　　from the thing itself! Take Asolo,
that long Virgilian country round about—
　　　　　　　half mystery and half
　　　　　　　morality, but then!
　　　　　　then the scramble of rural
　　　　　　royalty, with royal thoughts!
"It is, at bottom,
would you not say, sir,
　　　　a criticism of life?" I:
　　　　"Rather take it at the top,
　　　　　　burning ever upward
　　　　　　to its blank point of bliss."
　　　Sumptuous, of course, the dinner,
views from the villa entrancing, as you know:
　　　the valley full of mist and looking
like a sea of absinthe, distant hills rising
　　　　　　　from it, forming the shore
　　　　　　　of Purgatory, past
　　　　Acheron. And the Russian
　　　　Duchess looked on indifferent,
staring as she ate,
watching the Brenta
　　　　　as if she were but watching
　　　　　the Grand Duke's body pass by:
　　　　　　　"What is there, that you make
　　　　　　　so much of, in water?"—
leaving off the lobster—"I am quite
tired of it. There it goes: flow flow flow, always
　　　the same." She demands to see me here,
a Princess by birth, a Nihilist by trade!
　　　　　　offers a rendez-vous,
　　　　　　my dears, at her hotel,

48

that I may explain stanzas
she found *obscure*. I suppose
it is dangerous,
if you have not had
the advantage of dying,
to attempt a description
of death, and afterwards
there are, unfortunately,
obstacles in the way . . . though Ba came
not to believe in those either. It is all
rigmarole and rhodomontade, even
at the hands of a Grand Duchess practicing
mesmerism and miracles
on all sides. I sink to
precious trifling, yet better
than the fate of a fallen
rocket that likely
will be mine as well.
I neither hope nor deserve
to be loved by anybody,
nor much, nor at all, yet
I am very grateful
when someone is at pains to do it.
A great many such ladies of the first rank
were present at that dinner, and if
honeyed words from pretty lips could surfeit,
I had enough—though one
can swallow quantities
of whipped cream and do no harm
to an old stomach. They seem
to care so deeply
for what they call *art*:
I suppose it is like one
of those indelicate subjects
which always sound better
in a foreign language.
I am not interested in art.
I am interested in the obstacles
to art. One creature with queenly airs

and a snake, I vow, tattooed on her ankle,
  clung to me like ivy:
  whatever should she do
in order to become, say,
a poet? *In order!* Never
have I pretended
to afford anyone
  such literature as might
  substitute for a cigar,
    but so much I told her:
    "Don't twitter, though sparrows
all do; things happen, and then we get
a lark or a nightingale or even an owl,
  which last is by no means to be scorned."
Kay Bronson cannot abide, you know, the rule
  of an equal number
  in men and women guests.
    She says she invites her friends
    for conversation, not mating.
Even so, there are
surprises. Walking
  in the woods with my snake-lady,
  I said: "Let us sit here"; then,
    after regarding me
    steadily a moment,
  her pale eyes glowing like grapes,
she said: "You may make love to me, if you like."
  The old have death, and the young have love,
but death comes once—love over and over.
    Or is it to the old
    that death comes back and back,
  and love no longer at all?
  I told her, it was for poetry
I ate and drank and
dressed and had my being,
    but she would not let me go.
    To be quit of her and them
      is a godsend to me,
      for all the graying wreck

of nature here, where if not divine
it is diabolic. I said I was not well,
   yet well or ill, up at the villa
I am a man smothered with society
      of women, like a duck
      with onions. I will not
      be Victorian in their way:
      I would be . . . Albertian!
In the one year, Ba
died, then Albert died.
      Ours were the Great Marriages,
      I cannot help but think, for
         I know ours to be, still,
         the Great Bereavements,
      the weeds worn so long neither the Queen
nor I remember quite the flowers, I daresay,
   sprouted by now to something emblematic,
something gone out of the garden altogether.
         Wife to husband, widow
         to widower, ah, Pen,
      we remember the flowers,
      in thirty years forget the weeds!
I want nothing left
out, and nothing back,
      no, nothing ever again.
      Don't expurgate: exorcise
         your losses! In Venice
         we learn about losses:
      they affect us only till we have
lost altogether. Then comes a poisonous
   impalpability that simulates
a form beneath the flow of time's gray garment,
         and through the place we see
         is signified a place
      we never saw. Life is all
      salutation. No reply.
Drifting through Venice
after twenty years'
      such drifting, and year by year

seeing only the bruises
in the marble blacker,
the patience of ruin
deeper, every stone an image of
accumulated sea-change, it was all one—
one of my numerous visions which so
numerously leave me. As I came, my box
beside me and my eyes
too old for disbelief,
clouds soon covered up the sun,
as if too good to be seen,
granting a dead glare,
visions from the verge
shadowless in the steel air,
unaccountable, violent
against an ultimate
horizon. At that hour
the ends of the earth were closing in,
and I thought: my boy, my Pen, cold walls hold him
among shades and silences, mostly
darkness there, under a grim incessant sky
grayer with each moment
since Asolo. It was
a pale departure into
this perfect decrepitude,
suffering this dim
disgrace of daylight
as the noiseless town neared us.
Neared *us*! We could not even
creep to it, but Venice
rose up out of the sea
to meet us, a momentary shape
made significant by perennial touching.
Ah, Fanny, there are times I can guess
what you good young Americans must feel, times—
I feel them too—when we
are nothing but the heirs
of an humiliating
splendor. As you have taught me,

it takes a great deal
to make one successful
        American, but to make
        one happy Venetian takes
        a mere handful of life
        among old stones. Indeed,
    if there be disagreeable things
in Venice, nothing is so disagreeable
    as the visitors, jostling for boats
around one. Lady Gordon warned I should find
            a *bateau-mouche* plying
            the Grand Canal! I had
            no distaste for it, myself,
            but the gondoliers, finding
their custom lessened,
had all struck, and we
        could barely get a *barca*
        for love *as well as* money!
            Poor fellows, they shall learn,
            as others have, that steam
    is stronger than they. We left behind
those foreigners fuming round the Redentore,
    and I knew: what is dead or dying
is more readily apprehended by us
            than what is part of life.
            Nothing in writing is
    easier than to raise the dead.
    Do not let me wander, Pen—
I am not enough
myself now to be
        spontaneous. I must *scheme.*
        Last year, Eliot Norton
            (I have learnt to admire
            if not to endure him)
    showed me the letters to Jane Carlyle
and those from her to Thomas, before and since
    their marriage, both. He will not print them,
even to correct Froude's falsifications,
            will not violate *anew*

the prostrate confidence
of husband and wife, will not
be known as the one to do it,
at any rate. Pen,
such must not be my fate.
I dread but one thing: biography.
The truth which is in this box,
once unlatched, once published
to the world, is worth all
the tragedy of errors after:
time finds a withered leaf in every laurel,
age makes egoism more eager,
less enjoying. It shall be her words, my words,
no more than that, no less.
There are enough of them,
five hundred letters, by my count—
long ago. What our words are,
I am not certain.
It is done. Old love
is slow in going, but goes.
Some twenty years since I looked
at what is in the box.
Cowardice, call it that;
I do not know the name. Sufficient
for me, knowing they are there. Without opening,
I can say the words, some of the words:
"My power lives in me like the fire in those mad
Mediterranean
phares I have watched at sea,
wherein the light is ever
turning in a dark gallery,
still bright and alive,
and only after
a wary interval leaps out,
for a moment, from the one
mean chink, and then goes on
with between it and you
the blind wall." Perhaps because I can
recite that much, I do not care for the rest.

You keep them now, Pen, and once I am
gone, give them to Smith. It should be two volumes . . .
   Nothing but ourselves then,
   though that be too much now
  for me. Put the box away,
  high and dry. I am still here.

Now this is splendid,
what you have done with
  the stairs, Fanny, this is warm!
  It shows what *can* be done. If,
   as I have always said,
   these people are ever
  refined, it will be by fire. A few
coals do it: the life in us abolishes
  the death in things. I recall, last time,
how drear it all looked, and how I dreaded
   to feel the pale hush
   of the irreparable
  on all these blighted rooms,
  the relics of how many
Doges littering
your inhuman walls?
  A pressure of sanctity
  almost profane, disorder
   in the very daylight . . .
   All gone, now, and well gone
  behind us, or ahead—like the letters:
too far behind me to be endured, too far
  ahead to be dared. Let them rest here.
Ah, Venice! Pen, your Venice now, how it rocks
   all ambitions to sleep,
   floats a man to his doom,
  even when the secular truth
  is a stroll on the sandbars.
Again the delusion!
We are all under
  a net that covers the world!
  Or is it but the canal,

lapping in light on your
ceilings? It is nothing,
then, no cause for alarm, dear children,
it has passed, as all spells do, however cast.
The preponderance of some dissolving
force, mine or water's, need not be contended with,
merely endured, merely
survived. Strange, though, how close
the meshes were, everywhere
entrapping, overtaking . . .
If I am to go
out to the Lido
at all, I must go before
I am too sick to go, and
above all, before I mind
being sicker. Let me have
my cloak again, Fanny, and your man
to row me beyond these wicked walls. I want
to see the grass, if it be but gray
wires curling on the beach. I need to walk now,
without these palaces
pressing in upon me;
they make, for all their marble
pride, a valley of darkness—
at its end I see
vast uncertainty.
I want room now, not solace,
I must have the roar and release
of some open water,
even if it be black.
Then here, returning, then the firelight,
then, in the winter half of the world, to sleep . . .

1890
Further Echoes of the Late Lord Leighton

Knighted 1878; created Baronet, 1886; created Baron Leighton of Stretton, 1896; Royal Aca-
demician, 1869; President of the Royal Academy, 1878; Hon. D.C.L., Oxford, 1879; Hon.
LL.D., Cambridge, 1879; Commander of the Legion of Honour, 1889; Hon. Member, Berlin
Academy, Royal Academy of Vienna, Royal Academy of Belgium, Academy of St. Luke,
Rome; Academies of Florence, Genoa, Turin, Antwerp; Lieut.-Colonel of the 20th Middlesex
(Artists') Rifle Volunteers

"Ach, the women! Worse, the wives. And widows worst of all.
Madame Viardot—to hear that I went to Paris. Think
     what she has to overcome:
harsh voice, ugly face, ungainly person, yet contrives
to look almost handsome. Possibly on account of
     Gluck's *Orfeo*, into which
she enters heart and soul. She says it is the only thing
that after fifty performances has given her
     not a moment's *ennui*! No
chance of her singing such in England—I don't believe
a Covent Garden audience would sit through it.
     Speaking of ugly, I am

to illustrate the Evans-Lewes-Eliot woman's
new novel for the *Cornhill*—two 'Florentine' drawings
     for each of the twelve numbers.
Already she writes: 'Romola's face and hair are not
just the thing—how could they be? I meant the hair to fall
     forward from behind the ears—
I shall inevitably be detestable to you . . .' and here
the homely fabulist breaks off with these words: 'Perhaps
     we shall see one another
before you begin the next drawing. My misery
is the certainty I must be often in error.'
     Within the year I have had

analogous nonsense from Browning's wife—*wifely*
nonsense in fact, declaring herself 'satisfied but
for a want of strength about
the brow, which I must write of, for I can't trust Robert
himself with the message. I think the brow is feeble,
less massive than his; in fact
your temple is *hollow.* Yet how I thank you for
having put so much of my husband on paper is proved
by the very insolence
of my criticism.' And then another year finds me
designing a slab for the woman in the English
Cemetery at Florence—

talk of hollow temples! Not the faintest what to do
about my title. Father has a place in Shropshire:
*Baron Leighton of Stretton
in the County of Shropshire?* And the bloody motto?
Swinburne has a way with such things. His way. Advises
Dread Shame. Ambiguous. Well,
why not? And then again, why? What good can come of it?
After the R.A., what price a seat in the Upper House?
Still, the first 'arts' peerage since
Tennyson. That Painting should be lower than Letters
(no higher than baronetcies), inadmissible!
The offer was made. Accept."

The Queen sighed. She could not altogether approve, yet
forty years ago dear Albert had urged the purchase of
*Cimabue's Madonna
Carried in Procession through the Streets of Florence*—who
could guess what horrors would follow: *The Bath of Psyche!*
Not even the Prince Consort
foresaw that sea-water of the Lesbian grape could turn
so brackish in the cup. Yet public services weighed,
and a pure, unmarried life . . .
His last words: "Give my love to the Royal Academy."
The day before his death, the announcement became
official. The Queen had signed.

1891
An Idyll

for Mark Strand

A storm is coming, but the clouds are still
no more than a classic custard in the west,
no closer than the sun, still august, shining
through the dishevelled branches of an oak
as if there were no darkness gathering
itself together round the scene's edges,
although the gulls come sideways, suddenly
white against the cliffs, loud in their anger.
It is the Isle of Wight, and Tennyson's Tree
("like a breaking wave?" asked Allingham,
ever poetical. "No, not in the least,"
the poet replied, peering into the leaves)
under which are sitting two old men,
the Laureate and the Signor painting him;
and being read to, both of them, by Hallam
Tennyson out of a green book, *The Golden Bough*,
published this year of the first Electrocution
(America's riposte to Gallows and Guillotine)
and the last of Parnell: it is 1891.
The Signor? Craved a name more musical
than Frith or Stubbs, and markedly more human
than Lamb or Leech or Crabbe or Hogg, unmeet
for a Grand Mannerist—"I find the laurel
also bears a thorn." Was at some pains
in the presentment of a Mortal Form
to express the lower lid, although his eyes,
with a bister tinge around them, always looked
as if they were put in by dirty fingers:
portraits fuscous now, flat, leathery
Black Masters . . . At fifty had married a girl
of seventeen, to Save her from the Stage
(Nelly Terry—Ellen Watts—annulled);

at seventy, "Watts' *Hope*" a Household Word
and glory waking summer in his veins,
married again (she was twenty), the details
managed by Gracious Ladies, life and death
alike in the hands of older women. One
experience survived a thousand dinners out:
hearing some noise at midnight he remained
in darkness on the stairs, ready, stirred—
"it was the stubborn beat of wings, as if
some creature was attempting flight." Then came
a far-off voice, yet filling the air, that seemed
to cry, "Anima mia! anima mia!"—then
all was unusually still. Each time,
as even now, he told someone the story,
his blood ran brighter, like an opal warmed.
Hallam endures the venerable rudeness
(being rich in that patience the old require
of others and but rarely deserve of themselves),
reads again from the pages he cuts as he reads,
and the Signor, missing half the words immersed
by the murmuring boughs, contrives to scumble in
a clump of mistletoe from the Sacred Oak,
ghostly but quite identifiable
over Alfred's shoulder . . . She would often come
with him, in those days, to Freshwater,
his first great inspiration, beautiful
Nelly, her hair still down, in a red straw
mushroom, the dull-red feather on it full,
lying there among the kingcups, campions
and clover just the color of that plume.
Was it not wonderful that Alfred, lately,
should see her at the Lyceum, in his *Cup*,
one face, one voice outshining all the rest
in Godwin's dresses—Nelly Godwin now,
but Ellen Terry always. He had seen her
once more himself, in splendor, through the hedge
at Little Holland House, but she had outgrown
that look of a lily with a glow-worm inside . . .
The old painter pauses, watching the setters

roll ecstatically in those campions now,
Don and Grig, snapping at each other's fleas
till the even older poet orders them off:
"What do we know of their pain, do we know
aught of the feelings of insects? They may feel
more pain than we." Hallam lays by the book,
accustomed to the signs (whose very name
had been a sign of grief he was born to bear),
and his roused father continues, righteousness
subsiding into reminiscences:
"Charles Darwin himself—decades ago
it was, a tall yellow man, sickly, dull—
could not resolve my doubts, for all his wasps
and worm-casts which will someday bury Stonehenge—
sat just where you sit, Signor, praising 'Maud'
and marvelling at my 'Miniature Edition':
I want no Species Fame, I want the warrant
of immortality." The text has shaken
Tennyson, its tale of the grove, the tree
and the grim figure with a drawn sword prowling
day and night around it, impatient
for the king to kill him, even as he killed
the king . . . "I dream of kings," he interrupts
himself, turning to Hallam: "it is true,
I suppose, that such divinity is apt
to cost them their lives . . . Priam has appeared
to me in the night." Hallam sighs. If only
someone would help him. But Signor Watts,
half deaf, stares unheeding at the cliffs,
the Colored Rocks of Alum Bay, a smear
by this light, a stain—like something spilt.
"Priam and the rest. Not Arthur, though, no more . . .
You talk of wings, Signor: I have heard
time flowing in the middle of the night,
all things fluttering doomward, and I know
our modern fame is nothing—better have
an acre of land. I shall go down, down!
I'm up now." The Ancient Sage is blind,
the Signor cannot hear, a storm is coming.

"I feel myself to be a center, still,
and though, sometimes, of a dark morning,
I have doubts, I do believe I shall not
die."
            Who speaks? The Prospero of the Isle,
or only the Laureate? We must leave them there,
the light falters, and Mrs. Cameron—
whose photograph we have enlisted, enlarged
upon—turns away, the glass negative
held by the corners in her collodionized hands:
"Magnificent!" she whispers to herself,
"to focus them all in one picture—such an effort!"
Dark, short, sharp-eyed, we can hear her
very distinctly: "I longed to arrest the life
which came before me, and at length the longing
has been satisfied." Carlyle fumed, of course,
Browning said she made bags under his eyes,
yet there they stand, or sit, and the two old men
before us are with them: dead, immortal.
"The sun obeys your gestures," Tennyson
had told her, and her method is our own:
"Coming to a subject which, in my own eyes,
was beautiful, I stopped there, leaving all
the blur of Being on it." Away she strides
to her glass-house with the plates, both dogs
following her, and Hallam leads his father
and the Signor to the Hall. The sky darkens
moment by moment, and the oak, untenanted,
surrenders to the storm at Freshwater,
August 15, 1891.

1897

An interval between the House & the Grave, deeply desired.
—The Rt. Hon. William Ewart Gladstone

That summer at Bordighera, in a fashion
somewhat agitated, he confided his dreams—
    haunted by halls and lines of people,
horrors outright, the frequent burden of which was
a weak old man gradually bruised to death by clubs.
    "What is politics in England, John,
but a long Khyber Pass, with all the misery
of a passage in," he sighed, "and no passage out?"
    We were walking the beach together,
the air was sullen, all this coast from Menton
to Santa Margharita one mild Miltonic
    hell where the welkin glistens and reeks,
every surface swelters until Earth's face cracks,
and only the Sea is whole, running high along
    the sand, huge green masses of water
shattering to mere foam at our feet. In this heat
who would expect such a sea? Mr. G delights
    in it, has a passion for its sound,
would like to have it in his ears all day, all night:
"It is the truth of Dante's *Banquet*, my boy, where
    the noble soul is said to be like
a good mariner, for he, when he draws near port,
lowers his sails and enters softly, with gentle
    steerage." It is his way of speaking
I can catch, though I am separated from him
in the order of ideas by an interval
    that must be called a gulf. Forgive me
if I go too far—I am simply a funnel,
my local memory has always been vivid,
    I seem never to have forgotten
a circumstance, a scene, a single syllable,

for all my personal rank as a vanishing
        quantity—why else should Mr. G
have kept me with him past his years of employment,
years of Parliamentary meddle and muddle?
        "In the long run, John, we are all dead;
memoirs are as hateful to me as monuments,
but a memory like yours is another thing."
        Striding down the beach desecrated
by gold-necked bottles, lobster claws, bits of veal pie,
he would ask me to prod him into reckoning
        of what has been his life. Eighty-eight
years have deterred none of his senses, save perhaps
that of . . . reality: the man is a great white rock
        with a little moss on it, just so,
and the green sea-water beneath. One word of mine
suffices to release, like some bottled *djinni*,
        that affluent language he bestows
so effortlessly. Once, indeed, he admitted
speculating why the room seemed to fall silent—
        "only to discover I had stopped
talking. It was a genuine discovery."
The word, this time, was some trifling *bon mot* of mine
        on the Heir Apparent's appearance.
That was enough: "Three decades of Her Majesty's
crisp, incessant orders, John, have convinced me quite
        of the unfailing, the shall I say
hereditary antipathy of our sovereigns
to their heirs apparent. The single time I dined
        with the Prince and his mother, a swan—
very white and tender, stuffed with truffles as well—
was the best company at table, and the Queen's
        sole remark to her son (and myself)
was that dogs behaved better to the furniture
than in the past . . . the one improvement quite certain
        in modern times. Ah, my boy," he groaned,
"we are well away from Balmorality here,
the terrible Tartanitis which overtook
        the Throne in my time, hard upon

the Morte d'Albert. Remarkable statesman, mind you,
but the stock was weak. You recall the cousin, Ludwig
    of Bavaria? Talked with his eyes
tight shut. Drowned himself in the ornamental lake
with his doctor. No stamina in the family.
    Though the Queen is of the family,
and endures . . . Her words to me, when I took my leave—
simple perfection of perfect simplicity:
    'Often, Mr. Gladstone, I believe,
after a period of strenuous reform,
a moment comes, quite suddenly, when the British
    people tires of being, ah, *improved*.'
Thank God, John, I am quit of all such encounters."
And then, as we proceeded to the pier from which
    a superb view might be had, waves
hurling themselves over each other to the rocks,
he took from an inner pocket, with a sharp glance
    into my eyes, a green morocco
notebook quite glossy with wear. "I was but eighteen,
John, when I entered these words. Judge, if I have
    kept faith with those emotions of mine."
The diary was in his backhand, tiny script,
unchanged subsequently. "On board the *Queen of Scotland*.
    Rose to breakfast, but uneasily.
Attempted reading, first book of Herodotus,
not too unwell to reflect. Returned to bed, then
    translated a few lines of Dante.
Also, Beauties of Shakespeare. By evening, high wind
blowing. Quite ill, though still in bed. Yet could not help
    admiring the white crests of the waves,
even as I stood at the cabin's low casement."
He took it from me with a gesture to the sea,
    and we walked on, Mr. G gloating
in the huge force, the swell and beat of the rollers
on the shore, like a titanic pulse. As they ran,
    bounding toward us with bright persuasions
of grace and power, he wondered if we had not more
and better words for the sea than the French language:

"*flot, vague, onde, lame,* as against
breaker, billow, comber, bore, eagre, roller, swell
and surge." He quite shouted the words into the tide.
I have never seen him so happy.

1907
A Proposal from Paris

The recipient may well have been Arnold Schoenberg, though of course the latter's tone poem on the subject proposed was composed in 1905.

Herr Privatdozent, it is not my way
        to intervene
   in matters of this nature:
our livelihood
is, after all, our very life—I know.
        Yet so truly
   inviting is the venture
I would have you
embark upon that I must run the risk . . .
        As a German
   musician, hear my offer,
my *overture*,
which it must indeed be called. Yes, but first
        let me tell you
   how it has all come about.
I am writing
from our bedroom—*Jugendstil*, pink satin—
        overlooking
   Place Vendôme, where all the new
leaves cannot yet
keep the Column out there from suggesting
        what a column,
   my wife reminds me, always
suggests. Aside
from such obscenities, we are left quite
        undisturbed here,
   and for a French impresario
I must admit

Astruc has been generous, though perhaps
                imagining
        us both more susceptible
to coronets
than to *Kröner*, if you take my meaning.
                After last night's
        performance of *Salome*
(the last of five
by which I introduced my Prinzessin
                to her public
        here), I was to have the bulk
of my fee, but
found instead the *loge d'artistes* filled with
                loud duchesses.
        There was the usual furor,
and it may be
that in the confusion I let myself
                become somewhat
        overwrought. In any case,
when the trollope
who is Astruc's mistress and doubles for
                Emmy Destinn
        during the Dance requested
a solo bow,
I reminded her (and the company)
                that dancing was,
        really, an inferior art,
requiring no
special notice from a public applauding
                Frau Destinn and—
        yes, I said as much—myself.
"If anything,"
the harlot answered, "is inferior"
                —these are her words—
        "it is the masquerading
of a self-styled
genius who comes on stage every night,
                making his bows
        to a house that does not ask

him to appear."
At which my Pauline (you know how forthright
        she is at times)
    went up and administered
two ringing slaps
that brought the blood to Trouhanova's cheeks.
            "We have not yet
    sunk so low," she smiled, taking
my arm, "that we
need be insulted by the Seraglio."
            We left the house,
    and need I say, the francs were
waiting for us
by the time we reached the Ritz.—You will think
            I am forgetting,
    dear friend, but I bear in mind,
through all the din
and distractions of Paris, my purpose,
                which is to win
    you over to an idea,
or an *ideal*,
so tempting that were it not for the last
            of *Elektra*—
    her dance of triumph and death—
I am not sure
I should even afford you this Great Chance.
            The next evening,
    you see, after *my* series,
Romain Rolland
(a pacifist!) and some handsome jockey
            of a fellow
    named Ravel invited me
to the so-called
masterpiece of the new French school, revived
            at the Comique:
    Pelléas et Mélisande.
Nikisch, also,
was in the house, and how I look forward
            to *his* account

of the deplorable fraud . . .
After three scenes
I leaned over, pulled Ravel's sleeve; the man
                    (to call him that)
        is a kind of Narcissist
who reduces
all his needs to a few physical charms,
                    and even there
        in the dim *baignoire* I think
I could make out
that he was rouged and powdered, and I *know*
                    he was perfumed.
        Overcoming my distaste,
I questioned him:
"Is it like this throughout?" "Yes." "Nothing more?"
                    "Nothing." (proudly!)
        "Then," I permitted myself
to inform him,
"there's nothing in it—no development,
                    no melody,
        no consecutive phrases . . ."
"There *are* phrases,"
he had the effrontery to tell me,
                    "only hidden."
        At this, my French quite failed me:
"First and foremost,
I am a musician," I replied, "and
                    I hear nothing.
        Of course it is very . . . (here
I had to fall
back on our own) . . . *gekunstet*, but never
                    spontaneous,
        there is no . . . no *Schwung* in it
(I defy you,
Herr Privatdozent, to find a French word
                    proper for *Schwung*)
        —one might as well be hearing
only the words,
the prose of Maeterlinck."—And that, dear friend,

is why I write . . .
Knowing your gifts as I do,
I conjure you
to take this very subject, *Pelléas*
und Mélisande:
precisely in those places
where Debussy's
mood-murmurs misfire—the lovers' farewell,
then the murder—
there you will write one Big Scene
after the next.
I promise you there's music in the piece
after your own
passion for nobility,
for heroic
renunciation—the thing lies ready
to your hand, just
as it jostles mine, although
von Hofmannsthal
is waiting, and I dare not . . . You may guess,
the houselights up,
how Ravel melted away
like a pale wisp
of patchouli, and Rolland took me round
to Debussy.
What was it I expected?
One of Khnopff's heads,
or a Klimt: some Celt with periwinkles
of the abyss
in his eyes—here was a gnome
in a sack suit,
carved out of one thick black radish. They say
his wife's money
is what he lives on—like Wagner,
in blue velvet.
And how *could* this Dekadent tell the tale—
I remind you,
only to torment myself:
the lovers meet,

every shadow, every sound a terror
               when they embrace,
      and that is when she sees him:
"Golaud, Golaud—
where our shadows end!" but will not escape.
               Love is the death
      they share—does it remind you?
And Pelléas
takes her lips again, again, the stars fall . . .
               and Golaud falls
      upon the lovers, cuts down
Pelléas, then
crashes through the forest pursuing her . . .
               Let it be yours,
      my dear Herr Privatdozent,
since it may not
be mine—but never Monsieur Debussy's,
               promise me that!
      Pauline joins me in sending,
now as always,
our devoted regards. *Yours,*
      RICHARD STRAUSS

1915
A Pre-Raphaelite Ending, London

for Sanford Friedman

The speaker is Mrs. William Morris, addressing her daughter May, a spinster in her late forties.

Save it all; you do not know
the value things will come to have until
the world grows dim around you, and your things
—however doubtful in the changing light,
                    things are what you have
                    left. And all you have.
    Once the Zeppelins are gone
—and I shall be gone too, then, surely gone
out of this chair, this bed, this *furniture*,
there will be time enough to throw away
                    whatever is left.
                    Keep the papers here
    in these boxes where I have
kept them so long to myself—for myself,
till the Zeppelins . . . I am not certain
(how could I be, kept here out of harm's way?)
                    what Zeppelins *are*.
                    You would not expect
    the daughter of an Oxford
livery-stable keeper to know it . . .
Your father was not fond of animals.
He said once he might get to like a horse,
                    if he had the time.
                    Take care with the ones
    on top, they are photographs.
Read out what is scrawled there: "Dearest Janey,
Dodgson will be here tomorrow at noon,
do come as early as you can manage."

They have no backing
and break like dead leaves.
Often Gabriel painted
from these when he could not see me. He said
Mr. Dodgson knew what to leave out. Give
that one to me. No, it does not matter.
I want to hear you
say the words aloud.
"Absence can never make me
so far from you again as your presence did
for years. Yet no one seems alive now—
the places empty of you are empty
of all life." Of course
William knew of it,
but trusted. He had a deep
understanding of one side of life, and
invented the other. Remember how
he loved to list the things he owned,
grade and tabulate . . .
Why, he could not sit
in this room without an arm
about my waist—when others were by. Then
one time he burst out in a rage: "Is it
nothing but make-believe, am I no more
than Louis XVI
tinkering with locks?"
You know what his rages were—
I saw him drive his head against that wall,
making a dent in the plaster. "With locks,"
he said, "tinkering with locks, and too late . . ."
With locks, did he say,
or clocks? Clocks, I think.
How can a woman resolve
her marriage, save by lies? I have not learned
from others. I speak of my own life. She
stays at home, the man goes forth. A husband's
absence, a daughter's
envy, a lover's
suspicion—that is her lot.

What survives is the resistance we bring
to life, the courage of our features, not
the strain life brings to us. Each doctor says
                    a different thing
                    when I awaken
    gasping in the night. How well
one has to be, to be ill! *Tragic health*,
Mr. Ruskin called it. That is his hand,
I recognize the stroke. He gave me this
                    during a long walk
                    after Gabriel
    was cold in his grave, at last.
No one may see them till after my death,
and you must wait for that. William waited,
but I have not died. He came to Kelmscott
                    —the meadows flooded
                    that year, and the noise
    of water filled the air. "Jane,
I wegwet," he said—he could not pronounce
his r's, odd in a man named Ruskin. Then
a tortoise-shell butterfly settled on
                    my shoulder, but he
                    refused to notice.
    "I cannot admire any
lower in the scale than a fish," he said,
"I have the best disposition toward slugs
and gnats, but why they exist I do not
                    understand." He stopped,
                    though, to pick some cress
    growing by the path—and what
he regretted was that he could not bear
to destroy Gabriel's drawings he gave me
on the condition that I never look
                    at them in my life.
                    They must be naked
    drawings of me, beautiful
indeed if Mr. Ruskin could not burn
what he bought to keep the world and William
from seeing. There are his words on the seal:

"I should as soon try
finding fault with him
as with a nightshade-blossom
or a thundercloud. Of him and of these
all I can say is that God made him, and
they are greatly made. To me they may be
dreadful or deadly.
There is certainly
something wrong with him—awful
in proportion to the power it affects
and renders at present useless. So it was
with Turner, so with Byron." With this came
a great quantity
of ivory-dust
to be made into a jelly,
which it seems is an excellent physic
for invalids. Not even William failed
to guess the shame beneath the show
he had the habit,
months and years after,
of taking up the packet
and regarding its black seal with the eye
of an enemy. I was like Mariana
in the moated grange, listening too often
to the mouse shrieking
in the wainscot. "I
can't paint you but I love you—"
he said that when I sat to them, at Oxford.
He first saw me there, and his destiny
was defined . . . Gabriel called him a name:
Tops, the poetic
upholstery-man.
Their mothers all outlived them—
Gabriel, William *and* Mr. Ruskin.
It was an abyss then, an imbroglio
then and after. The reciprocal
life of "well persons"
grew impossible.
Moments come when the pattern

is laid before us, plain. And then we know
the limitations, accidentally
repeated, are the stuff of life. They will
                    return again, for
                    they are just . . . ourselves.
    Then we know that this and none
other will be our life. And so begins
a long decay—we die from day to dream,
and common speech we answer with a scream.
                    Put those things aside.
                    Here are the letters
    from Iceland, times were mended
for us both, by then. William was away
from the loud group of yellowing rowdies
who called themselves "communists"—and from me.
                    And he wrote, always,
                    lovely letters—if
    you did not have to hear him
say the words, as though he were breaking off
bones, throwing them aside—it was, through him,
an ancient voice speaking, or a voice from
                    a previous life
                    jerking the words out
    of a body which it had
nothing to do with. Take one from the lot,
they are all the same, though like no one else:
freeing ourselves we forge our own chains.
                    "I lie often out
                    on the cliffs, lazy
    themselves, all grown with gold broom,
not athletic as at Dover, not gaunt
as at Shields, and through the mist of summer
sea and sky are one, while just underfoot
                    the boats, together
                    stand immovable—
    as if their shadows clogged them.
So one may lie and symbolize until
one falls asleep, and that be a symbol
as well." Take the last one. I remember

the last words the best.
"As for living, dear,
people like those you speak of
don't know what life means or death either, save
for one or two moments when something breaks
the crust, and they act for the time as if
they were sensitive."
William's mind was set
on things more significant
than human lives, individual lives . . .
During the last illness, Dolmetsch came here
to play Byrd to him on the virginals.
He broke into tears
—of joy, only joy,
at the opening phrases
of a pavane. Then he saw white bodies
moving, crowned and bound with gold. That faded.
I went for the post, and when I returned
he stifled the blood
streaming from his mouth
and held fast to my gown, one
of his designs I had worn all those days.
"The clothes are well enough," were his last words,
"but where has the body gone?" Is there more
besides, in the box?
I thought not. Will you
do as I say, save it all—
the rest of the things are mere images,
not medieval—only middle-aged:
lifelike but lifeless, wonderful but dead.
These are mine. Save them.
I have nothing save them.

FINDINGS

Beyond Words

Song is miraculous because it masters what is otherwise a pure instrument of self-seeking, the human voice.   —Hugo von Hofmannsthal

He was a man whom words obeyed.   —Richard Strauss

His last month was July, the Summerland
    he called it, when one son
(the older boy) had taken poison: then,
    quite suddenly, he died too.

    Look—through the crooked window
he could never open, between branches
    of an old sour-cherry tree
bright with fruit—orderly there on the desk,

letters from his old ally and foe,
    paperweighted in packets
by two Offenbach scores: *La Belle Hélène*
    beside *Orpheus in Hell.*

    "You know this inmost aim, this
arrogance of my nature," he confessed,
    "to produce out of myself
a whole theater, a repertory:

not works, but rather a literature."
    In a real sense the man died
of responsibility, the sustained
    pressure of remembering

    what had long been dismembered—
Europe, the wide land. Deep secrets hide
    in surfaces, he knew, where else
could they go? and the spells we desecrate

run from mouth to mouth, unguessed, exhausted.
    He fell, then, the Conjurer,

and all the puppets with him into whose
    sawdust he poured so much blood.

    Speechless they lay where he lay,
corpses who once had proved that what lovers
    or friends mean to each other
is made clear by exchanging magic rings,

the presentation of a silver rose . . .
    All gestures were ruined now:
the Madman's knee in Zerbinetta's eye,
    Sophie with the awful nurse

    hanging on her, Mandryka
sprawling, broken, obscene really, like them
    all at this remove—merely
the others of *him*. That much of dying

could be rehearsed: for we are not ourselves
    until we know how little
of our selves is truly our own. He knew,
    now, how little and how much,

    the Magician who leaped from
the father's into the son's body and
    back, changing like clothes The Forms.
You can see the papers still, by this light,

though not the thread of script: it is too dark.
    Branches move at the window
and bitter cherries like dead tanagers
    brighten the grass where they lie,

    shed the night before—droppings.
They sweeten, rot and dry. In an early
    poem he said, "and yet, to say
'evening' is to say much." It is evening.

From Tarragona

Dear Señor Parrilla (now I know,
    after an instructive shock
at the Alhambra-Palace, whose bar
    furbishes the neon fact
in lavender Moorish uncials:
    your name means grill-room! a fair
description, I should guess, of our times
    together, those thrice-weekly
sessions which closed upon a prospect
    of the alternative forms
taken by the imperfect subjunctive),
    Dear Arturo Grillroom, then,
a word—though merely indicative—
    for your efforts: *gramercy*,
that is my word, an archaic thanks
    to suit the sheer helplessness
of *any* language here, any term
    to match the time. Whatever
Spanish you managed to teach me stales
    as I sit here on the beach
before the town, watching it pour down
    the hill, motionless and still
perpetual. Even the oldest
    phrases of gratitude wilt
in this terrible light, this glower
    of centuries—hence my silence:
I speak to hold my tongue and my peace
    (it is the aporia
of the living muzzled by the dead)
    in the face of so much war
remembered or at least remodelled:
    La Cruz de los Caídos

elbowed aside by Roger de Lauria,
    Alphonso the Bellicose,
Jaime el Conquistador, even
    Saint Paul (who converted it
to Christ when upwards of a million
    souls could be saved in the town) —
statues rough with salt, green and ideal
    above me on the *Balcón
del Mediterráneo*. Above
    them, Catalan ruins prop
the Carlos Quinto donjon, and at noon,
    which is now, the *Copona*,
Archbishop Coponan's famous bell
    cast from melted Roman coins,
strikes in the cathedral (Romanesque,
    Gothic, then Lanceolate,
Flamboyant, Plateresque, finally
    Churrigueresque) built on the site
of a Mosque where the Temple of Jove
    once stood. Augustus lived here,
I see his scepter's shadow falling
    over the Judería
renowned for doctors and bookbinders
    (some sixteen thousand volumes
crowd the Casa Consistorial,
    all in four dark rooms upstairs).
What words, teacher, for the Pelasgic
    Enclosure, Cyclopean
walls beneath the Scipian fortress?
    I write to tell you there is
nothing to say, and no news from here.
    The sea washes up to my
American feet as I stare down
    the beach to the menhirs left
by the Long Men of Medol Quarry:
    Behind me, in the Museo
Diocesano, are rusty hooks
    now rotted from their wooden
handles—their owners had no houses,

but lived in the cliff fissures.
Like me they had no . . . words? left nothing
    for history but middens
which contained red pottery, antlers
    used as picks, ox-blade shovels,
a few bushels of shells, the bones of
    wild boar and goat, of roe-deer,
fox and badger; of three kinds of birds
    and seven kinds of fishes.

Giovanni Da Fiesole on the Sublime, or Fra Angelico's *Last Judgment*

for Adrienne Rich

How to behold what cannot be held?
Start from the center and from all that
lies or flies or merely rises left
of center. You may have noticed how
Hell, in these affairs, is on the right
invariably (though for an inside Judge,
of course, that would be the left. And we
are not inside.). I have no doctrine
intricate enough for Hell, which I leave
in its own right, where it will be left.

Right down the center, then, in two rows,
run nineteen black holes, their square lids off;
also one sarcophagus, up front.
Out of these has come the world; out of
that coffin, I guess, the Judge above
the world. Nor is my doctrine liable
to smooth itself out for the blue ease
of Heaven outlining one low hill
against the sky at the graveyard's end
like a woman's body—a hill like Eve.

Some of us stand, still, at the margin
of this cemetery, marvelling
that no more than a mortared pavement can
separate us from the Other Side
which numbers as many nuns and priests
(even Popes and Empresses!) as ours.
The rest, though, stirring to a music
that our startled blood remembers now,
embrace each other or the Angels
of this green place: the dancing begins.

We dance in a circle of bushes,
red and yellow roses, round a pool
of green water. There is one lily,
gold as a lantern in the dark grass,
and all the trees accompany us
with gestures of fruition. We stop!
The ring of bodies opens where a last
Angel, in scarlet, hands us on. Now
we go, we are leaving this garden
of colors and gowns. We walk into

a light falling upon us, falling
out of the great rose gate upon us,
light so thick we cannot trust our eyes
to walk into it so. We lift up
our hands then and walk into the light.
How to behold what cannot be held?
Make believe you hold it, no longer
lighting but light, and walk into that
gold success. The world must be its own
witness, we judge ourselves, raise your hands.

From Beyoglu

Dear Anne, counting here and now I can discover
    ten boats, no—a dozen boats.
  In this light or lack of it, in this
unlikely emptiness of air that lets me look
    miles up the Bosporus, miles
    down the Marmara to Kadiköy,
miles across the Horn to Usküdar, some dozen
    boats—lighted, each one, if not
    by light revealed—are set like moving
jewels in the water, shiftless, still; or perhaps
    it is the sky they're set in,
    plying up where further jewels fly
from Yesilköy to Ankara and all points East;
    the last few minutes lost me
    the horizon—there is no telling.

Before, when there was—say an hour ago, at least—
    a door in the minaret
    level with our balcony opened
and out stepped a man in shirtsleeves cupping both hands
    round his mouth. Whereat the air
    rang with calls to prayer, who could believe
how loud? There are little rings of light bulbs now
    just where that muezzin vanished
    once he'd bawled the sunset out of sight,
and all the world that is not Turkish—Turquoise!—turns
    ultramarine. Every light
    is a jewel, like the twelve boats—
even this balcony (to them) another gem,
    jewels the kind you love, Anne,
    the kind we saw in the Seraglio:

Amber drops labelled Tears of the latest Phoenix;
  Draconites engendered
 in the colorless brain of serpents;
an Amethyst whose liquor, at night, thickens to
  Sapphires which will melt the wax
 they're sealed with, even by moonlight;
cloudy Emeralds glistening in a glass as though
  slaves had licked them into shape:
 stones, jewels, lights! only farther off,
these, mocking sea, sky and the now invisible
  promontories. Atmosphere,
 in Istanbul, mimics History—
changing the sky, chaining the sea, leaching out all
  local color from the land,
 leaving dust and ash: the moon at noon.

This afternoon, our third, was a disaster here.
  Anne my dear, everything
 here is a disaster: closed, under
restoration, bricked up, broken, sadly lacking,
  reconstructed, brought down, now
 in disuse, utterly gutted, quite
ruined, badly weathered, reinforced, past repair,
  toppled, razed, formerly vast,
 slashed, scarred, contaminated, stripped,
stolen, sacked, defaced, vandalized, once resplendent,
  damaged by earthquake, lost, burnt,
 interrupted by the Sultan's death,
unexcavated, filled in, whereabouts unknown—
  we returned, without a word,
 to the hotel, twilight and the view.

But at night these ashes glow, this dust kindles; like
  the Sultan's topaz, sallow
 then suddenly red, the moon turns Greek
fire, catches. While I watch I *hear* the past appear:
  the moment the moon rises
 or the city, on its pyre, sinks back

to Constantinople, then to Byzantium,
    S in the room behind me
  switches on the radio, full blast,
and a music fierce as the muezzin's fills the air—
    Finlandia. Dearest Anne,
  do you remember the year we were
Vikings? Monday after Monday, Miss Petersen
    started off with *The Silver*
  Songbook, Sibelius, "O land of lakes

and azure streams a-flowing." Sure, von Karajan
    conveys it better, the true
  Viking from Vienna. But the truth?
The trouble is I can't tell, Anne, can't tell the truth
    from travesty: children
  shrilling Sibelius in a ring,
supposing the black Finns to be their blond Vikings—
    we were those children, we sang,
  we suffered, we were there. Where were we?
Wasn't it real, is only *this* real: the complacent
    "stirring" orchestration here
  and now, and the moon, and Istanbul?
Are all those mornings' silver singing gone, when you
    and I were Great Lakes Vikings?
  They come upon me, and I am theirs.

Such music summons me to my own devotions,
    imperative as any
  howls from the minaret. How to find
a place for the past once it turns on you, and how
    to believe the present play
  of lights and placid sea? My dozen boats
have left the harbor basin black, till one ferry
    edges out from Galata,
  from the bridge they break in two at midnight,
and as it trusts itself to darkness, my answer comes—
    nor is it, you would prompt me
  from the songbook, as if we ever

lacked masters in displacement: Vladimir, Marcel!
  There is another world—in
  this one; the past is in the present

or nowhere. Mostly that, I find, in Istanbul:
  a nowhere city faint
  beyond finding, a site for Baudelaire,
"hospital whorehouse prison purgatory hell"—
  until the moon turns it on
  with a sound like Sibelius, grace
beyond argument or need granting the vision.
  Unsounded, true Istanbul
  contains itself in glory, all trash.
"The year we were Vikings" is here with the Blue Mosque,
  a dim splendor depending
  on a light, a sound, a memory
given, not gained. *Nothing is left, but nothing leaves*:
  that is the Holy Wisdom
  masquerading in Turkish Delight.

Even *Finlandia* comes to an end, but with it
  comes a kind of solace, Anne,
  a final comfort: the Finns are Turks!
Mongol types who share a language—Ural-Altaic—
  "characterized by vowel
  harmony, agglutinative forms
and uniformity." Which sounds like poetry,
  even like a poem, no?
  once we know Sibelius was born
in Turku, Finland. S turns out the light, our room
  ceases to be a jewel;
  the ferry from Galata misses
Seraglio Point. It is dinner-time. Love, Anne dear,
  from the European Side,
  from Beyoglu, where I am.
  RICHARD

TWO-PART
INVENTIONS

After the Facts

JOHANN CHRISTIAN FRIEDRICH HÖLDERLIN, 1770–1843

I
Villandry, "Les Douves" par Azay-le-Rideau,
December 28, 1822
My dear M. Prüfe, do you not recall,
            in reply to yours,
a letter from the late Louis Destourd,
Mayor of Villandry, Deputy from Blois?
I myself recall it, though I never saw
            the text at the time,
for it has become the sad (though inspiring)
duty of his only daughter to dispose
of the lamented M. Destourd's effects,
            among which I find,
with some emotion, your inquiry preserved.
To that, as to any solicitation,
his answers were doubtless satisfactory,
            as far as they go,
yet my father left no orders that the case,
by the mere occasion of *his* rejoinder,
must be judged—say, by his daughter—to be *closed*.
            Therefore I resume—
though responsibility, even were he
alive, would no longer be Papa's *alone*,
for since the period of your interest
            I have myself turned
wife and mother, thrice over: need I remark,
it is my *maternity* which has tripled!
I remain married, with a felicity
            to which I believe
that of my sons attests, to the *same husband*,

95

Henri Fourières, a fervent patron of the arts,
indeed a perfect virtuoso upon
        the *arpeggione*,
and it is consonant with his character,
as with his accomplishments, that he spurs me
to speak of the events of long years ago
        (before our marriage),
regarding which you wrote so purposefully
to poor Papa. It has occurred to *me*, as well,
that my narrative, my impressions, my words
        may be of some use
in restoring to his proper genius
a poet, as you intimated, forlorn
in the prime of his prophetic mission.
        Mad or even masked
as "Scardanelli" (the one clue you afford),
I would succor a man who discards his own
identity   let me describe to you more
        circumstantially
than Papa ever could or *would* (my father
was the son, necessarily, of another age—
an age perhaps of clearer vision, clearly
        one of drier eyes),
more *flagrantly*, as Papa would have phrased it,
the Episode I figured in to such effect.
Discover to your mysterious "patient"
        my recollections,
for one memory makes us all remember,
and I am certain what so amazed me, then,
is with him, now, wherever his mind may be.
        I have plagued *my* wits
to "place" the man—between your Schiller and your
Schlegel, though surely neither: too young, too fair,
yet the eminence you intimate was there.
        Will you not name him?
It had been one of those autumn afternoons,
ageless, unswept, apparently infinite—
weather which to reminiscence seems a rule
        of life in those days.

At first I scarcely glanced up from the volume
(the Cérieux edition, I have it still,
of Sénancour's romance, or is it nonsense
        so to qualify
a work of such laborious melancholy?) . . .
As I say, I was not inclined to leave off
reading to Papa, for I supposed the sound
        no more than the cry
of our peacocks, more strident at that season,
in fine weather. How like my father it was,
to cultivate the white variety alone
        and fondly insist
the creatures supplied by harshness of accent
what they lacked in luster! Granting it was so,
the present intonation was too gentle,
        too *lamentable*
to be the clamor of our particular birds,
and I suspect a sort of curiosity
conquered my reluctance to lay by the tale
        of poor *Obermann*.
So I stood up (in white muslin, sprigged, white silk
ribbons on my straw bonnet, white string gloves, too
—white was my color then, all in white, and one
        crimson cabbage-rose),
took Papa's arm, and with him passed down the steps
of our terrace to the great basin below,
advancing with some concern, as I have said,
        but no real alarm.
There, uttering at intervals the eerie
ululation I have just alluded to,
then falling silent, though the fountain guttered
        a grief of its own,
there, beyond the basin, stood, or stooped, or knelt
—I cannot through the curtain of forced water,
as through the fabric of Time itself, be sure
        of the man's posture—
a sad and shabby Stranger who showed, when we
circled the margin and ventured to approach,
by the misery of his apparel as by

the mist in his eyes,
that he was none of our neighbors, nor indeed
an inhabitant of our nation. With no
surprise, no deference, no vestige even
            of obsequity
in his demeanor, the Wanderer addressed
himself to my father, though his gaze was fixed
on me, as if I were some white misgiving
            in his darkened mind.
I shall never, I know, forget what he said—
though I must break off, my dear M. Prüfe,
before I have fairly begun, in order
            to bring you the scene
in all its *enchantment* (the one word to choose):
our basin was quite embowered by a whole
people of Grecian gods, marbles we had bought
            from "the Canova
of Blois," Théophile Clore. In pale attitudes
of power they ringed the pool, figures white
against the dingy water where the Stranger
            knelt (I see that, now—
had I dropped my rose?) ensorcelled as we came
upon him—it was like a play! knelt before
the statue of Pomona, I think, gasping:
            "It is Aglaia!
But the water should be brighter, like the Spring
of Erechtheus. It is unworthy of the gods
to see their images in a dark mirror.
            But we are not"—this
with a terrible sigh—"we are not in Greece."
"Are you then a Greek?" asked Papa, gesturing,
"and are these your gods?" "These? Neither mine nor yours.
            We have come too late
for them. It is the world which is divine now,
and that is why there is no God. The divine
has no name, only the gods are named, like these,
            and they change their names."
My father was a man of principle, not
a man of faith, and would have pursued the point

(it is no common thing, to hold such discourse
         with a Wanderer
in one's park), yet even as he made to speak,
the ragged man rushed on: "To be what we are—
that is to be divine. But the gods are dead,
         the world is alone
and knowledge—knowledge . . ."—here he fixed upon me
eyes that seemed to draw my own into a pool
of dim oblivion—"knowledge is only
         knowledge of our death."
By these words it was apparent, to Papa,
the speaker was a German; he asked his name.
Thereupon the man fell again to his knees,
         his face in his hands
(which I had occasion then to remark: thin,
pale for all the dirt and curving at the tips
as if they would scoop the darkness hovering
         round the blue pupils)
and promised to tell us . . . the next day! "It is
difficult for me, remembering my name.
To escape a city is one thing, to choose
         a road, another."
These were his last words, for with them, as if
summoned *by* them, one of our peacocks appeared,
crest trembling like a lyre, coral claws oddly
         raw upon the moss,
and with the hollow clash of an opening
parasol, spread his perfect fan before me,
white quills quivering, each one an inducement
         to admiration.
Faced with this . . . rival, the Stranger turned away,
and I never saw him again. Nor have I
forgotten what I *heard*: that night I wakened
         to a horrid scream,
never explained, from the servants' hall, a scream
like the peacocks' (though they do not cry at night).
Papa, next day, said the lunatic had fled,
         but in my own mind
I cannot yet reconcile that Wanderer

saying, "the gods are dead, the world is alone,"
with the howling of the night, if that was he.
       "He"—I mean the one
you desired my father to identify,
though with no more designation who he was
than the calling of Poet. *Will you not name him?*
       Nor have I yet solved
the riddle of his departure, the gaze
he gave me (that I gave him back)—then nothing
but a shriek at midnight, and the man was gone.
       Almost, I incline
to call it jealousy of a white peacock
paying court to a white girl. What is the use
of trying to fit the two visions together?
       All of us have been
children though we may not know what we knew then,
nor have at the same hour the wisdom of those
who are at the end of their days. M. Prüfe,
       perhaps my father's
emphasis upon that night's disorder has
prevailed over what was said the day before,
in the circle of the gods, and in sunlight,
       as the white peacock
pronounced *his* judgment, and the Stranger spoke
of our immortality, or of what is not
immortal, merely fate. If I have redressed
       the balance, do I
earn thereby an answer to your Enigma?
Never, as you may discern, have I broken
faith with my bright recollection, for all
       the days dividing
me from that strange encounter. Thus I remain,
with passionate hope for the recovery
of a mind so *memorable* I believe
       it cannot forget
what it wrought as well upon your importunate
correspondent, MARIANNE FOURIÈRES, *née*
DESTOURD. May I depend on the indulgence
       of a prompt reply?

II

Tübingen, the New Year. My dear Madame,
you have gone to some trouble, and you have
(in the circumstances) my gratitude
for your letter. I fear it comes too late.
Evidently you paid your visitor
the extravagant compliment which no
ordinary woman ever pays a man—
that of listening to him while he talks.
I cannot say the person you describe
(when you give him a moment from your own
preoccupations and predilections)
is the patient in my care. Certainly
he differs altogether from the fool
represented in your father's account.
That is immaterial. Such glimpses
as you afford when it is not yourself,
your father or your finery you bring
before us—on stage, one might almost say—
fail to supply the means whereby I might
awaken in the man who answers to
"Scardanelli" those associations
which would bring home to himself a poet
absent so long in mind if not in flesh.
Men are like trees: last to go is the bark,
and it is indeed the rind of a man
living with us so long in Tübingen,
heedless of every bodily function,
refusing to have his fingernails cut
and speaking—when he speaks—in Italian,
a language he has by no means mastered.
His social existence is more like that
of an early Christian than of a man
of the Nineteenth Century, and if much
must be excused him, there is much to be
excused. As you appear to realize,
it was my hope, in writing to your father,
that when faced with what had been his words
—spoken while he was yet the Laureate

of our earth, our sun, our moon—the poet
might recover what had been his alone:
acceptance, after all, is that final
act which enables us to see clearly.
Alas, earth is no more than an old sun,
and the moon a dead earth. Many a time
I have shown to Signor Scardanelli
(as he must be called) manuscripts of his,
written at twenty. At twenty, Madame,
the Poet is always right. At sixty,
the Doctor is never wrong, and to these
confrontations his response is one blaze
of invariable babble, the rough
scratching of filthy talons on the page,
and then the poor creature begins to sing . . .
It was long my notion that what appears
nonsense in these "performances" of his
would recover itself into poetry
and more, but it is all monstrous, grotesque,
gross and degrading. You write, let us say,
from the brink of prurience, of prying
at best, nor can you have a conception,
when you speak of his pale hands, his blue eyes,
even of his responses to questions!
what it means to minister to this man.
If he could ever regain acquaintance
with what he had spoken upon the edge
of darkness, from whose fall our dimensions
rise, then indeed might some resumption come.
The Cup, the Poem, the Light are all drunk
in darkness—how else could they be taken?
But we are beyond the edge, the margin
where you and your father met a Stranger
who may or may not have been my patient.
I read him out those portions of your tale
in which his own grievous utterances
were given. Nothing availed. With a burst
of derisive laughter, he who had once
been Master of our German Muse, who had

dedicated his odes to Schiller and
his versions of Sophocles to Hegel—
this man, my dear lady, closed his eyelids
(reddened now by nights of staring dullness)
and murmured but one phrase, so utterly
belied by his own condition (as by
his Italian comedy) that it dismays me
in the mere report: "la perfezione
è senza lamento." The rest dithered
away into incoherence. Perhaps
my little experiment did no harm—
surely it did no good. Nothing changes,
all is changed. I am obliged, nonetheless,
for your telling of an episode to which
you bring the talents of a telling pen,
indeed. Your narrative shall be added
to a memorial volume the Friends of
the Poet are compiling in witness
to his life among us. What the witless
Scardanelli makes of these matters
is no matter. You have had, dear Madame,
a privileged or a preposterous
meeting—the risk of your choice remains
with you. Though futile to its possible
subject—or object, as he must now be called—
its record is of consequence, and I am,
as I was to the late M. Destourd,
your debtor, faithfully,
      JOACHIM PRÜFE

Infirmities

No use having an executor, Horace Traubel,
    literary or the other kind
    unless I can show you what to execute.
Losing every damn thing all over again, Horace.
    I need you: this floor's become a *flood*—
    dive in! See if you can't come up with something:
letters—tied in green ribbon—from an "Abraham Stoker."
    Wrote to me from Dublin, years ago . . .
    Now he's coming to see me, or to let me
have a look at him. Either way, I must lay hands on
    those letters . . . I know they're here somewhere.
Mary Davis is no help at all. Once a week
she comes to clean house, that's what she calls it, forages
    through my mail as if it was haystacks—
    only thing she could find down there's a needle!
No, in *that* pile, Horace . . . Letters from the seventies:
    I recall the first one came as if
    for my birthday—fifty . . . long past now. Some things
you don't forget. Keep looking Horace: a young man's hand,
    twenty, he said . . . Middle-aged by now.
    (I thought so at forty, know better today.)
That's it! the green ribbon—green never fades. I chose it
    for Ireland. Just read out the top one,
    then you'll understand why I kept the others.

Put this letter in the fire, if you like,
but so you do, you'll miss the pleasure of
this next sentence, which ought to be that you
have defeated an unworthy impulse:
You are a true man, Walt, as I would be
myself, & therefore I would be to you

as an apprentice is to his master.
You have shaken off the shackles, therefore
your wings are free. I wear the shackles still
on my shoulders, tight—hence I have no wings.
I write to you today because you are
different from other men. If you were
the same as they, I would not dare to write.
As it is, I must either call you Walt
or not name you at all—I have chosen
the better course. I thank you for the love
& sympathy you've given in common
with my kind . . . I have read your poems, Walt,
aloud to myself with my door locked
late at night, & read them on the seashore
where I could look round me & see no more
sign of human life than ships out at sea,
& there I often found myself waking
from a dream with the book lying open
beside me . . .

". . . on the grass . . ." Stop, Horace. I remember what comes next,
        and I need to hear it, too. But first
what *you* need: this Stoker fellow's here! Coming
today to Mickle Street. Now when he rings, you let him
        in, Horace, then leave us two alone.
Stoker thought he was writing to me, of course,
but it was really to himself. I answered—warmly,
        I always do, to the personal.
I wrote with my whole heart. Now read me some more.

        . . . If I lie out on the grass,
those days come back to me with undying
freshness. I look among the stalks or blades
& wonder where the energy comes from—
that fond hum of Nature, never ceasing,
for ears that can hear. I guess at what is
below the brown uneven earth that seems
so level at a distance, so rugged

in reality. At such moments comes
the wisdom of those half-forgotten thoughts,
the rudiments of all philosophy . . .

That boy was my reader, no doubt about it. We need
        our readers, every one. Now we'll see
    what this man's done with that boy. Today's letter—
oh, I can manage to find a letter that comes today,
        Horace: today is easy to find;
    it's yesterday I tend to lose . . . Stoker writes
different from the way he used to. Guess we all do that.
        Sorry to have lost what was in his
    early messages. Lord, what I've lost in mine!
He sounds polite enough now, of course, but determined
        to settle the business of the day.
    Explains he's come over here with Sir Henry
Irving, Irving the actor—they knight them over there—
        manages the Lyceum theater
    for him in London, brings the whole troupe
here on tour. Says "Sir Henry" has contracted to play
        New York, Philadelphia, Washington . . .
    I played Washington, in a manner of speaking,
before Washington played me—played me out! . . . Stoker has
        his reasons for coming today, says
    he needs me—needs me *again* is what he says.
Maybe so. You let him in, Horace, send him up here
        to me, and if he don't come back down
    in half an hour, you collect him. Half an hour's
all I can stand of any man's "needing"—even mine!
        Now read some more young Stoker, till
    the old one gets here.

I know about the grass because for years
I could not walk, though no one ever put
defining names to the disease I had.
Certainly till I was about seven
I never knew what it was to stand upright.
But I was naturally thoughtful, &
the leisure of long illness gave the chance

for fruitful thoughts later on: healthy ones.
All my early recollections are of
being carried about in people's arms
& being set somewhere or other—
on a bed or sofa, if in the house,
or if the weather was fine, on a rug
outdoors, or even right out on the grass . . .

. . . There's the bell! Stop right there—
"on the grass," of course. I know the sound of my own bell:
      One thing I still recognize. All right,
    let that be your signal, Horace. Go downstairs,
let him in, send him up. We may have something to say
      to one another . . .
                  Welcome, Stoker—
welcome, Abraham! Let's greet one another
as old friends, as indeed we are . . .

Sir, I cherish your friendship, but the name
a friend must know me by is changed: it's Bram,
Bram Stoker I call myself, sign myself,
now that I endeavor to write . . . fiction.

                  I overlook the change
    of name—dislike it, actually.
Stoker was born Abraham, and he should be
Abraham still—has the breath of humanity in it,
      and Lincoln too. Can't "Abraham" write
fiction as well?

Surely you'll sanction the change, Sir: you too
must have known a like need for a new name.
Were you not called "Walter" before the Leaves?

      You show an old man his place . . .
Glad to be there. The years might have blurred that need. The man
    Stoker repeats, no—fulfills the boy!
You took a shine to me over in Ireland,
when you were at Trinity. I value your good will:

maybe you've remained of the same mind,
in substance, as at first . . . You see, I prepared
myself for your visit by reading those old letters
of yours. Appears from what you wrote me,
if I understand you rightly, that we share
infirmities. Most men do, of course. Sometimes I think
it's all they share. All they *can* share. But
our weaknesses, yours and mine, set in
at opposite ends of life: old age has withered me,
nowadays they put me out to grass
on a blanket, just as you lay there in your
own childhood. The grass is the same—for you in your first,
for me in my second, most likely.
Still and all, I get up, get dressed, get outside
most days. Live here lonesome enough, but in good spirits . . .
You find me . . . Well, how do you find me?

I'm honored, sir, by your welcome, and
happy you still recall the impetuous
and perhaps importunate outpourings
of a faltering youth to Walt Whitman
many years ago. That makes it easier
to come to you with my questions again.
I would not tax your strength for all the world,
and my own duties—surely I explained
that my obligations to Sir Henry
will not permit me to trouble you long
—there was, in fact, some difficulty
finding my way to Camden and to you—
but I'm gratified to be here at last.
How do I find you, sir? I find you just
as I hoped you would be: that wonderful
mane of white hair over your collar, that
munificent mustache over your mouth,
to mingle with the mass of flowing beard—
you know, you are rather like Tennyson.
You quite remind me of him as he was
at the Lyceum—you don't mind that, do you?

Mind! I like it! Why, I'm proud to be told so.
I like being tickled! Irish flattery is best—
        found that out when Mr. Wilde was here,
had all the sauce an old stomach could swallow.
Still, what a broth of a boy he was! Younger than you,
        I guess—you ever know him, back home?

I knew his mother, Lady Wilde. She kept
a sort of salon in Merrion Square—
in fact it was there I first met my wife,
one of those Saturday at-homes. Florence
—that's my wife—was a friend of Oscar's too . . .

Hah! You're married, and respectable,
and an author of "fiction" into the bargain . . . Not
        often such a man comes to me with
questions. Young Wilde asked some—a *salon*, you say?
That explains a lot. All about art they were, art with
        a big A. I spell it small, myself . . .
If you haven't much time, put your questions, son,
but let me get mine in first. What sort of fiction is it
        that you must "endeavor" to write?

Well, usually I dash things off, not
much more than typed-up drafts, to pay debts,
you know, or to earn some extra cash. But
lately I seem to have come once again
under your spell, sir: I too have a sort
of poem I must write—oh, it's in prose,
of course, but you understand that—and
there are characters to speak the lines, and
in a sense they revolve around one man
who rather resembles you, sir. He too
has long white hair and a heavy mustache,
powerful bearing, something . . . leonine.
He too longs to pass through the crowded streets
of mighty cities, to be in the rush
of humanity, to share life, change, death—

all that makes us what we are. Is this not
Walt Whitman's "call in the midst of the crowd"?

I don't know that it is. Tell me some more, "Bram,"
let me hear what you want to do with me . . . *Leonine?*

Yes, masterful. You know: the king of beasts.
I've written quite a lot about the man
modelled on you. In my narrative,
all others serve him, or come to do so . . .
I can even recite for you the way
Count Dracula (that is my hero's name)
is addressed by one of his followers
when the Count is introduced: "I am here
to do your bidding, Master, I am yours,
and you will reward me, for I shall be
faithful. I have worshipped you long and far.
Now that you are near, I await commands,
and you will not pass over me, will you,
dear Master, in your distribution of
all the good things that are within your gift? . . ."

I don't much like this talk of Masters
and Counts. What is it he's done, this Dracula,
that everyone is so eager to serve him? Does he serve
others in return?

It was you, sir, who gave me the clue, you
who spoke of adhesiveness, that union
beyond any binding together of bodies,
a universal solvent in the blood . . .
I found it in Leaves of Grass *long ago,*
and to what I found have tried to be true.
It was your own poem, your own words
which guided me, and which will guide me still.
Surely you will remember "Trickle Drops" . . . ?

Make it a rule
that if I wrote it, I don't remember it.

The *Leaves* is not a sacred book, but a growing thing.
            The text is in a state of constant
        transformation. To see what I've changed *from* what
to what, Horace keeps the old book here—you find the poem,
            Abraham, read it to me yourself,
        then maybe I can link my lines to your Count . . .

        The privilege of reading Whitman's words
        to Whitman's ears is beyond presumption . . .
        Here it is, in "Calamus," the teaching
        I have tried to make into a tale . . .

Oh, in "Calamus," is it? Then I don't wonder. That
            was what they wanted me to cut out.
        All the English critics urged me to it: "Your book,"
they said, "will go into every house in America.
            Surely that is worth the sacrifice?"
        It would not be any sacrifice. So far
as I care, they might cut a thousand. It is not that—
            it is quite another matter. When
        I wrote as I did, I thought I was doing
right, and right makes for good. I think that all God made is for
            good, that the work of His hands is clean
        in all ways, if used as He intended. No,
I shall never cut a line so long as I live. Read
            me the news from naughty "Calamus."

        "Trickle drops! my blue veins leaving!
        O drops of me! trickle, slow drops,
        Candid from me falling, drip, bleeding drops,
        From my face, from my forehead and lips,
        From my breast, from within where I was conceal'd,
            press forth, red drops, confession drops,
        Stain every page, stain every song I sing, every word
            I say, bloody drops,
        Let them know your scarlet heat, let them glisten,
        Saturate them with yourself all ashamed and wet,
        Glow upon all I have written or shall write, bleeding drops,
        Let it all be seen in your light, blushing drops."

Yes, that's right: we put that in ahead of
"City of Orgies." I mind that well—the same fool English
said it was "a pity not to cut
certain passages," and I knew just the ones:
"Trickle Drops," then the lines that come at the end of
"City of Orgies": ". . . These repay me,
lovers, continual lovers, only repay me."

Then you follow me, sir, as I do you . . .
to the point where the Count dismisses
the Vampire Women to claim the bleeding
youth for his own: "This man belongs to me."

"Vampire Women"? No such thing.
And is your Count a vampire too? Inspired
by Walt Whitman and a *bloodsucker*?

I want to make the voluptuousness
of death equal to the deathlike nature
of love. Like you, sir, I dare my readers
to acknowledge that the mystery of
sexual love is worth dying for . . .

. . . Not "like me," Stoker!
Only worth *living* for, that's *my* mystery,
if you can call it such. Take your Count back home with you,
let Sir Henry have him. I've heard of
his ways. Heard how they're going to settle
the Bacon-Shakespeare dispute . . . Going to dig up
Shakespeare and dig up Bacon, then let
Sir Henry recite *Hamlet* to them. And the one
who turns over in his grave will be the author! Heard
that one, have you, Abraham Stoker?

Frequently, sir. And many others too,
in all the years of my service. You see,
I am indentured to Henry Irving
in the same way I once tethered myself
to you. By doing so, perhaps in both

servitudes, I've learned that close relations
between two people, any two, always
afford vampiric exploitation. Sir,
I fear you find my expressions . . . misplaced:
no one, I now perceive, may pluck the heart
out of Walt Whitman's mystery, who lives
according to the Eleventh Commandment
of Modern Times . . .

As if ten weren't enough. I don't hold much with
commandments, Abraham. What in Hell's the eleventh?

"Thou Shalt Not Be Found Out"

That's one I'll obey . . . Abraham, here's
Horace, he'll take you to the Mickle street car:
you're sure to find your way with him . . . Goodbye, son,
there's no bad blood between us two now,
am I right? Please to give my best regards to
Mr. Wilde when you see him next . . . Another fine Irish
(whisper this) man of art. Endeavor
to write your own fiction, young fellow. Good luck
with it. Nothing to do with me . . .
Night, Horace. Leave a lamp.

The Lesson of the Master

for Sanford Friedman

. . . Edith Wharton was here, an angel of devastation in her wondrous, cushioned,
general car.   —Henry James

PARIS–VERSAILLES, 1912

No,
    not out the window.
There is a receptacle under the seat:
if the tray is full, please empty the ashes
    there, Mr. Roseman.

> *And if the receptacle is full,*
> *I suppose we could open the door.*
> *After all, Mrs. Wharton, they're not* his.

    Indeed they are not!
His I hold here, and shall not let them leave me:
they will not go until the urn itself
    turns to earth again.
Ping!
    don't snap at our guest,
he's only doing as I ask. Lie down, Pong,
lie down! Orderliness about *my* ashes
is an action, Mr. Roseman, not a passion,
    as you might suppose:
I have not replaced the carriage-and-pair
with a Delage merely to litter the road
    with my own leavings.
Need the Bois de Boulogne be ashen behind
my poor little cortège, as well as before?

> *Not until Ville d'Avray. Rain and mud*
> *it "needs" to be, in order to be*
> *reality, orderly or not.*
> *Once we get to Ville d'Avray, Corot*

has the last word—he is the last word
in ashes, don't you think, Mrs. Wharton?
All that gray and silver, all that blur!
Until then, of course, the ashes are
yours—so many, or so much (what does
one say in the case of ashes? much
or many? A writer ought to know . . .)

My cigarettes leave
many ashes. The ashes of a man are
much . . . too much to bear alone. Too much for me.
That is why I asked for company, Mr. Roseman:
    I need another
presence here, now, if I am to reach Versailles
in countenance to face the cemetery;
till then I do not want to be quite alone.
    I want you to help . . .

            . . . To help bear the ashes? They are yours
        as well. All that he left, the leavings . . .
        Provided I can fill a function,
        I am pleased to help you—emptying
        is a function like any other,
        except filling, of course. And I can
        empty as fast as you can fill—almost.
        How much you smoked that other time, or
        at least how many, snapping up one
        gold-tipped Egyptian after the next!
        Even then you would not wait to grow
        an ash before you ground out the glow.
        In fact, when I first met you, I thought . . .

Met me—you met me?

            . . . At Howard Overing's, in London.
        Isn't that why you asked me to come?

No, I asked Mr. James particularly
to suggest someone I had not met, someone

whom I did not know.
On such a journey—this is not the first time
I have escorted to a cemetery
    what are called remains,
though it will be the last, as long as I remain—
the last remainder, as Mr. Scribner says . . .
    Someone whom I know!
On such a journey one may say anything,
and prefers, of course, to say it to no one
    in particular.

> *I am no one in particular,*
> *Mrs. Wharton, you don't know me; I*
> *know you. I know you in general.*

    You know my novels,
you mean: you have read me? That is not the same . . .
One reads most writers to escape knowing them.

> *No, I mean I spent an afternoon—*
> *last year—with you in London. Of course*
> *you don't remember me distinctly,*
> *individually. How could you!*
> *I was one of the shadows, a mere*
> *hypothesis of furniture: the one*
> *Overing introduced as "a friend*
> *of Gerald's"—and we were all his friends,*
> *you, and Mr. James, and the rest of us,*
> *the shadows . . . Who could remember that?*

    I hope Gerald could . . .
Over the gate of Hell must be written HERE
EVERYTHING IS REMEMBERED. I am in
    no more than Limbo
since Gerald died. Forgive me, Mr. Roseman,
I do not mean to be rude, but since we did
meet, as you say, why on earth should Mr. James
suggest you be a party to my sad errand . . . ?

I haven't the faintest idea.
Perhaps because on earth an errand
means a mistake as well, Mrs. Wharton.
I don't pretend to know Mr. James's
reason — he has so many. Or so much?

Well, he *meets* so many. He meets more and more
people: reason enough to make more and more
mistakes — in order to be more and more alone,
I sometimes think. Gerald used to say he had
been spared only —

        — to be by-passed. Gerald was not spared.

    How did you know that —
how do you know what Gerald said of Mr. James?

        Mrs. Wharton, though you may not recall
        meeting me, I was presented to you
        as Gerald's friend. Men speak to their friends,
        and Gerald spoke to me. Even of you
        he would speak . . .

    He would speak of me?
To you? Gerald discussed me with his . . . his friends?

        As you know, he rarely
      let his good things go unrepeated.

    They bore repeating.

      Were you bored? I never was, Mrs. Wharton.

    Nor I, Mr. Roseman.
If you must, then, they are *worth* repeating, those
    "good things" of Gerald's.
As I suppose what he said of me to be
    worth repeating: now.

Surely. He called you "the self-made man"—
it became the phrase for you among
his friends. Don't you find it becoming?
"Edith Wharton is a self-made man . . ."

     Inevitably
the case, I'm sure you can see, when one starts life
as a woman. To men of my father's world,
     which was Gerald's world—
my great-grandfather married a Mackenzie—
to men of that world, who made it a bold choice
to have *books* in the room called the library,
     women were a toast,
or they were nothing: a woman never went
out if she expected men to come to her.
Authorship was regarded—though *regarded*
is scarcely the word—as something between
a black art and a form of manual labor:
     either enterprise,
for a lady, equally unsuitable.
That is why I owe so much—owe everything
to Gerald. He found me when my mind was starved,
and he fed me till our last hour together.

Yes, Gerald was a great feeder for
late hours. Spanish hours, you might call them,
they were that late. When we were in Spain,
he used to say . . . Well, you know what he said.
And it helped you—it fed you, fed your mind?
So you were not, entirely, self-made.

     Entirely selfish,
you mean? Perhaps—perhaps not. I never had
your opportunities in Spain to find out.
We saw each other here, Rue de Varenne,
     and when the end came
I promised him the grave in Versailles. With mine,
     when it is my time.

*I have never seen the American
graveyard in Versailles, but I suppose
the associations would please him:
how far-sighted you've been, Mrs. Wharton.*

One sees beyond the senses. I hesitate
to imagine what the life of the spirit
        would have been to me
without Gerald Mackenzie. Had it not been
for him, I should have turned out to be
no more than another of those lectured-to
ladies who mean to have the best culture, quite
        as they mean to have
the best plumbing; they like to let culture run
over them as the hot water does, you know,
        without much effort.

> *And you made an effort. Much effort,
> in fact. Certainly you did not leave
> Mr. Wharton because he lectured you—
> you were a lady who turned out
> otherwise: you turned out many books.*

I turned into them, if you must have the phrase.
        They were an effort
my husband could not endure, even before
his illness—before we had to live apart.
No distractions: he was quite given over
to the New York of families and fortunes.
A trivial society gains significance
        from the life it gags.
Money-making in New York is so strenuous
that men and women never meet socially
        before dinner-hours.
If I was a failure in Boston because
I was thought too fashionable to be serious,
        in New York I failed
because I was feared to be too serious
        to be fashionable.

But you did not fail—you left. If that's
failing, then Gerald failed, and Mr. James,
and even I—then all of us failed!
And certainly Gerald never failed—
he pulled up his stakes for higher ones:
that was one of his "good things," wasn't it?
Something of the kind. If leaving is
failing, then which of us failed—to leave?

Not Teddy—Mr. Wharton. He was a success, there.
Too much of one ever to leave his New York,
though Gerald called him "Teddy Bore" for it—did he
    repeat that one too?
Wonderful to bores and children, Teddy was;
you really should have seen the man with children!
Now to me the Devil frequently appeared
in the shape of a child, but he could never
deceive me as to his true identity—
I was always aware of it, and eschewed
    all contact with him
under that disguise . . . Teddy could not endure
my disbelief in children. Nor could Gerald
endure Teddy. When I had to make a choice,
I chose my books and Gerald—I chose my books
    because of Gerald.
I chose to make something of myself: a divorce
is a great creator, as I was to learn.

"Marriage, divorce and death make barren
our lives." Swinburne—wrong, as usual:
you had all three from Teddy Wharton, and
lived to tell . . . many tales. You made up
a new kind of life for yourself, then?

    I was left alone
with time: I became what is called an author.
Not a poet, like Swinburne. Poets write something,
authors write about something. My dear young man,
whatever we manage to do is merely

a modification
of what we have failed to do. So when we fail,
it is only because we have given up.

> *But you have given up nothing! All*
> *you had is within reach, Mrs. Wharton—*
> *like Ping and Pong, like the ashtray there . . .*

. . . and the ashes here.

> *Exactly. You must have read my mind.*

I read what is legible. Little enough.
        Until now, you see,
Gerald was not within reach. To me he was
a man who could take nothing from another,
but gave, gave only, as he would give to me,
        and gave to the end.

> *What was it you wanted him to take?*

What I had: myself. By the time I had made
something to give him worth the taking: nothing.
        Freedom is nothing,
it was nothing to Gerald, only to me.
But if you have made something, you need someone
to offer it to—the freedom you have made
        by making up lives,
even if it is only your own you've made.
And you need to do something visible,
you need an act you can see as a result
        of the thing in you.

> . *Gerald—I told you he was my friend,*
> *Mrs. Wharton, I know this about him,*
> *just this much, but I think it is more*
> *than you have made out for yourself—he . . .*
> *Gerald was attached to anyone*
> *not for what they were, but for the things*

they prevented . . . It enabled him
to give, as you call it, to give in . . .

Prevented . . . You don't have your share of the robe!
    It always grows chill
in the car—February makes rides a choice
between icicles and asphyxiation.
    I feel it myself—
pull it over your knees. Ping, get off! Don't let
    the dogs bully you:
Gerald always said they bullied me. Only
because I let them. During the last decades
of the Empire—during the Decadence, in fact—
the Emperors had a craving for human
    curiosities;
whenever one was found, he, she or it was shipped
to Rome (for they mostly came from Egypt). Once
they found a boy who understood what birds said—
now I have always been like that about dogs,
    since I was a girl:
I am a devoted animal-lover
who dislikes all animals but dogs . . . Gerald
always says—said—Gerald always . . . That is true,
    he valued what kept
back the big things, and a pound of prevention
was a fortune to him. We knew the same man,
I see, if not each other. Wherever he was,
Gerald led a wife with a want at its heart . . .

                . . . What did you say, Mrs. Wharton? Gerald led . . .

. . . or perhaps a wound. A wanting life, or wounded;
I never guessed, he never gave me the chance
to know the difference. I waited, I worked:
where the mind burns, the moods loom, Mr. Roseman.
    I was a woman
becoming what I made, melting into print,
and those loose flames of mine fed a single fire . . .

At Gerald's altar? So you never
learned, so busy were you tending to
your . . . You never knew about Gerald.

What I knew about Gerald I never "learned,"
    dear Mr. Roseman,
do you mean to educate me further, now!
The only corpse of any real consequence
is the one ripening—the one preparing
    itself within us.
What is there left to learn about a dead man?

> *Well, you know so much else—so many*
> *other things. Sometimes other people*
> *are right, preposterous as it seems,*
> *Mrs. Wharton, and you can learn from them.*
> *As you can when they are wrong. I am*
> *at a loss—quite happy to be there,*
> *but that is where I am, at a loss*
> *to tell if you left Teddy Wharton*
> *for literature or for Gerald . . . ?*

And whom would you tell?
Literature and Gerald were one learning,
Mr. Roseman, one gift to me—one given, if you
    must be personal.

> *What could be more to the point than being*
> *personal when you are talking about*
> *a person? Both of us knew Gerald—*
> *I have my doubts if it was "the same man,"*
> *as you say. For instance, he taught you . . .*
> *Gerald taught me nothing. He gave me*
> *nothing I could be said to possess.*
> *What would be worth having? Knowledge is*
> *not what you have but what you are . . .*

And what were you, the two of you, may I ask?

As you see, we must be personal.

We must . . . not. I retract my question, Mr. Roseman.

> *Oh no, don't. Don't retract anything.*
> *I see, now, it is why I am here,*
> *why I was suggested for the job:*
> *your question, and my answer to it.*
> *We were what you failed to be—to become,*
> *you and Teddy, you and Gerald: one.*

Stop! Georges, arrêtez
la voiture. Il faut que les chiens sortent.
Essayez d'éviter les flaques, je ne veux pas
    qu'ils rentrent tout mouillés.
I have asked the chauffeur to walk Ping and Pong.

> *I understand French, Mrs. Wharton;*
> *as you understood English, just now.*

Go on, Ping, go with Georges. Mr. Roseman, I—
    I will not hear this.

> *You will not hear because you know "this"*
> *already, Mrs. Wharton. How many*
> *years has it been since Teddy died: eight?*
> *Eight years, during which you waited for*
> *Gerald Mackenzie to marry you—*
> *waited, writing in that costliest*
> *of cabinets, the kind of life*
> *which can be changed at any moment . . .*

What do you know about change of life? Have you
    changed yours, Mr. Roseman?

> *It has been changed for me. Those eight years—*
> *Gerald's last and in a sense my first*
> *eight years, in which our lives overlapped—*
> *during that time of ours, Mrs. Wharton,*

you deluded yourself by waiting
for a decision you yourself had made
long since. You are, therefore you go on . . .

So do you, Mr. Roseman, you speak with all
    the authority
of an outsider. And indeed you are one.

Let me go on, let me tell you this—
you won't mind because I don't matter,
isn't that the case? It will help you,
later on, when Gerald is . . . One thing
Gerald said—oh, not "always," but he said it,
he said it when he knew his own mind—
was that women are for men who fail.
Gerald did not fail—he descended,
perhaps, beneath himself in order
to be on top of others, but never
failed. That is why you could not figure
as you expected in Gerald's life:
being a woman was an abyss
which might suddenly swallow you both . . .

How would *you* know anything at all about
    being a woman?

I am a woman, Mrs. Wharton, for the same
reason that you are a man: "self-made"
at thirty-five! I am a woman just
because I am a man. How could I
help knowing? Besides, you help me
know: you wrote books so that I would know . . .
Our Gerald was not a man to think
differently of a book for having
read it, but I am. I read your books,
and I learned what Gerald never taught
me. Because I read your books I think
differently of life—and women.

You speak in riddles, Mr. Roseman. I don't see . . .

> *Come now, Mrs. Wharton, you see clearly—*
> *you see what you believe. If you are*
> *a self-made man, you must not forget*
> *those of us God made. What did you make*
> *of Gerald's friends you met at Howard's—*
> *all those appreciative listeners!*
> *What do you make of Mr. James! Surely*
> *you know what we are and what we do.*
> *You may not have known the niceties—*
> *did you visit the house in Cairo,*
> *did you take the yacht to Syracuse,*
> *and when Gerald was ill, were you there?*
> *So much for what we are, what we do:*
> *you did know that, Mrs. Wharton, didn't you?*

I know what *you* are, Mr. Roseman, you tell me
    enough to know that.
Nor am I tempted to put you and Gerald
and Mr. James in the same basket of crabs
because you do—or say you did—the same things.
You are men who do not need women—that is
what you say, that is what you are telling me,
is it not? That is what you smile and tell me
    Gerald was. No need . . .
One learns not to need by needing, it would seem:
    that is how I learned . . .
Here are the dogs. Merci, Georges, non. Cette fois
prenez-les avec vous. Maintenant, je crois qu'ils vont
    dormir tout de suite.
Mr. Roseman, we may resume our expedition
(for such it is turning out to be, a voyage
    of discoveries)
with perhaps a different sense—with a new
dispensation of each other. You are a . . .

> *. . . I have been telling you what I am,*
> *Mrs. Wharton, so that you might not have*

to say as much to me. I would spare
you the needless expense of . . . of
what has already been expended . . .

You call it spending!
You are, if I am correct in my assumption—
you are a Jew, Mr. Roseman, are you not?

Oh yes, Mrs. Wharton, and my father
was a banker, too—a Jew Banker!
You are correct in your assumption.
Will that make it easier for you
to realize just why I am here—
to reject your realization?
The Chosen People are commonly
treated as a people chosen for
the sake of somebody else . . . I do not
look for uncommon treatment from you,
that would hardly be fair. It is hard
for either of us to be fair now,
thanks to Mr. James . . . To be sure, I am
a Jew, you were saying, do go on . . .

I shall, Mr. Roseman.
Each of us gets—Gerald always used to say,
though doubtless not to you—the Jew he deserves . . .
When you claim I know what you are, what you do,
in that triumphant tone of yours—quite heroic—
I think you had better understand: I have
    never thought of them,
doing and *being*, as one and the same thing,
the way I thought of Gerald and literature—
    so mistakenly,
you force me to realize . . . Women, Mr. Roseman,
women defend themselves against what they are—
    that is what they *do.*
Some do it by marriage, I have defended
myself otherwise . . . too long for you to take
from me the Gerald I knew, the Gerald who

invented me—for whom I invented myself,
    if you enjoy that
way of putting it. You take Gerald from me
    and replace him with
a preposterous caricature who behaves
as people behave in the newspapers,
some newspapers, and Elizabethan plays . . .

> *Mrs. Wharton, I cannot take from you*
> *what you never had. Even Shylock*
> *could not do that. What I am saying*
> *is that Gerald led another life . . .*

There is not another life for anyone, not
    even for Gerald.
He is dead, once and for all. And for good, now.
I suppose there is another way to live . . .

> *That may be life, or what you call life,*
> *Mrs. Wharton, but it is not living—*
> *it is pretending . . . You liked Gerald*
> *to pretend, and he liked pretending.*

    Please do not go on.
To the brazen all is brass. We have nothing
in common, not even memory. Memory least of all.
    How dare you speak of
"our" Gerald as if . . . as if you had the right . . .

> *I told you I had my doubts when you,*
> *Mrs. Wharton, said we knew the same man.*
> *Certainly we have not lost the same*
> *meaning from our lives. How dare I speak!*
> *You know, Mrs. Wharton, you confirm*
> *my first impression of you, last year,*
> *as you sat there, smoking, in London,*
> *Ping on your lap, Pong at your feet—like*
> *two foxes fallen from the little*
> *wreath of dead red furs round your shoulders,*

with the afternoon light turning you
into a sort of sibyl, circled
by your own oracular vapors:
I listened to you talk, and I heard
all the harshness of a dogmatist
mingling somehow in every sentence
with the bleakness of an egoist
and the pretentiousness of a snob . . .

Is that what you heard?
So you're something of a novelist yourself—
    a novelist manqué.
How incorruptible youth is, when it has
failed to be interesting! You slash at me—
    out to draw blood now
with all the weapons in your reach, Mr. Roseman,
the mean and merciless ones which lie behind
    losses. What have you
lost? A slender man, tall, with tight skin, clear eyes,
who could not keep his hand from trembling when he
    poured a glass of wine.
Very well. I chose Gerald—you lost him.
I am quite prepared to surrender my choice:
    you still have your loss,
and you call me names for it. How do they help?
    Were you never taught
that humor is the fun we refrain from making?
What Gerald gave me was the capacity
to become independent of what he was.

        As well as of what he did, Mrs. Wharton?

And of what he did.
I see that as well—manqué see, manqué do.
You are too young to be much interested
in a universe in which we have to die;
    that is why you speak
so . . . so knowingly. I am old enough, now—
    call it middle-aged—

not to be interested in much besides.
The years are sad, the days jubilant . . .
You speak knowingly: I speak in ignorance.
        Better not to say
what you know. There might be some reason for your
knowing it. As there is for your saying it.
        One glance at the long
itinerary of our . . . relationship,
Gerald's and mine, long and wrong as it has been,
gives me the presumption of a Cassandra.

> *Yes, a Cassandra in a smart scarf*
> *you drape round a gray toque with that odd*
> *coquetry of yours, emphasizing*
> *your eyes until you resemble some . . .*
> *some wanderer in a wedding-veil.*

        If I do wander,
it is what brings me back to you, Mr. Roseman:
        I am not a Jew,
so I wander differently from your way;
Jews—it is what I wanted to say just now . . .
        I am not so harsh
as you would have me, nor so unresourceful,
if indeed I am a sibyl, a Cassandra . . .
        Let me try once more:
Jews feel that wherever they happen to be
is home because they are there. My dear young man,
to me anywhere would seem strange that did not!
I shall try to speak as both of us deserve,
        or as Gerald does.
This is what I mean, the important detail
which escaped you in the charming genre scene
I offered and you so cleverly described:
        I am in motion.
I have all that people are valued for, but
little that could make anyone love me . . . You see,
        I have always been
everyone's admiration and no one's choice.

It is I who have done the choosing . . . Gerald—
    As I have always
done the moving. Gerald did not love me. No.
Affection and desire—those apparently
were his poles, and we divide them between us,
    you and I. We stand
for different parts of life—of Gerald's life.

> *Love, Mrs. Wharton, was in the center,*
> *somewhere—anywhere, between us two.*
> *Gerald kept it all for himself,*
> *the way trees keep shade in the desert.*
> *We have a geography of the spirit—*
> *all Americans do, even when . . .*

    . . . Even when we fail
to live up to our geography, as we have.

> *But as I told you before, Gerald*
> *did not fail: in his geography*
> *he must have had a Great Barrier Reef*
> *of the soul, and behind it he kept*
> *his heart—in a kind of cold storage.*

Cold storage, deplorable as it may be,
    has done far less harm
to hearts than more promiscuous exposure—
than tropical mildew and dry-rot. I think
Gerald's life—or what it now appears to me
    I know of his life—
must have been lived so . . . so vicariously
that only reminiscence could make it real
    to him. To me, now.

> *At last. So we have come to the core*
> *of our trouble. Not that I am a Jew*
> *or that Gerald and I took part in*
> *those nameless sins which, when named, always*
> *turn out to exclude the name-caller.*

The trouble is that Gerald was not
the mere inspiration you believed
or were determined to believe him —
the chalk-egg that lures the hen to sit —
but a . . . Mrs. Wharton, if you look past
the desolation of an empty place,
you see he was a burden to you!

To me . . . "mere inspiration" is a burden;
        memory, prison.
Oh, the terrible energy of the dead!
What water falling was to Theocritus
in Sicily: nearest to the visible
        divine . . . A burden!
Without the urn, the ashes I hold would weigh
        —how much, I wonder?
Gerald's death cannot define him, merely end
a life that seemed active, and even crowded,
        but . . . negligible,
a kind of brilliance made up of limitations,
        my limitations,
you understand . . .
                    We must be at least beyond
Ville d'Avray by now—look to the left: is that
        the spire you spoke of,
Corot's church, and Saint-Cloud lying behind it?

            Yes, Ville d'Avray. They call this the Bois
            de Fausses Reposes. Versailles is over there . . .

A perfect nook in which to knit a novel,
        if you can reach it!
How wretched all these banlieu thoroughfares are—
we never really escape the boundaries
of Paris, get beyond the pale . . . or the dark.

        The way we escape America.

Yes. For all the drawbacks of our street-cleaning
and the excesses of our architecture,
    we do get away—
we Americans *want* to get away from
our diversions even more quickly than we
    want to get *to* them:
convenience is the tenth muse of our life . . .

> *You speak so differently, Mrs. Wharton,*
> *the moment you are released—relieved,*
> *I might almost say, or I must say—*
> *from Gerald. You become a different*
> *woman: it is a strange mutation . . .*

    A different woman?
You cannot turn a pillar of society
into a pillar of salt without bringing
    down the synagogue.
And it is a strange journey. For me, Gerald
in the flesh was merely a preparation.
    The truth—later
the truth becomes apparent: once you regard
someone as lost to you, then he . . . only then . . .
You are never truly together with him
until he is dead and actually inside you.

> *So for you Gerald's death was simply*
> *a kind of childbirth the wrong way round!*

    Nothing is "simply" . . .
I told you I distrusted children, as I
distrust all victims—they win in the long run,
    if they should get one.
Born victims: children. I do not want a sense
of the past, as Mr. James keeps calling it,
    and the future is deaf—
we must not count on the future to bestow
    meaning on our acts:

if we do, all action becomes impossible.
I want a sense of the continuous life.
I—is there something wrong, Mr. Roseman?
          What are you . . . ? I see.
I suppose one comes to grips with grief only
by seeing it come true in others . . . Take this . . .

> *Thank you . . . Mrs. Wharton, I did not*
> *expect that. Tears are not in my line.*

          Nor mine, my dear man,
but I am better prepared—women must be.

> *You brought it all back . . . Unhappiness*
> *wonderfully aids the memory:*
> *I was here—in Paris—with Gerald.*
> *You remember, he escorted the heir*
> *apparent of Siam around the Louvre . . .*
> *The prince asked no questions, never looked*
> *right or left through all the galleries*
> *until they stopped, and we all stopped too,*
> *in front of some primitive Pietà.*
> *Then his highness spoke for the first time,*
> *asking what the group represented.*
> *The curator of the Louvre explained,*
> *"It is the figure of our dead God*
> *after His enemies have crucified Him."*
> *The prince listened, staring, but Gerald—*
> *Gerald burst out laughing—couldn't stop,*
> *peal after peal of awful laughter*
> *echoing through the Louvre . . . Then his face*
> *went blank, and our procession moved on.*
> *Do you understand, Mrs. Wharton, why*
> *I thought of that just now? Do you know?*

No, Mr. Roseman, I don't know. But I have
begun to learn something I needed to know.
          . . . To learn something else.
We shall be at the cemetery before

much longer—Georges cannot take the car inside.
    They will be waiting,
the arrangements are all made—one does not leave
such matters to chance. I want to change them now.
Please! The urn, I want you to take it from me—
when we stop, get out and give it to the man
waiting at the grave. *I'll* wait here in the car.

You don't want to get out? You won't come?

I want you to put Gerald's ashes in the ground.
    We are, all of us,
distinctly marked to get back what we give, even
from what we may name inanimate nature.
    Take the ashes now.
When you come back, we shall decide what to say.

To say to each other, Mrs. Wharton?

    No, to Mr. James!
He has made his experiment in fiction—
    he has turned his screw,
as I suppose he would say. What shall *we* say?

I shall say nothing. People are far
more tolerant of artists, Mrs. Wharton,
than artists are of people, I find.

Silence, then, for Mr. James: it is the one
telling punishment. And for ourselves as well?
It might be premature to meet. Let us keep
    each other as last
illusions . . . Here's the drive. And here's the urn.
I leave the last of Gerald in your hands, Mr. Roseman,
    where so clearly he . . .

Thank you . . . Edith, if I may. Thank you.

Thank you, Mr. Roseman.

Won't you call me by my given name?

I never heard it, I think, Mr. Roseman.

It's Gerald, Gerald Roseman, Edith.

. . . That is the first time I have laughed in a week . . .
Our story, the one we shall spare Mr. James,
is what the American public always
wants: a tragedy with a happy ending.

A silent one.

A Natural Death

for Françoise Choay

SUMMER, 1947

I
Pesaro.   Professor Hemming, I am in the wrong
   period! None of which is left now. Only
      what came before or will come next
            remains to be seen.
   There has been no *rapido* from Rimini
      since the War; a bus lets you off (you
         and the pigs and hens) at noon.
Noon in Pesaro,
      do you know what that means? A yellow
         darkness to illustrate all
            shadows—not darkness,
               not yellow either:
         a light that shows up
      every pimple on your skin,
   but not one color of the spectrum.
I just made it to
   San Domenico (1390), and came out blinder
      than the bats inside. A sacristan
         drew me a map, though he *dreads*
            all Americans
(we bombed the Foglia bridge): lucky for me the Villa
   is on this side. Of course I would have to walk.
      I walked, on what they call a *spiaggia,*
the lunatic fringe
   of the sea, polluted with green leather froth;
      the snakes drop into it as you pass—
         they look like arrows swimming,
            even wickeder
   than on land, if that hot slime *is* land.

It will be worth it, I thought,
    slithering past them
(though all I could see
    was boxes, inland,
    piled up there by cave-dwellers
who could not find a cliff)—worth it all
        to reach my first real
Sandro di Fiore: not a sketch, a blueprint,
    But the Thing Itself, on the Villa
    grounds, the great Scena Marina . . .
        Professor Hemming,
there was no path, no signpost: I had to jump across
    cracks in the dry ground, as if the earth had split
    open like a dead pomegranate.
Sand shot up in shrouds,
    then fell back. Suddenly nine birds went
    over, like one triangular piece
    of metal trembling only
        around the edges.
I am not a coward, you know that,
    and a girl who's on her own
    in Italy learns
to put up with things.
        But these were not things!
    These were . . . omens—ominous.
Still, I kept on, until the Villa
        came in sight, by five,
and though the dazzle on the water was not
    so needle-sharp, the stored-up staleness
    of the day simmered round me,
        sour, blistering, dumb.
Sforza built the Villa, Dossi frescoed it, later
    (1493) Lucretia Borgia poisoned someone here.
        And in the park, my poor lost *Maestro*
was allowed to make
    his Sea-Theater, sixty-three years ago.
    Sforza . . . Borgia . . . Delle Rovere . . .
        Their stones still stand, for them Time
        is at a standstill,

their heartless marble persons beckon
and their history begins.
This place makes you want
to have old lovers
back, old victories,
good things you may have done once.
They do not seem to matter here, where
nothing matters past
the past. I took the wrong hero then, the wrong
Alessandro. Is that why nothing
is left? There was the Scena,
made too late to last:
not Renaissance but wrecked, whitewash graying in salt air,
oleanders growing out of what had been a wall—
I just don't see what could have been *done*
in this . . . this refuse.
Sandro said: Realism was just exposure;
Art, revelation. What was revealed
inside these palings, what shown
in this arena
dumped out of daylight
by a clump of stakes,
where all Mystery shrivels
from the malice of comparison?
Professor Hemming,
one last hiss upon the living shore, and then
the sea died out (when it is warmer
than marble, it looks somewhat
harder). In this world,
God only and the Angels may be spectators. We
have our work to do. *Theater of the sea!*
I left the recent ruin to the tide—
short work, I should say.
Next time you hear, it will be from Bussaco,
where I hope Di Fiore and I have
better luck. *Best,* CYNTHIA

II

Bussaco.   Your letter, Professor Hemming, was here
    waiting for me. Wonderful news or fond hopes?
      I wonder. With each "new" building lost,
            is Fiore living
    more likely to make good such losses to me
      than Fiore dead—drawings and gossip?
      Remember that interview
with Victor Horta:
    advantages of leaving off leaves
      and flowers both, retaining
        nothing but the stem!
              Sandro saying: "Sap
      is the grammar of all
    ornament," and Horta kicking
Sandro's cane and asking: "Does it still run through *that*?"
I can imagine
    how you must be cringing at the chapter now—
    "Fallacies of Organic Theory . . ."
      Having no stone to turn to,
        hearsay is a help,
Professor Hemming—what can you do with nothing but
    the truth? If our old man is alive, I know
    I must sound him out, and I will, but
"life" gets in the way.
    There is enough on record, and wrecks enough,
      as I began to write you: The room
      they gave me in Coimbra makes
          any *Spanish* inn,
    for all they say, seem like the Statler.
      Again I had to walk, ten
        blank kilometers
to where Bussaco
      begins. Like a wall
    the woods rise against you, cork
    and Lusitanian oak, laurustine,
        giant arbutus,
and what they call maritime fir. No sunlight
    gets down to you—nothing but trunks, boles,

saplings plastered together,
endless erections—
what else could you call them? In 1622 Pope Gregory
prohibited women from entering the woods.
It makes enchanted ground, thousands
of acres of it,
a kind of male Mystery Cult, those trees up
and up, and no hope of lying down;
even the dead trees stand up
against each other,
propped on the living ones, no falling
here except for water, springs
suddenly making
the dark columns loud.
And at the center,
Sandro's huge folly, erected
for the queer count who never got there—
assassinated
—and forgotten, like him, since 1914.
You know how I got there? A white dog
ran past me with a white bone
in its mouth: a sign.
I followed. It is an easy step to take, calling
something divine because it cannot speak.
Anyway, I followed and I came
to what might have been
Sleeping Beauty's castle house before the Prince.
I stood there staring—all I could do
was stare at what had turned into
a single treetrunk—
of course it was streaked and stained with vines
that hung like so many shawls
but could not hide it:
Fiore's hunting lodge!
a whited sepulchre,
dead white, nothing to see there
but another part of the forest
gone to its white end.
The first death is red, then black, the white one last:

white things are always an afterthought,
doubles or seconds of real things,
parodies of them,
like that mad White Mass conducted by time and darkness
before my eyes. I'll never know what Sandro
had in his mind (nor am I so sure
Sandro had a mind):
not hunting, that I *am* sure of, and—God knows—
no lodging here. Professor Hemming,
I am sick and tired. Of course
it was easier
getting out of that
phallic labyrinth
than getting in, but what is
the good of it all, going on to Var—
even if the church
is really there, for once, not washed out to sea,
or victimized by vegetable
penis envy? I suppose
the good is getting
onward and upward
to Bloemenwerf, one building
famous enough even for Flemings
to preserve. Grant me this: never has a research
fellowship been harder earned. If he is alive,
I guess I'll have to tell *il Maestro*
what is left of him:
I don't know whether to extend sympathy
or spank him for what I've been through.
I'll decide between here and
France. *Best*, CYNTHIA

III
Les Gorges du Céans (Corniche du Var).   Professor Hemming,
I cannot wait, although our letters will cross,
most likely: I hope mine reaches you
in a proper state,
before it is quite wizened and must be steeped
in water like anemones from Grasse.

The fact is . . . No, sentences
starting with such words
are always lies. Not fact but *finding*
is why I must write: I came
across the red corniche
(summer service of
La Compagnie du Ski—
a private railroad-car is not
an acquired taste: one takes to it then
and there, straight from Nice),
expecting another of Fiore's dead secrets
confided to the public and very
faithfully kept, but instead
I can see it now,
actually there! preposterous pillars and cones
of the Chapel Penitent, thousands of feet
above my window-sill, but in sight!
And it is a sight:
ten fingers of the earth, imploring stone, hands—
the strange and still religious nightmare
from which there is no waking
save in sleep. The prince
died from the bite of his pet monkey
and was succeeded by his father,
King Alexander,
who was mad enough
and nearly rich enough
to let Fiore turn the world
back to Will. It looks that way from here,
as if everything
possessed the power to transform itself, or else
be transformed. Professor Hemming, you
were right after all, thank God!
I'm going up there
with my camera now, and a man to take the measurements.
What the money of a guilty Balkan king
and the genius (it *was* genius, yes)
of Alessandro
managed to make, will be the making of my

dissertation, as you foresaw. More
tonight, once down. *A bientôt . . .*

Your letter was here when I got back.
Professor Hemming, *got back*
from what? From chaos,
nothing but stones, sweating grooves, lizards, lumps of a cliff
populous with ravens that kept crying out,
ravening obscenities, no doubt—
tragedia buffa!
Not penitence but dissolution, no trace
of the shaping spirit, no index
of a man's hand. Amazing,
to have your letter
to come back to then, counselling hope
hard upon that blind grotto—
grotesque!—out of which
the hot wind whistled,
as if to keep up
its spirits. "There is no joy
in the world but the joy we have *had*,"
you write, "the only
issue is by forfeiture, by *losing* something."
Professor Hemming, I can renounce
what I never had, but could he,
can he, at ninety-four?
A miracle, you call it, Fiore's being alive
(more of one, I think, your finding out
where he has gone to earth)—but can I
meet a miracle
on its own ground, disclosing to an old man
who once said, "Never copy the old
but never forget the old,"
that he no longer
exists, everything
gone? Surely you see
a somewhat rusty irony
in telling me first to ferret out
Fiore where he lies,

and then that the Bloemenwerf Town Hall was bombed
by *both* the Luftwaffe and the R.A.F. —
the one public edifice
up in flames, or down
in ashes, casualties of war quite casually
disposed of. Dear Professor Hemming,
I'll go to Paris, Rue Guénégaud,
but I will not give
the word to Fiore — I can ask what he *meant*,
not what they *mean*, and I can record
his answers. No more — enough.
Fondly, CYNTHIA

IV
Paris.   In order to tell you anything at all
I must tell you all in order. Taking life
as it comes, what it comes to is this:
things we never get
over. I will *send* over my saga now,
and together we can sort it out
later — like Thea and Tesman.
Tonight, then, let me
simply translate, transcribe, temporize
and testify . . . It is hard
to live up to our
daily disasters
and fatal not to.
The Rue Guénégaud is dim,
dirty and so dull you cannot tell
anything about it
but the truth. Behind her pane, a concierge screamed
faint instructions like a boiled ghost
whispering invective — six
stories to Fiore,
whose door was opened by a string tied to the bedpost,
and in the bed lay an ancient man who looked
exhausted by his own head of hair:
white hair gray with dirt,
yellow with age, and eyebrows that were the skins

of some small mammal just not large enough
   to be used as mats. My *pneu*
         was lying open
   where someone had left it (not his nurse!
   Nursing he called "a tribute paid
      to sexuality
by those who object
      to the usual means")
   and where *he* left his . . . what?
   When I think of his dinners and how
         he ate, I wonder
he and his cats were not sick together every day
   for their dessert! All that dingy afternoon
   he would smile into my staring face
      with an amiable
awareness I was there, and yet with a sort of absence:
   I was all there for him—he was not all there
      for me. I took it down, every word
(*that* much was all there)
   in Gregg for which I am forever grateful,
      having shown since high school a certain
         idiot flair—though I know, now,
            why it is we call
our tyrants *dictators*. I asked him, first,
      if he had written memoirs
         of a life so long
by any measurement,
         even by shadows.
      The voice that answered verged on
   a rustle, the sound of cloth ripping
         or water running—
some incessant impulse nearly audible
   in the next arrondissement:

I never wanted to remember   if I did I might keep the future from
happening   the past encroaches   each hour is made new by forgetting
yesterday   forgetting   there is no difference between being no longer
and never having been   what matters is to come widowed to our joys
I am proud of what I am not what I have done   was it all to end in a

counting-house on top of a cinder-heap   memoirs   in the world of
memory we do not see things splendid as they are   we see nothing   I have
not lived in my time I have lived through it   there is a choice in this world
we must choose between time and eternity   what you make is only the
means of disowning the past   and of course as you will learn my dear once
you disown the past you have no defense against the future

that was
when I could ask (for I had
no heart to *tell* him)
about the dismembered sites: Pesaro, Bussaco, Var.
"Not what you remember, then, but what you meant,
what you had in mind when you made it—
a building . . . a place
like the Sea-Theater?"

in mind child   I had nothing in mind   it was in the body I had it in the
body I made it to be inimitable like the sea closing even as it opens
leaving no trace   I'll tell you how it was   D'Annunzio took me on a
yacht   there were islands in the mist   "now watch that one" he told me
and ordered a cannon to be fired   he was always firing firing   gulls by
the thousands mounted like veils from the island up into the sky   circling
overhead   and calling calling   that was my Scena Marina child   I did
not make it for the mind   nor has the body fallen as pious people suggest
so much farther than the soul   I wanted to make one dance there one
dance of arms white arms the rest darkness and out of that the voices
accompanied by arms   life itself passing like the weaver's shuttle in and
out of that wonderful web of women   the white moments of life   I could
not make them do it   my theater sank into a vortex of jealousy   fraud
and falsehood   there will always be insanity in the average   average
women who wanted to succeed   success   whenever I came near it near
success the more beauty I saw in what is called failure   failure is not in the
nature of things   failure is the nature of things

Professor Hemming
that sounded like my cue: "the nature
of things"—and Fiore sounded
in a telling vein.
I said I had been

to Bussaco, and just the name was needle enough:
I had struck an artery!

you went there   you saw it you saw Bussaco   well of course that was not
life   that was not a theater   that was a tryst   another thing   my dear
would you hand me that   no there the bedpan I suppose you would call it
love   when the Count mentioned that he wanted a hunting lodge it
sounded like an offer of the last straw   but that was only his pretext his
prevarication   he wanted a place in the forest where he met his passions
that was his name for them   a man with the expression of a collie-dog into
which has entered the soul of Casanova   and I gave him love I gave him
there in the heart of Broceliande you have been to the forest you saw it
here my child would you take this down the hall   the last door you'll see
the place   I gave him passion you know the story of Pelléas and Mélisande
my dear I see that you know everything   you found it   and the part in
the story where Pelléas stands at the tower it is in the third act   he cannot
reach her and she cannot reach him they strain to touch one another and
then Mélisande leans down out of the broken tower and she lets down her
hair   it is a kind of rapture a terrible rapture and Pelléas stands inside
Mélisande's hair that is what I made for him I let the Count stand   even
alone   even by daylight inside Mélisande's hair   I wanted to show him I
wanted him to find out what comes of "passion" when the will is not
frustrated but extinct   when there is no cause and no consequence when
there is only the moment and the moment brings   not terror but freedom
freedom from memory   I knew it the instant my design was done we are
all deluded like Mélisande by our innocence   and we are all corrupted like
Golaud by our experience   there is only relinquishment   my dear girl the
most poetical thing in the world is not being sick   we are suspended
between nature and nothingness in that place where we have the truth of
our bodies   it is not poetic   it is the truth   only truth can be exaggerated
nothing else will stand the strain   as I became an older man I became a
newer artist   and the end of art my dear you know what that is the end of
art   it is the recovery of paradise   when the Count took holy orders I
decided to go off to Aleppo and give up art too   art seemed to me to be full
of regrets whereas Aleppo is only full of fleas   but I did not go   you have
to entertain the pang and taste the bitterness for all they are worth   you
have to know what has happened to you

imagine,
what it must have been like, then,
knowing what I knew,
hearing (listening
at least, for I was
writing much too fast to hear)
imagine my despair knowing I would have
to tell him the truth!
Not until I had made him talk about Var,
not until then, I resolved, and asked—
had he ever revisited his
Chapel Penitent
since its construction?

I never go back   I do not want to see them again   they have existed
the undiscovered regions of art Fuseli says are dreams   when I look for
existence I look for it in myself   the sands drift in   the buildings are
remembered   that life never lets go   nor do you want it to   it is part of
this room this bed   its towers and domes are the architecture of these
bedclothes   the dead   we are always debtors to the dead   we feel they
have not had their chance   that is what the King felt   as if life had given
us unfair advantages   he tried all the mediums   voices squeaking
where the missing collar-stud has been for thirty years   the passionate dead
act within us   they are not messenger-boys and hotel-porters   even
Alexander found it so   the dead who really live   the dead whose presence
we know we hardly care to call back or even speak of   that was what I
could give him   you know how a Greek woman's dress was rinsed in brine
and then pulled lengthwise and slowly twisted until it looked like a bundle
of knots   when it was dry and the knots were loosened it had the secret of
clinging to the body   every limb revealed forever   that was the garment I
made for the body of this death   I made it of stone   and when the King
came to Var he knew it he recognized it   my dear you are forever asking
what I meant what I mean   you tell me you were there and you saw it
why do you ask for meaning   I never put two stones together to mean
anything   for a while at first meaning simplifies and then it supersedes
the world   when Alexander came to Céans I was telling you he looked up
to the chapel at the top of the gorge and he gave one great cry "leave me
with my dead" he moaned and that was all   reality becomes perceptible

child only for the man who accepts death it is not a thing you can learn
how could you my dear you keep writing with all the self-assurance of a
duchess writing writing   a duchess with two lovers

It was always duchesses,
kings and counts for Di Fiore—
those were the terms he employed,
for *they* employed him.
Perhaps that gave me the notion, Professor Hemming;
I was at a loss again, but I wanted
to give him something, comfort him
for all those losses
he did not even know he had suffered yet.
I wanted to thank him for being
alive, and I gave
what I had to give:
an *Aureus* of Hadrian,
a phoenix on the reverse,
a coin I've carried since I was in school.
He could not see it
for himself, and when I told him what it was
his withered fingers were caressing,
I thought he would fling it at me!
Something in his face
faltered then, but his voice did not falter,
and if his mind dismantled a little,
he could master it:

this is a Roman coin   Rome of the Antonines   it is the reign of the Beast
competing accounting ruling remembering   under Rome a man could
endure anything without virtue not this   do not give me this   it is the
past   it is all I have ever opposed you have seen my buildings you know my
work she read me your letter   you know what I've done it is beatitude of
creatures I "meant" the processes of plants not this money not this death   I
merely discovered an old secret   the past need not exist   life can be lived
without the history of itself   or it cannot perhaps   who said life was to be
lived   endured   no ecstasy endures it grows and it dies out   not this
order not this coin it is no currency it does not move or change   I do not
serve the law   it is not history or even knowledge but a kind of incoherent

gratitude   no purpose but ecstasy   art must go out   take it back my dear
take it away from me it is not the earth only history

Not once, I think, in all the dismay
of that dreadful downward wake—
the Sea-Theater
dissolved at Pesaro,
the Lodge overgrown
at Bussaco, the Town Hall
in cinders at Bloemenwerf, at Var
the Chapel stone dead—
not once, Professor Hemming, had I lost heart
or hope of recovering Fiore
from himself, till he returned
my coin that had been
a talisman for me, a sign I was keeping faith
with all we have been, with all we might have been.
I heard my own words before I knew
I had spoken them:
"*Maestro*, I did not mean to disappoint you.
I did not mean to tell you at all,
but you say you want to know . . .
And now that *I* know
what your expectations are, perhaps
I can give you satisfaction.
They are no longer
what you made them to be,
they are no longer.
That is why I have troubled you
for meanings." And I told all of it,
what I had found there,
or not found, in Pesaro, Bussaco, Var,
and what your letter consigned to fire
as well—at the cost of one
miserable coin
I spent Fiore's lifework as I might have spilled
his chamberpot. Professor Hemming, if I was
hurt and then humbled by my own spite,
I think I was *horrified*

by what happened then:
                    the old man took hold
                    of that ridiculous string
              until he could grasp the bedpost,
                         grimaced a little
         but rose up, bolt upright now, until his eyes
           —cloudy, colorless, a statue's eyes—
                 stared into mine, and a chill
        or charge or tremor
              ran through what must have been all the bare bones
                 (and only bones) under the nightshirt,
        even his hair shook . . .
              Then it all ended, and Fiore was speaking,
                 though the figure in front of me seemed
                    to have no connection with
         the words I was hearing, the words he must have spoken!

*they are gone then   gone now   irrecoverable as a sunset   when there is
no triumph to show then night becomes the triumph   darkness purposeless
it has come   and I was right to come here   why do you suppose I chose
Paris   dying slowly here of hand-to-mouth disease   there was no road
until I took this road   every great city has twelve hundred inhabitants
Paris is the sole exception   Paris has not twelve hundred but one-hundred-
twenty   I came here to be found   I leave the rest where they lie   or had I
better say where they fell   it is only when you have   given everything that
you can give more   that you have more to give   it is inadmissible for a
man to leave   the trace of his passage upon earth   give it all back   the
elements   the compassionate sea   and the fire   and the ground   and
the growing air   as you described it   we must survive what we have
made   it is not ours   I have survived in Paris   my body separates me
nothing more than that and an indefinable fragrance of perpetual female
possession   I waited for you   and I can wait for you no longer my dear
because you have arrived   a phoenix on the reverse   easier to love than to
mourn*

                    I know he was still
              looking into my eyes, I know he was
                 still alive then, for the change
                    began there: *his* eyes

filled and overflowed,
his body fell away—only it did not fall,
it faded out, until I could not see
the little landslide of bones
under the bedclothes.
The head rolled over
and the face was gone. Even
the hands were erased. I was alone.
Professor Hemming,
that was the death of Alessandro di Fiore,
and I think I brought it to him.
I think he waited for me
to bring him that death.
It is not what I came to do, halfway across
Europe, it is not what I meant to do,
but it is what I have done. Destroyed
or delivered him—
I don't know which. I need the distance,
I need time. I need your help.
I send you all this:
please keep it for me
until it becomes
mine. *Yours*, CYNTHIA

FELLOW
FEELINGS

Decades

for Hart Crane

1   *Crane's Canary Cottage.*   I have turned four,
and the tablecloth between my mother and me
(my father opposite, of course) invites
pollution of its pure canary note
by a nest of shiny knives and glasses—"not
for fingering." This is my first meal *out*
and I must behave, on my father's sharp orders
and yours—your father's: it is their bill of fare
we pay for, and who knew how much it cost,

that April evening as we ate? My mother
ate my father, her leftovers mine till now:
I failed like yours—your father—to defend
myself against the opposite sex, my own,
that night the news came, Mother's Day for sure,
that April something, nineteen thirty-two,
when Wheelwright said you turned to *Fish Food* (he
turned it to advantage in the very first
of all your elegies, asking final questions:

*what did you see as you fell, what did you hear
as you sank?*). I fed to find the answers, for
that was a sacramental feast. Dear Hart,
our mothers ate our fathers, what do we
eat but each other? All the things we take
into our heads to do! and let strange creatures
make our mouths their home. Our problem is not
to find who remembers our parents—our problem is
to find who remembers ourselves. I love our problem,

it becomes our solution: unbecoming, it dissolves.
I was four, you drowned. Now you remember me.

II   *Laukhuff's Bookstore.*   I am fourteen, I live
on the Diet of Words, shoving a ladder around
high shelves while the German ex-organ-maker
smokes with a distant nightmare in his eyes
("You have heard of Essen," he murmurs, "you never
will again": it is nineteen forty-three),
his body on hinges, his elbows hovering wide
over the *Jugendstil* bindings (Werfel, Kraus . . .)
like a not-quite-open penknife. "Hart Crane?

He came here to marry the world . . . You understand?
Maritare mundum: it is the work of magic,
Mirandola says it somewhere, to marry the world . . .
And not much time to do it in, he had to read
all the books, to marry the world, *then* to burn . . .
It is one kind of greatness to grow old—to be
capable of growing old, like Goethe;
it was Hart's kind to refuse. You understand?"
Laukhuff is asking *me*, laughing through smoke

his postponing, renouncing laugh. No, I don't—
that much I do. I climb down, clutching *The Bridge*,
and hand it over. "Will I understand this,
Mr. Laukhuff? Should I buy it?" "Cross it first.
You won't, but there is a certain value, there is
poetic justice in the sense of having missed
the full meaning of things. Sure, buy it. Spend
all you have, your mother will give you more."
The German penknife closes with a click.

Marriage, Hart. The endless war. The words.
Cleveland was our mother-in-lieu. We left.

III   *Les Deux Magots.*   I am twenty-four and free,
now, to finger knives and glasses—no cloth
to be stained, nothing but cold zinc dividing
me from your old friend opposite, your coeval,
the Fugitive convert who cases the loud café
evasively while I lay my cards on the table:

I tell him of myself, which is as much
as to have asked him pardon—Shakespeare, no less!—
but he winces at what he hears, and what he sees:

your Montparnasse is dead, my Saint-Germain
dead-set against the capital of gaiety
you shared in the twenties. Gay it is, though,
and so am I, to his disparagement
expressed, dear Hart, in terms of our *decadence*
as the flaming creatures pass. "Such men," he says,
"fare best, as we Southerners say of foxes, when
most opposed—none so spited by their own,
and yet I see how proud these sick cubs grow!"

There is a silence, colder than the zinc
between us. Hopeless. I have lost heart,
as I always do when I rejoin the Fathers,
lost the pride of my "proclivity,"
and the penalty and disgrace of losing is
to become part of your enemy. Have I lost you,
Hart? I need you here, quarrelsome, drunk
on your permanent shore-leave from the opposite sex,
opposing shore, the loss, the losses, the gain . . .

There is always a chance of charity when we are dead.
Only the living cannot be forgiven.

IV   *Sands Street Bar & Grille.* At thirty-four
I am older than your ghost I follow in
under the Bridge that hisses overhead.
Dark enough here to make ghosts of us all,
and only a great layer of ghosts knows how
to be democratic in the dark: no wonder
you gave your hand to Walt, always on edge,
on the beach of embarking, the brink where they fall
into the sea, these castles of our misconduct . . .

Your ghost, anonymous, cruises among ghosts,
our neighborly disgrace. Was it from this

you made your Bridge, reaching up to Walt
and down to me—out of this River, this Harbor,
this Island and these, these sexual shadows, made
an enviable failure, your dread success?
I do not believe in exceptions—if you did it
then it can be done; show me your toys, ghost,
show me your torments out of which you rise,

dripping in your bones, from death to be
a trophy of disaster. What did you learn,
steeped in the great green teacher of the gradual,
when all you knew was sudden, a genius in need
of a little more talent, a poet not by grace
but the violence of good works? I still do not
understand you, but I stand under you here,
marvelling at the shadows where apprenticeship
is not vocation, of course, only voyeurism.

Albatross, siren, you haunt me far from home.
It is dark. Here not seeing is half-believing.

v *Garrettsville.*   By forty-four I know
your beginning *lost at land*, your end *at sea*:
sometimes beginnings can be more desperate
than ends, patrimony more than matrimony,
and middle age the worst despair of all.
I do not find you here, or in the bars,
or Laukhuff's, or that yellow restaurant—
not even on the beach you walked with Walt,
hand in hand, you told him: *never to let go.*

But that is where you find me. Take my hand
as you gave yours to him. We suffer from
the same fabled disease, and only the hope
of dying of it keeps a man alive. Keeps!
I press your poems as if they were Wild Flowers
for a sidelong grammar of paternity.
We join the Fathers after all, Hart, rejoin
not to repel or repeal or destroy, but to fuse,

as Walt declared it: wisdom of the shores,

easy to conceive of, hard to come by, to choose
our fathers and to make our history.
What takes us has us, that is what I know.
We lose, being born, all we lose by dying:
all. I have seen the Birthplace—a strange door
closes on a stranger, and I walk away.
Soon the shadows will come out of their corners and spin
a slow web across the wallpaper. Here
is where you met the enemy and were theirs.

Hart, the world you drowned for is your wife:
a farewell to mortality, not my life.

Personal Values

My dear Magritte, I have been ill. Again.
By now of course the symptoms are well known,
Signs which are taken or mistaken for
Wonders by the broken-winded mind, blown
Is the word all right, though all wrong is more
Like it: blown up and at the last gasp down
Until I cannot call my soul my own

During such uncalled-for occasions when
The torn mind turns into the body, then
Turns out, instants or ecstasies later,
To have been literally taken in.
Taken—was it always as well known—where?
You know, but you're not telling, not even
Telling tales out of school—André Breton

Himself could never persuade you to own
Up to what he called your "magic reason":
You refused to tell tales *in* school either.
In any case or, to be casual, in mine,
Each time the fit approaches, I repair
(To be fitted, you might say) to the one
Room there is no earthly obligation

To share, the place in which to be alone
Par excellence, par misère, a site no one
Has named properly because it must pair
The washing function with the wasting one,
Lore of the toilette with the toilet's lair.
This is where the thing chooses to come on,
Yet once I get inside, the room has gone,

Nowhere to be found: the four walls open
Up and away—the sky! Against which, seen
As if for the first (or last) time, appear
The comb in the corner, the soap near the green
Toothbrush glass, one huge matchstick on the floor
Where Marie must have missed it, all obscene
With enormity, much too big to mean

What the scale of mere habituation
Managed to confer upon them or shun
By not conferring. I wait for my seizure
With the patience of . . . a patient, at pains
To discover the glass beyond me, over
My head, the soap escaping by design,
The totem matchstick—like the comb, a sign

Of my illusions made illustrious: icon
And idol, texts of a new religion.
As I wait for the next spasm to spare
Or despair, dear René (which means *reborn*),
I send all my thanks for your more than fair
Copy of my condition. *Merci*. Where
Else could I find my life's illustration?

Howard's Way
A Letter to 102 Boulevard Haussmann

Mon cher maître, could even you have mastered
such dissemblance?
                    Given your gift for luring
the accidental and the inevitable
to lie down together, what would you have done
with these disparities — could you have parsed them
into a semblance of sense?
                              Mind, that phoenix,
kindles its own fire: identity at stake,
it does not depend on the world for fuel —
must I? Dear Marcel, did you?
                              Suppose I rehearse
how it went with me last night, how far it went
beyond my means: I write what I recover from
what I have chosen to forget. I put it
to you — perhaps you can put it right for me.
No one knows the ropes better, what lines to draw,
what chords to strike, what strings to pull — and knowing,
for better or worse, would tell.
                                  Now just suppose
You had accompanied me, had paid a call
in answer to a call, a summons from hell —
as any place is hell, at the other end
of a telephone wire, that is not heaven.
Suppose you approached, with *your* urbanity,
my city's most publicized apartment-house
looming grim at the Park's edge, grimy and grand —
sufficiently grand to be used for shooting
horror-movies.
                (I know, you cannot have heard
of horror-movies. Or can you? *Fantomas*

was shown in Paris, you saw *Judex*, *La Proie* . . .
Seeing is believing—we are what we see,
and if what we see and believe is silly,
only what we could see, could believe is not.)

Horror-movies then, and there—could you believe?
in the redoubt Dakota, so huge our word
apartment takes on a meaning all its own,
the converse of togetherness (now that word
you never heard of, thank God. We mean well, but
the ease with which we say what we mean—horrors!
sounds like the most affable of lies).
                                        To the dark
Dakota then you came, suppose, and instead
of visiting its most Proustian denizen,
the leading lady famous not for her roles
but for her first appearance in a Southern
hamlet, also the birthplace that very year
(and the hideout since) of the one novelist
we've had who takes after your own hidden heart—
though knowing another man's secret is not
the same as having to live with your own . . .

Suppose, then, rather than visiting "the girl
next door" to our great fabulist, you had found
yourself and me outside another door, one
to an attic room, really a *chambre de bonne*
(more likely, in the Dakota, *de mauvaise*)
bestowed by that lady on her kissing kin,
the man who called us, whom we are calling on!

He famous as well: the poet-pornographer
freshly returned—restored—a pilgrim from Nepal
and beautiful, still beautiful, or worse still
you could see that he had been beautiful once.
He admits us, the old beau, with a hard look,
as though wondering how much we cost. (*He* cost
a lot, and can afford to be entertaining

only to strangers: entertainment at best
is merely lust compassionately disguised
as the will to please.
                              Master, you *are* helping!)
Pattering across the parquet, his blind pug
attacks. "Down, Principe, down! Oh dear, do mind
that pile of poo." We bestride the pool of pee
by inches, whereupon we are well inside
a room filled (or emptied) by a flickering
blue light. There are others here, oblivious
of Principe and us: all their faces turned
one way, washed by a reflected radiance—
mysterious little male presences, looking
just like pressed flowers.
                              We sit down too, we watch.
On the screen, persons inconceivably wound
around each other commit by noose and knout
actions of ecstasy and passions of pain
on a hairless Oriental boy, a child!
though is that a child's body? relentlessly
acquiescent to the penetrations of
a gray-haired man . . .
                              All at once another man,
corpulent, with the face of a polite snake
(the man who uses all the instruments) comes:
there is a sudden struggle, until both men . . .
The child's hand flutters, though they hold him down, and
two fingers thrust across the screen in protest
or appeal: black talons, inches long.
                              No one
speaks. Not a word. Only the reel chatters on—
the bodies exchange a last seizure, comic,
anonymous. To forgo identity
as these do, first give up the fear of falling—
most of us cannot, for who would need to rise
if we were not afraid of falling?
                              By this

light or lack of it, the little audience
has the look of men watching and unaware
we are watching them watch: a look as though
they were not in their own bodies, but in ours . . .

Something breaks, the screen goes blank, and here we are
sitting with a dozen men in a room so
nondescript no reasonable person could
possibly make love here, or commit suicide:
keeping up appearances is not difficult
once you have seen through them—you told us, master,
merely hold them from behind, the way you hold
a shield, and appearances protect you quite well.

Introductions follow: the guest of honor,
a tall, gray-haired man of ash and addictions
whose first forbidden book everyone devoured;
the later licit ones are, of course, unread:
the one way we can survive is to become
imitations of ourselves—for otherwise
experience touches us and we must change.

Beside him, his sarcous secretary whose
pale eyes are so wide-set that like a serpent
he can look straight ahead only by turning
his face from side to side.
                                        And across the room
a third person is identified, though hardly:
a living idol, fourteen perhaps, and so
symmetrical he need not have a self . . .
                                                        "This
is Inda, I brought him back from Katmandu."
I hold out my hand as he does, the idol does,
and then I feel the nails. So he is the child,
those are the men—he suffered, they were there then,
here now: gray hair, snake-eyes . . .
                                                Horror-films, indeed—
we take off our sex and have . . . clothes! I cannot

bear this. Master, is art the image of life?
Is life?

       "Act your age," you urge me and, outraged,
I answer: "What is acting? I should act yours,
you mean—one more obscene performance . . . "

                      You
take your part by holding your peace. You are not
there, you are silent—have you left me?

                  Rudely,
I admit, I stumble, almost running, out,
unready for that recognition scene . . .

                  Down,
away! where winter opens the clouds above
the Park and beyond the trees. There are the stars,
unsteady constellations—blue movies all
right, or all wrong: a world whose beauty is just
a jangle to our ears, a blur in our eyes,
an entanglement about our feet . . .

                  I move
by darkness as *they* moved by light: Howard's way.
Crossing the city to send you this, I am
awed as the meanings converge, syllables
I cannot dispel, alien oracles
I cannot receive: Dakota. Katmandu.
                        RICHARD

The Giant on Giant-Killing
Homage to the bronze *David* of
Donatello, 1430

I am from Gath where my name
in Assyrian means *destroyer*, a household word
by now, and deservedly. Every household needs
a word for destroyer—nothing secret in the fact,
nothing disgraceful about a universal need—
     and my name is a good word.
Try the syllables on your own tongue, say *Goliath*.
It sounds right, doesn't it—powerful and Philistine
and destructive, somehow. It always sounded like that
to me. *Goliath!* I shouted, and the sun would break
     in pieces on my armor.
The world, as far as I could see, was the sun breaking
on things, making them break. So I was hardly surprised
when the world came to an end because the sun broke *through*:
no pieces, unbroken, whole—no longer flash but flesh.
     The end came as a body.
You see, I am past the end, or I could not know it:
look at my face under his left foot and you *will* see,
look at my mouth—is that the mouth of a man surprised
by the end of the world? Notice the way my mustache turns
     over his triumphant toe
(a kind of caress, and not the only one), notice
my full lips softened into a little smile. You see:
the triumph is mine, whatever the tale. And the scene
on my helmet tells the true story: a chariot,
     eight naked boys, wingèd ones,
and the wine, the mirror, the parasol—my triumph
inherits me. He holds my sword. He is what I see,
that is why you see him: the naked boy without wings.
There is a wing, but it happens to be my helmet's
     and inches up the inside
of his right thigh stiffening to allow the feathers

an overture, covertly spread, to that focus where
nothing resembles a hollow so much as a swelling.
That focus?—those. Find one place on his fertile torso
　　where your fingers cannot feed,
one interval to which all the others fail to pay
their respects, even as they take the light, the shadows.
It is why the sun broke through me that morning—no stone
could lay Goliath low. See it still in the boy's hand?
　　No need for a stone! My eyes
were my only enemy, my only weapon too,
and fell upon David like a sword. The body is
what is eternal; the rest—boots, hat ribboned and wreathed,
even the coarse, boy's hair that has not once been cut—
　　a brevity, accidents,
though it is no accident when it is all you have.
Almost I think his face too is an accident, dim
under the long pointed brim. Call it an absence then,
an absence where life is refreshed and comforted
　　while the body has its way:
a presence, a proof emptied of past and future, drained
of obligations pending. Climb across the belly,
up the insolent haunches from which the buttocks are
slung (there, that is the boy's sling), scan the rhyming
　　landscape of the waist between
the simple nipples arched by his simpler, supple arms—
even the vulnerable shoulderblades, the vain wrists
are present but not the face, not David's mouth that is
the curved weapon used to kill a smile. And the carved eyes,
　　what are they seeing? Only
the body sees, the eyes look neither down at me nor
out at you. They look away, for they cannot acquit
what is there: the eyes know what the body will become.
It is why they are absent, not blind like mine, not blank
　　as iridescent agates.
They see the white colossus which in eighty years will come,
unwelcome: marble assertion of a will to wound
against which no man or music can survive. It is
what giant-killers must become. Michelangelo . . .
　　They become giants: no head

of Goliath kisses those unsolicited feet,
no one is there . . . Yes, I go, I have gone already.
I would rather mourn my going than mourn my David.
I am the man Goliath, and my name in Israel
        is also a household word,
every household needs the word—perhaps there *is* a shame
in that, a secret about such universal need—
but it is a good word, my name; try it on your own
tongue, savor the hard syllables, say *Goliath*
        which in Hebrew means *exile*.

Vocational Guidance,
with Special Reference to the
Annunciation of Simone Martini

Ordinarily
when the Messenger, otherwise known
as the Angel, makes himself
known, the rest of life absorbs his arrival—
or the rust of life;
not that we tell lies,
but we shall always be in terror
of the truth. Habitual
disorders suffice to hold fast to the small
change of small changes:
the dog keeps doing
undoable harm to the Bokhara,
your mother has called, again!
and that letter from the bank is anything
but reassuring.
Events are enough—
what Baudelaire calls *la frénésie
journalière*—to mitigate
an inopportune disclosure, to muffle
Angelic demands.
For Mary herself
the moment was unmanageable;
according to old masters
the Virgin resorted to household effects,
a dither of forms
in a minor world
where whatever is the case is lower
case, a means of avoiding
the garbled message: was it Give or Give Up
Something Capital?
You know how it is.
Not yourself for days (we all have spells),

you need *things* around the house
to help out—objects of *virtù* to shield you
　　from the articles
　　　　　　of a faith that goes
against the grain of mere existence.
　　With some degree of success
you make your way into the gradual warp,
　　pleasant evasions
　　　　　　in which the masters
specialize, plastic as all get out—
　　when there He is! utterly
demanding, utterly demonic, speaking
　　unutterable
　　　　　　truth *and* consequence
of truth. Disaster, even triumph—
　　no matter what the Angel
says, it is the Angel saying it: how can
　　that be anything
　　　　　　but gibberish? How
can you bear it? Only by binding
　　an extra strand of daily
confusion around your Messenger, turning
　　text into texture,
　　　　　　praise into no more
than prose, a general excuse for
　　reading languidly between
the lines when an Angel pronounces your fate
　　in brisk iambics.
　　　　　　Mary was finding
her comfort in Deuteronomy:
　　"With the smooth stones of the stream
is thy portion, there thy lot," when Gabriel
　　lighted before her.
　　　　　　Simone saw it,
and not all the plausible veneers
　　of Siena can rival
his unvarnished truth (though many times restored)
　　in the Uffizi.
　　　　　　It might be your life:

no vainglorious architecture
vaults into, no garden leads
your eye out of, the picture. Lilies, a bench,
and the two of them
up against flat gold
and cold marble—no getaway, no
domesticity, unless
you call the still-fluttering plaid stole knotted
at Gabriel's throat
a domestic touch.
Even the scarf draped behind
Mary can be misleading:
it looks more like wings, when wings are the last thing
in the world she wants:
wings are terrible,
they take up too much room, too much air,
they speak volumes. Gabriel
speaks only words, marring the gold but making
right for Mary's ear—
words are terrible.
No olive-branch he bears, no wreath
he wears can ease this meeting,
and Mary—Simone Martini's Mary,
you can see, abhors
her bright Intruder.
She was just . . . she *was*. Sulking now for
the rape of that imperfect:
"I was reading when I heard . . ." Why is he here?
Who needs an angel?
A glance at her hair
and Gabriel's (identical gold)
explains. It is Simone's
method, this auburn pun, his way of saying
we ourselves summon
Angels. Unwilling?
Unready? Giving rise to second
thoughts . . . If it had been enough
to brood over books, she never would have seen
her Visitor;

resentful, reverent,
Mary at this moment discovers
that she wills him to appear—
even the wings are part of her—no use tugging
the long blue mantle
away from the Good
Tidings into an almost abstract
or Japanese pattern of
refusal. Pay those bills, call your mother back
and clean up after
the dog: no dodging
the moment when you meet the Angel,
when he announces what you
have known all along. No second-guessing:
"Father, let this cup
pass from me"—his words
must enter the porches of your ear,
hammer strike anvil, until
the choice you have made, as Simone shows,
comes, unfurnished, home.

Venetian Interior, 1889

for David Kalstone

Stand to one side. No, over here with me:
out of the light but out of darkness too,
where everything that is not odd or old
is gold and subjugates the shadows. There,
now you will be no trouble and behold none—
anything *but* trouble, at first glance,
last chance to see what I say is worth a look.

This whole palazzo is the property
of a middle-aged and penniless dilettante,
Pen Browning (Robert's son), who has made terms
—palatial terms, in fact—with towering
premises afforded by the tact
of his New York heiress, Fannie Coddington
Browning, dutiful daughter-in-law, doubtful wife.

Yet who would not be full of doubts, perplexed
at having to define Pen's talents and finance
his tastes? Their Ca' Rezzonico itself
is dubious. The ripened fruit of centuries,
rat- and roach-infested, peeling, rank,
withers with each tide that rots the piles,
though apt withal to weather these tenants as well . . .

He is painting from the model: *Dryope*,
undressed of course but draped against the draft
in a looping swathe of silver-printed stuff
that seems to move, glistening over flesh—
it *does* move! lapped in its silver mesh are coils
of a python wrapped in loving torpor round
the *contadina*'s undistracted torso.

The afternoon is numb: Dryope sleeps
in her pose, the python slips a little
down the umber slope of her thigh, and Pen,
inspired, slaps a dashing curlicue
across his canvas. "I had the Jew come by
with this brocaded velvet yesterday—
I bargained some old clothes against it, Fan,

so you needn't ask how much it cost in dollars."
To whom does Pen speak, his eyes intent, his hands
"working busily"? Beyond his "subject," look
past the unimposing *Dryope*, look through
the tufts of pampas grass extending up
to the tufa vault whose patination casts
a pall of watery splendor on the scene—

if you manage to overlook the sumptuous junk,
jasper urns, a suit of Japanese armor,
two stuffed bears, on the divan bearskins too—
there, or in this atmosphere let me say *lo!*
on that very divan Robert Browning lolls,
a short and foreshortened colossus with feet of clay
but the hardest imaginable cranium, among

his son's possessions slightly ill at ease
though well bestowed on slippery pelts, and plays
(against the wealthy Fannie—see her white shawl?)
at draughts with agate pieces, red and green,
like a page from some old parchment of kings and queens.
In approbation of his son's economies
the old man smiles now—but does she? The skull

interfering with our view of Fannie is,
I believe, or was the Mahdi's which Pen keeps
beside his easel (Victorians could make
anything into a tobacco jar). "I took
my pipe through Cannaregio on a long tramp
yesterday morning, right into the Ghetto,
looking for likely faces, which I found!

Didn't you say, Father, a satisfactory Jew
is worth a dozen Gentiles? The one who sold
that velvet to me is sure to be ready by Spring:
for *Lear*, you know, or *Lazarus* at least . . ."
Pen chatters on to charm the python, not
Dryope or Fannie who look up
only when the poet, roused, exclaims—

as rapt before himself as a child in front
of the Christmas tree: "A satisfactory Jew!
Setting mere Rothschildsplay aside, Pen,
I never saw but one in all my life:
Dizzy, I mean—the potent wizard himself,
at Hampton Court a dozen years ago,
murmuring at the Queen's ear like a wasp

who hoped to buzz his way into the diamonds . . .
With that olive cast and those glowing-coal-black eyes
and the mighty dome of his forehead (to be sure,
no Christian temple), as unlike a living man
as any waxwork at Madame Tussaud's:
he had a face more mocking than a domino—
I would as soon have thought of sitting down

to tea with Hamlet or Ahasuerus . . ."
As if on cue, the poet's high voice fades,
the lights on his tree go out. Yet we have seen
enough and heard enough: the secret of losing
listeners—did Browning never learn?—
is to tell them everything. We lose details.
The Mahdi's skull and Fannie's coincide . . .

The scene blurs and the sounds become no more
than exaggerated silence. Stand with me
another moment till our presence is
sacrificed to transitions altogether.
Time will not console—at best it orders
into a kind of seasonable chaos.
Let me tell you, it will not take much

longer than a medical prescription—
I can give you ingredients, no cure . . .
Visitors to the palazzo used to speak
of the dangerous ménage—the menagerie!
Yet the Costa Rican python that cost Pen
(or Fannie) sixteen pounds was the first to go,
untempted by the rats of Rezzonico;

Dryope followed Dryope underground,
the girl carried off by a chill and buried
at San Michele, the great daub interred
in the cellars of the Metropolitan . . .
"Dear dead women, with such hair, too,"
we quote, and notice that hair is the first
of ourselves to decay before—last after—death.

In a year Robert Browning too was dead, immortal;
in another, Fannie dropped her shawl and took
the veil and vows of an Episcopalian nun;
and Pen? Oh, Pen went on painting, of course—
buono di cuore, in yellow chamois gloves,
obese, oblivious, dithering into debt
and an easy death. The sale of what we saw

or saw through in Venice *realized*, as they say,
some thirty thousand pounds at Sotheby's.
I told you: first glance is last chance.
Darkness slides over the waters—oil sludge
spreading under, till even Venice dies,
immortally immerded. Earth has no other way,
our provisional earth, than to become

invisible in us and rise again.
Rezzonico . . . Disraeli . . . We realize our task.
It is to print earth so deep in memory
that a meaning reaches the surface. Nothing but
darkness abides, darkness demanding not
illumination—not from the likes of us—
but only that we yield. And we yield.

Purgatory, formerly *Paradise*

for Abby and Bernard Friedman, fellow travellers

He is used—these are his words—to wander about
in his pictures at will, Cardinal Bembo wrote,
perplexed but extenuating, to the Princess,
Isabella of Este, *so that what thing is*
in his mind may satisfy those who look at them.
What thing . . .
                    The sun (is it the sun? the source of light
in any case, some definitive disclosure
seems by a sorcery to lie in stone, stuff, skin—
light falls from ourselves!) sinks behind us, suspended
in a visionary paralysis, almost
as if the proper spell, pronounced, would bring it back,
would keep the world at such a pitch of elegy
that looking is a kind of listening. Almost,
yet as *we* wander about, our shadows lengthen,
reaching to the right, though only here, close at hand.

Past this enclosure where we are, from cliff to cleft,
from what looks like the immovable Grand Hotel
on a far hill to the unmoved lagoon, nothing
darkens, nothing dies: it is the containing life
continuing Out There, forever beyond us.

I called this marble paling an enclosure,
this plain balustrade around a tessellation
(serpentine, carnelian, alabaster set
fast in a magical geometry that makes
radiant what is merely red and green and white),
but there is a gate down to the water lapping
beyond a low gray wall, and the gate is open.
We may go away—some of us are going now,
losing the light that was in us.

Look to the left:
see him? Lowering as he leaves, maybe a Moor
in his silver haik and fur-trimmed caftan, going,
his face resolutely turned from us (toward Mecca?)
like some discarded hope, receding . . .
                                    Who is he?
Perhaps the elder brother—Gentile—who paints
for the Sultan in Constantinople. He goes.
The open gate lets us in and out, we are not
held captive here on our high terrace, we are free
to pray, unless we are holding a sword and scrip,
or unless our hands are tied behind our white back
so that the arrows in us become our prayers.
Are we praying, though, or playing? The naked boys,
babies but boys, explicitly boys, are playing
without a doubt. They are playing with oranges
gathered from a tree—for there is a tree here, though
its dark foliage seems to loom beyond the pale
that confines us—*that does not confine us*: we are
free, I tell you . . .
                        The tree is confined, it grows
in a pot, stemming from its sinister chalice—
clay? stone? lead? who can say? Some substances elude
distinction: the unmelting pot stands pat, stays put
in the center of the starred pattern; more than that,
I think it is the center of the ringing world,
the omphalos of earth. You can tell from the tiles,
from the figure they form, that it is the Center.

One boy has shaken the tree, two others take up
the fallen oranges—he is still shaking it,
braced against the trunk, staring into the branches,
but his effort is fruitless, the fruit has fallen
to the . . . ground? no, to the warm mosaic granting
what Dante calls a place where all times are present.
On a pillow near the navel of the world (look,
even from here you can see it is green velvet,
that pillow, just as you can feel the tiles are warm)
sits another boy, golden as the naked three

but wearing a linen shirt. He does not look up
from the orange they have given him—even so,
judging by their gestures—determined, solemn, gay—
I know they will give him all of the oranges.

Everyone old enough to speak words is speaking
at once—praying, after all? Who is "everyone"?
Not yet to have named them is the weakness of our
wandering method—*in mediocritas res*,
as it were . . . Of the seven people with us, five
press their palms together, surely they are praying,
men and women both, old, young, and used to praying.
But not the man with the sword—he glowers after
the Moor whom more than likely he has driven off;
this man is angry, his red mantle shows as much,
and the great sword upraised: Saint Paul is not praying.
Near him and outside the balustrade but looking in
past his fervent hands, an old man in a gold robe
watches the children—no, he is watching the Child,
and if he is too old to be the father, it is
that kind of look: Joseph might come in through the gate
but does not. Job is inside, naked, white-haired
next to the white-armed Sebastian, also naked
but for the arrows. Their lips move, the old martyr's
and the young one's, but they stare, murmuring, across
the enclosure with no eyes for the glorious
selfish children—all they can see, through the branches
of the empty orange-tree, is the group of three
women.
        Of course that throne catches the eye, carries
up four carpeted steps of fine-carved stone, carries
higher to the horn-of-plenty holding highest
a wonderful red parasol. It means nothing
to the woman in blue who does not know she sits
on a throne; she will not look up from her prayers,
she may not even know there is a woman, crowned
and crimson-gowned, kneeling on the step at her feet—
and Catharine looks up no more than Mary.
                                        Only

the woman nearest of the three—nearest to us
as we wander—looks at the children, at the saints,
at everything. She sees what we see. Her lips part
and she speaks out of her prayers—is she praying?
I think she has no place in this performance, which
is called a Sacred Conversation. Look at her:
she wears no crown, she stands aside in a white shift
under a black shawl. Surely she is not a saint,
not a virgin, not a child: she is what we are,
all the rest that widens out of faith (or narrows:
for us, faith is always at a disadvantage,
a perpetually defeated thing which survives
all its conquerors) into a gold, given world,
one without convulsive or aspiring moments,
one. Whereby it is elusive, Out There, beyond
our claims to grace or disgrace: eternal, profane,
a profanity at which she stares. We stare too . . .

The lake plays hide-and-seek with us, we find it there
pressing round the corner of its cliffs, turning cold
boulders in a childish, hushed, expectant way, and
we keep feeling its banks are too big for the lake.
Something lived here once, there are huge holes, doors, even
stairways cut out of rock down to the rising depth,
so that if the water repeats: *I take*, the rock
replies: *I give.*
        A stone's throw across the channel
an anchorite, creeping out of his grotto,
stares knowingly at a startled centaur: life here
is a likelihood of life, call it a final
acceptance of monstrous possibilities, a world
where men—old men, old and tired—are not appalled
by such untoward encounters, but where myths are.
It is the one victory men win over myths.

Behind the centaur, under a wall reminded
by the light what even broken marble can be,
the goats are sleeping together with the sheep, while
their drover waits in his cave for the relenting

darkness; he stares into a gradual evening,
pondering no more than grass, maybe—green grass,
but a green that keeps a secret. The Cross up there
on the clifftop is no more to him than the centaur
trotting down the beach: for the goats, neither exists,
and the light has never heard of Jesus, only joy.

Farther on, further in, the prospect develops—
is that a town? At least the road starts there, curving
up from the lake where it leaves the ghost of itself
curving down, and life—what passes for life—passes:
another drover, someone with a donkey going
home, and a meeting between two human beings;
they are too far, or we are, to see more from here
than their meeting. They embrace: not as lovers do,
or enemies—just two human souls in a frank
community of pain. Then the road moves up, past
the sixteen buildings to the wilds.

                                         All this she sees,
the woman in black and white, bare-headed, alone.
And we see it, the world without a Sacred Book,
a world where neither the negligence of the rocks
nor the endless care of the waters can prevail,
but only that act by which a man wrests something
out of death he knows will return there, to its home.
Death is not home to us, even if home is death—
why else are we here, free on our frail balcony
while that world is bound in being? Patience is home,
and suffering and change, the pang of things past, the prong
of things to come. We bear our poverty within us.
Out There it is . . . out there: God stays in His machine,
and we—we breathe and live and are permitted here.

Longhi notes *that the trees brushed in against the sky*
on top of the precipice rising to the right
are a sixteenth-century addition. Who knows?
The inscription on the frame has also been called
a forgery: *Opus Ioannes Bellini.*

MISGIVINGS

Thebais

for Cynthia Macdonald

In the next small room we find Starnina's panel depicting the lives of saintly hermits in a landscape which shows the artist to have had a highly developed understanding of nature. Starnina (1354?–1403?) remains, however, an enigmatic figure; Berenson does not mention him, and the attempt to attribute this picture to the young Uccello was never convincing.
                                                                    —*Guide to the Uffizi*

There are, by my tally, just a hundred
of us here, monks living and dead, maybe
more—without a jeweler's loupe, who could tell?—
nor am I sure the dead ones count, except
to suggest a symbolic enterprise
to the living (more about that later) . . .
We are all over the place, even up
in a tree, even down in the dragon's
mouth—look over there on the extreme right,
just beyond the white-walled village, see him?—

your common or yellow-bellied dragon
waiting for one of us to wade across,
above the double bridge, where the water
thins to a more negotiable gold,
though why that dragon fails to negotiate
the stream in our direction I can't guess—
all the other animals are here, beasts
of burden, birds of prey, one dancing bear,
and there comes Brother Anselm from behind
the ragged hills, riding on a leopard!

I always said there was something showy
about Brother Anselm, he could never
be content like the rest of us to ward

off jackals, herd our long-horned antelope,
or discipline a fox which has just gnawed
through the neck of Father Eustace's hen—
do you see anyone else riding? No,
we walk, even on water, or else we are
transported, as by devils, through the air
to bleak caves with little more than a bell

and a basket to make our wants known. Wants!
We farm, we fish, and Brother Fred can bake
(if you call that baking). Once in a while
someone remembers us and sends real bread
from town—you might suppose those two in red
gowns were angels, up where George the novice
is reading to the new abbot (we read lots),
but they are merely rich ladies who hope
to have it both ways; every now and then
they stay the night, listening. Then we feast,

and that brings me—feasting does—to my point,
or at least to my line. Any depiction
of human life—and Lord knows, ours is that,
if "human" means warfare with what is not—
goes to show nothing exists by itself,
not even the eminent thunder rattling
Saint Antony who has just wrapped Saint Paul
(of Thebes, dead at 113)
in a yellow mantle he had himself
received from Athanasius, attended

by one of our reverent lions (rather
a desert specialty, that); not even,
between the pines, some intricate red roofs
which correspond to a red-silk binding
of the sermon read over a red-silk bier
of our patriach of earthly arcades
in the opposite corner; not even . . .
But it is hard for me to put you in

the picture over here: there have been no
enlargements made of the entire left half,

we must abide by a general sense of pink
and delicate architecture reproached
by certain precipices only, for
as the Preacher saith, better is the sight
of the eye than the wandering of desire.
And it *is* better, this unrequited
attachment of ours to things in general,
this long perspective we might call tragic
if we did not, like Starnina, call it
love: taken out of scale, taken close up,

it is holocaust. I say Starnina
"calls" it love, by which I mean he labors
to label what he shows, and thereby
calls it love, these coenobite practices
he discovers to us in little boats,
on large boulders, among lilac buildings,
for love is shown in violence, supreme
love in levity. Which joy, once a meager
publicity of pagans, is for this painter
a giant secret of his anchorites

whose world is an adventure, not a scheme,
and our differences from each other
an absolute sanctity. Nothing
exists by itself . . . Who is the man, anyway,
this Starnina of ours? One Gherardo
of Florence, who being nobler in blood
than in nature, by Vasari's account,
brought more harm on himself than on his friends
thereby; and more harm still would have brought
if he had not dwelt a long time in . . . Spain!

where he learned gentleness and courtesy,
so that on returning, those who bore him

hatred received him lovingly. Spain then,
or the desert behind Thebes—any place
of trial is inconceivable without
a semblance of self-exposure. And then
disappearance. Maybe we are not his
at all, because there was no Starnina . . .
Look! a man may vanish as God vanished,
by filling all things with created life.

A Commission

for the composer Dan Erkkila

Of course you will cut dead anything
    that savors of Richard Strauss
and the stews of Mitteleuropa—
    already there has been far
too much fantastication and self-
    indulgence, too much brocade
of the Great-Gold-Curtain variety.
    Let us have no Big Scenes, no
revelations that come down (stage) to
    some diva uneasily
divested of every last sequin
    until there she lies, winded,
a stocky body in a body stocking . . .

No, getting her clothes off has nothing
    to do with the requirements;
your job is to make certain the girl
    has good reason to get dressed!
For months she has been running around
    the palace in no more than
a necklace, pestering the staff and
    embarrassing visitors
with her endless whining: "Watch me dance!
    Watch me dance!" Now you must make
an occasion for her to put on
    finery, robe after robe,
until she startles everyone, swagged

and swathed: the image of her mother!
    Not until the very end,
though, is the resemblance apparent—
    you have to devise something

(ten minutes is what I have in mind)
   austere: not only a holding
back from pleasure, but a suspension
   which is a source of pleasure
in itself. Which is why I suggest
   you go back, or go sideways,
to the music of other cultures . . .
   our own has relied too much
on the passage of time, capitalized

on the lure of foreward movement. Now
   I want you to overcome
or disregard that sense of direction
   toward a final cadence.
A flute should do it, two minor drums
   and those brass finger-cymbals
the child stole from one of her mother's
   maids when the Romans arrived
and caused so much confusion at Court.
   And that's all—easy enough,
I'm sure, for a man of your resources
   (let these intentions be made
audible, not these calculations) . . .

Oh yes, one thing more. Just at the end
   I need a tremendous touch,
not so much loud as a contrast of
   loud and almost inaudible:
thanks to your work, you see, the gestures
   of taking on have *taken*,
that is the ritual your little set
   of variations (you did
have something of the sort in mind, no?)
   incarnates, so when Herod
has her strangled, it is for turning
   into Herodias, not
for that business with the head about

which he couldn't care less. Compose me
    a cadence of last resort,
if I may say so, the finality
    we lack in Salome's dance
with its circular realizations—
    especially if we start
with no more than a sliding scale
    from the flute (hard to improve
on Strauss there, but you can find something
    even more inevitable,
even simpler) . . . The moon is red now
    and the stage is dark, except
for Salome, dead in her robes, that woman.

HOMAGE TO NADAR

for Susan Sontag

Charles Garnier

If no one had heard of you, it was hardly
    your fault, more likely a foretaste
of the stubborn obscurity still to come—

    graduating with a Grand Prix,
you buggered away your hopes in Greece, begging
    permission from the puzzled Turks

to measure intervals between the pillars
    of Zeus Panhellenios, coy
yourself about the purpose but doggedly

    coloring the friezes faded
past recognition while Aegina lay ripe
    for the taking under your hands:

the boys, the nymph and her polychrome marbles
    were no preparation for fame,
nor a dozen water-colors "well received"

    at the 1860 Salon . . .
Who was more astonished than yourself, next year,
    when *your* Opéra was chosen

from all their monumentalities? But if
    we have accepted everything
we have missed something—war. Until that came too,

and your monster had to abide
thirteen years and a German occupation
    before it stood revealed—exposed—

to history and your doom: preposterous
    success and silence to the end,
which included your plans for the Casino

    at Monte Carlo and sculptures
commissioned from Doré and Sarah Bernhardt!
    Chance and Art, superior sports

between your wars and ours, diversions made you
    immortal, loved and forgotten.
Your coat bulges below the Order of . . . what?

    and your hair is beyond disorder:
did they wear steel-wool wigs in the Paris of
    Napoléon III? You regard

what Nadar called the objective straight on, young
    still, and with the intrepid stare
of a very brave ram, cornered but not cowed.

Sarah Bernhardt

Often enough you were naked under the cloak
    in those days; gentlemen drank
and waited, murmuring deprecations

    till the cloak dropped and your arms
which would dishevel the world—those white serpents,
    Hugo called them—were exposed,

thin as your legs, thin and white, but rusted here,
    then here, the rest white and hard . . .
Not yet: you have not yet had success on the stage,

    and if you were a mother two
years back, Maurice never knew his father—
    did you? A nun, you wanted

to be a nun, and became a sculptor, one
    craning female torso sent
each year to the Salon, ardent clay ladies

    in postures of possession.
Mortal will is already your mode, undressed,
    uncombed, probably unwashed—

you are the child he wrote in French for, Oscar
    who understood your crying
need and overheard, just thirty years too late,

    the voice of Salome, pure
gold bangles on a tin wire pulled to breaking,
    and of course the wire did break.

You seem to be regarding, on cue but still
    offstage, in the studio,
the resonant hells your talent sanctified

    for decades of unbelievers.
And taught your century its lesson, dying
    in *La Gloire*, your last *relâche*

attended by a house of fifty thousand:
    dazed Paris, unforgiving,
relented for your farewell tour of duty

    which was to doubt if either
the Heavenly City or that wan shade of it
    our dreams have perpetuated

can function, flourish or even form unless
        it include its opposite,
unless in heaven there is hell. Divine Sarah.

Victor Hugo
The deathbed portrait

You made darkness your own secret and declared
        "no one keeps secrets better
than children." Yours kept theirs best of all, dying

        or delirious before you—
no: you were always mad, but always alive
        until this pious keepsake

showed you had no secrets left to keep, lying
        dead as Charles and François, mad
as Adèle, merely one more carcass in your

        century's series of clean
old men who look like God. Yet cover yourself
        with light as with a garment—

even your beard, still growing under eyes grown
        still, becomes a burning bush.
Yourself! Who troubles now to identify

        such remains, consequences
of a theory condemned, like every theory,
        to masterpieces or else

to oblivion—who finds you out today?
        Swinburne was your last zealot,
Gide regretted, and we—we doubt everything

but the frenzied *aquarelles*
which prove real silence is the end of language,
not just the stopping of it.

No darkness here, no secret save the impression
of being a personage
who became extinct without ever having been

a volcano . . . Your face is
Faust's but with the light of hell gone out of it,
replaced by magnesium

and an embargo from heaven, Daumier said,
because you insisted so
on calling God *cher maître*. Ancient of Days

and innocent of days, take
this day our daily darkness for who you were,
the chiaroscuro lesson

taken but never given: there is only
one pleasure—that of being
alive. All the others are a misery.

Honoré Daumier

The absurd has its reasons which the reason
absorbs: now the outlines throb
when you draw, and the decade of sight left you

will leave you diligently
vulnerable to the long littleness of life,
who revealed so little else—

for you humanity was definable
    broadly by its weaknesses
or narrowly as your crayon could encroach

    upon the printed province
of that other Honoré who found the fraud
    in your tiny lead sculptures:

"This man has a touch of Michelangelo
    in him trying to get out!"
You gaze into the future which is darkness

    gathering at the far end
of Nadar's studio, as if you understood
    that from now on you must force

the edges of things to fulfill their centers—
    to you it is apparent
that the first portrait was a skull. No wonder

    you can paint nothing, these days,
but Sancho and his Don, flesh and the mad bones
    coursing across a bright plain

which is hell with hope in it, the real hell.
    Shadows are wanted; you work
by too much light to believe the visible—

    we need to keep in the shade
of Something that is greater than what we see
    and that we don't want to face

all the time. You will provide manner with fact
    and let matter, thus obscured,
dispose of itself. What you have kept will earn

    its keep, not theory but thirst,
one vision sustaining you twenty blind years:
    it is a truth that all men

are tragic, even a sublime truth; it is
　　a truth equally sublime
that all men are comic. And you never lied.

Jacques Offenbach

Your great days are gone, great days are always gone
　　and only the clothes remain
to prove how rich you were and if German once

　　or even Jewish, still French
by Imperial decree and the Emperor's
　　own tailor. Yards of sable

cannot smother apprehensions—bankruptcy
　　hovers like the next good tune,
and you strain your ears for that inspired stammer

　　which precedes all melody . . .
Henceforth there will be no major breakthroughs but
　　some marvellous backsliding:

the vogue has grown too vast for suave allusions
　　to Verdi and Meyerbeer
—your magenta period—hence a skeleton

　　in pince-nez and puce knit gloves
prepares one more time to rape the double-bass,
　　a cantor's son from Cologne

now "the little Mozart of the Champs-Elysées"
　　according to Rossini,
who should know. Your face is a cold rooster's, old

cock fresh out of sunrises,
and you take off your pince-nez as carefully
        as if it were a dragon-

fly, breathing brimstone on the lenses. To the pure
        all things are rotten, and you
have made music so profligate it is no

        wonder more Germans would come
to Paris and suppress it with cannonballs.
        Whereupon the foam died down.

Not even the New World can indemnify
        Orpheus from your underworld;
miracles of wit and monsters of moral

        obtuseness sufflaminate
your hopes for *Hoffmann* (never heard) by one last
        succès d'animosité . . .

Genius balked only because you could not bear
        to be alone with talent:
the will says *free* and the world says *lost*.

Gioachino Rossini

How much you could have told me, Maestro, about
        wigs (who needs to know it all),
wearing here a sleek horsehair effrontery

        over frizzled white sideburns,
brazening the vast fraud past vanity *or* art,
        even wearing, sometimes, two,

one on top of the other—for warmth, you claimed,
    extinguishing cheeky stares
by a "speaking likeness," this hard look that says

    I know I'm making a fool
of myself, but what else have I left? Vale-
    tudinarianism

lasting twenty years has its lesson to teach:
    a man must begin to love
in order to avoid falling ill, as Freud

    subsequently reported.
Gift or giveaway, *success* and its sequel,
    silence, equally immense,

round off every corner of your countenance,
    and behind those lizard lids
the words *genius* and *failure* represent

    nothing really existing,
only a stage of understanding ourselves.
    Not that you breathed such words, for

breathing came hard—they are what you would have said
    had you been bribed (by Wagner,
say) to defend yourself. Instead you merely

    changed wigs and smiled, satisfied
to speak by means of some brief exhalation,
    much as a Mohammedan

might spit, and by writing more tiny pieces
    with your left hand (though *for* both);
as if to inquire, by that very restraint

    of ecstasy which makes all
leisure possible—no instigator now,
    merely an institution—

"Where is the life that is not a new defeat?
        Yet where is the life that was
not always meant for a kind of victory?"

Richard Wagner
A disputed portrait by Nadar Jeune

No props—for once we have you unstaged, ideal
        genius at forty without
wadded-silk dressing-gown, wine-velvet beret,

        a villa filled with idols.
You stare off-camera at—what? Here at least
        there is more than meets the ear

cocked, this moment, for Frau Wesendonck's praises
        and for Cosima's prayers—
so much more ardent, at sixteen, than Minna's:

        a few infidelities
will bring far less sorrow than the long-drawn-out
        disloyalty of desire.

What we see is what we dream you must have been,
        boldly readying yourself
for what Baudelaire called the greatest honor

        a poet can have: to do
no more and no less than what he intended.
        Until your will had been done,

the difference between sanity and hysteria,
        illusion and reality,
had always been a matter of time: what was

real, what was sane, had always
lasted longer—only truth was continuous.
    You would alter that, transform

our fears and even our fatigue, you would force
    time to change shape and by cold
legerdemain, from Ortrud to Klingsor, make

    event, mere happening, into
duration, having discovered the center
    of our every appetite

is in its metamorphoses. Wait, though—dates
    conflict, the size of the plate
is wrong, and you hated Nadar; for a man

    just over five feet, could these
long shanks be yours? Experts shrug, and we are left
    with the old dissatisfactions:

complete understanding of a dream includes
    the knowledge that it is one,
and such knowledge wakes us up. This is not you.

Charles Baudelaire

You were the hero inherent in Eros—
    "builder of cities" all right
but saboteur as well—wherefore you despised

    such indispensable prey
as readers who failed, despite your example,
    to pluck themselves a garden

from the garbage of the past. If we look hard
     at things they seem to look back;
out of a writhing greatcoat you stare at us

     with that splendid impatience
which is the deepest French virtue, "taken"
     by your lifelong friend between

hyperboles—at one extreme, lilac gloves
     and black curls to your collar,
at the other, Jeanne's insulted beauty and

     bald paralysis—but here
implacable, holding fast to a passion
     for exactitude. Today

you published ten poems you wanted to call
     Lesbiennes until advised
by Hyppolite Babou to name them *Fleurs du Mal* . . .

     Why not? you are so busy
with your current Poe translations and puzzled
     by favors to be curried

from George Sand, "poor dear dreadful little lady,
     always having a crow to pick
with Jean-Jacques!" You look at things, though, look until

     you don't know if they are you
or you they: it is the moment when what was
     ruin becomes a model,

Paris a synonym for both. Arbiter
     of ennui, you rummage on:
Mexican idols, a gilded Buddha, rag dolls

     might as well be our true God,
offensive concretion of the temporal
     process. We cannot erect

the New Jerusalem until we destroy
    Babylon; what do we use
in the building, you asked, but the same damned stones?

Edmond and Jules de Goncourt

Fiction was no help, though folly more than fact
    was what you found diverting
and made more than that for us—made it something

        halfway between dirty and
    divagation, incidentally making
        yourselves, into the bargain,

    masters of a vipers' nest coiled underneath
        every page, masquerading
    as footnotes. Fancy discovering you both

        so handsome here, yet for once
    indistinct—the blur is surely not Nadar's
        but some morose confusion

    of your own—say the confession of "two lives
        never parted in labor
    or in pleasure," knee to knee, white hands guarding

        cavernous crotches. Of course
    one of you went first (syphilis at forty: so
        you must have been parted once

    in pleasure), while the other just went on
        with the *Journal*, year by year . . .
    Writing together, your task has been shedding

one kind of glory to take
up another, yet it was child's play to you,
    and you took a child's delight

in it, pouring vinegar on troubled waters
    with a sort of awed contempt
while, during the dark discipline of Paris days,

    all your bibelots rattled
in the Rue Saint-Georges each time Baron Haussmann's
    wreckers struck again. Meanwhile

you needed nothing but each other; well, you had
    each other—no one reads you
now, and no wonder: a man writes to say, *I*

    am not the only one, and
you were two. Then Jules died, and you, no longer
    "raising your eyelids as if

taking off your clothes," in Gautier's words, you,
    Edmond, sat down again to write . . .
Come dust now, come shadows, for the world is dead.

Gustave Doré

This is your last thin moment. Work fed you well,
    wealth followed and fondled—no
wonder the Goncourts mocked your pink face, "the full

    moon in a magic lantern."
England, at least, could be persuaded to switch
    the lantern on: Biblical

landscapes the Salon regularly refused,
    huge leathern daubs, sold out
in the London shop you bought to show them in.

    And all the rest, save Maman,
was a cheat—smart young men who aped your mufflers
    and marvelled at the magic

would not withstand your ardors. As if something
    was out of scale . . . How the size
of things disappoints (your Ancient Mariner,

    even your Wandering Jew
were tiny tempests in the vast black teapots
    you brewed them in), not because

they are so small but because the mind itself
    is so huge. The engravings
persisted at a heat so white it would melt

    the very heart in your mouth.
Soon you had illustrated two hundred books,
    and no one came to dinner;

Maman was dead; the ink dried in its well;
    your Strasbourg was German now . . .
And at fifty, having prevailed on the world

    to see its classics your way,
you blew up, eclipsed by your own garish luck.
    You swallowed too much, even

the one boy who stayed (for brandy, you pleaded):
    le gigolo malgré lui . . .
When nothing was left to eat you had to die:

    as long as some reality
remains outside us, we are still alive
    come hell or high water, both

of which came with remarkable frequency
        until fire was just fussy
and the flood frivolous. Then the page went blank.

Théophile Gautier

My God, you're my age and look at you: a wreck!
        Lank across the "ruined brow"
and rippling to the ripely crusted collar,

        rusty locks to which no nose
but yours has the key—your cheeks furrow away
        from it as though from a prow

till the rancid wake of your beard rusts out in
        the shallows. You have been had
feature by feature, all fine once, all foul now,

        till only your eyes, sandbagged
against what overflow? stare from the leavings
        of wine, women and hashish.

What are you wearing? White leather, it looks like,
        a gown from Turkey, throttled
with a scarf, below the scurf, from Liberty . . .

        When the divine beds become
mortal battlefields, this flesh is the result:
        you had no need of heaven

or of hell either, but lived instead on chaos,
        reminding us *improper*
was first used of humans in your 1850s . . .

I guess I love you even so,
for beyond the national satisfactions
    of the mouth, beyond in fact

the daily business of revelation, you
    symbolize the paradox
assaulting us when we learn that history

    is merely experience.
Your hands are not seen—they shake too much to show—
    but it is a prejudice

to suppose instability must be sad
    or trivial; only those
who can still love their faults make good confessions,

    and yours are good as the Devil,
who is always the other thing than God, God
    gone to the Devil. No, not love,

it is envy I feel, contemplating you,
    your fate consumed by sacred
couplings in a burning world—consummated.

George Sand

You were comrades, *compères*, Nadar had even
    named a balloon after you,
so when, that afternoon in his studio—

    though you were sixty, beyond
seduction or at least beyond seducing,
    irreproachably chaptered

at Nohant in a rustle of no more than
        imaginary copulation—
when he asked you to sit for him as Racine

    you went along with the gag,
if it was one, wrapped yourself in red velvet
    and a Louis-something wig

left around for fancy-dress parties, and lo!
        disclose yourself a classic
in precisely the moral drag you managed

        to forgo for a lifetime
of thriving on what others call intuition,
        though it is in fact no more

than a subtle human power of noticing,
        or attention, or simply
trust in experience. Neither the *grande dame*

        your dreadful novels flouted
nor the *grande amoureuse* you flattered yourself
        your lovers were not up to,

you still belong with the subversive poet
        you take off or put on here,
for you have discovered that to make choices

        is nothing, to take them less—
to create choices is everything. The ones
        you created were a trap

Racinian enough for your disguise: releasing
        inhibitions is quite as
compulsive, repetitive and hysterical

        an operation (and opus)
as repressing them. Perhaps a genius
        though never a gentleman,

you pose with a flamboyant frumpishness past
    the dull coquetries of sex,
serenely heretical, efficient, real.

Nadar
A portrait by Nadar Jeune

for Rosalind Krauss

You will be obscured by a cloud of postures
    and a roster of great names,
but here, in your high thirties, you can hardly

    be more distinct, distinguished
by hair, hope and the heroic resolution
    to present life with an image

unretouched—had it not been the fallacy
    of centuries to *correct*?
Edited, glossed, conflated, expurgated—

    what was left to believe in?
*All men are mad when they are alone, almost
    all women*: that was your text

and your testimony, the acknowledgment
    of a balloonist whose pride
it was to announce that countless things have been

    seen and remain to be seen,
and for whom humility was equivalent
    to seeing things as they are,

opacity being a great discoverer.
    Why else is it your portraits
loom likelier for us now than all preening

identifications since?
Because you made your Act between consenting
        adults a Sacred Game

wherein the dead god is recognized, the change
        being from darkness to light
and revelation—the god reborn. You were

        our demiurge: from a world
where chaos and cosmos are superimposed,
        from a world where anything

can happen but nothing happens twice, you spoke
        your *fiat lux* or *fiat*
nox to bring forth the creation of nature

        against nature within nature.
Now you have sixty years in which to retrieve
        the visionary from the visual,

then fade into the once and future classics,
        leaving us to enlarge on
what cannot be divided, individuals.

LINING UP

Lining Up
Pasadena: the Museum Vestibule

Better stay where we are: here at least
we have, however odd, what passes
      for a roof over our heads,
and even if the walls are nothing
more than glass, they will be nothing less;
      how else take in so clearly
these citizens coming upon us
in radiant raiment, the motley
      of Southern California?
Where else but in Eden could we find
our freedom only by losing it—
      such nakedness, and such clothes!—
leathers "treated" to be tractable
as silk and velvet supplanted by
      aniline facsimile,
shades of medieval shades louder
than the flaunts of Florence! Our neighbors
      add themselves to the straggling
file we stand in, parti-colored lives
clustered, strung-out, singular, alone,
      these burghers of L.A., some
eager to sample what is promised them,
others uncertain why they have come—
      not turning back but turning
aside, as if reluctant to face
engagements they suspect are lying
      in wait for them up ahead,
although disinclined to loiter long
over an obstacle in their path,
      avoided and already
behind them: *The Burghers of Calais*,
such more-than-life-size Others looming
      monochrome and lame, naked

bronze which has gained a life of its own
—green and grisly, but a life of sorts—
        by merely being outside . . .

We are safe here; you feel safe, don't you?
for all the sudden menace of a sky
        variable to the point
where no one evidently knows how
to be prepared for what is in store . . .
        Well, no one alive; *they* know,
the Six made over to their ruin
by Rodin, who a hundred years back
        (before there was a museum
in Pasadena) found them waiting
for him in the chronicles of his
        fellow snob and countryman
Froissart, recorded without favor
or much fear (five hundred years before
        there was a Pasadena),
men who brought themselves to break the siege,
"stripped, barefoot, ready for the hangman":
1)   Jean d'Aire offering the keys
which drag his muscles down to string,
ecstatic as he moves, Calais saved,
        to a death an hour away;
2)   Andreu d'Andres encircling his despair
within both arms as if the body
        were the pain it knows will come;
3)   Jacques de Wiessant striding, neck outstretched
to let his eyes see *how* it will come
        before the lean flesh can learn;
4)   his brother Pierre beckoning—to what?—
under his crooked elbow he looks
        back to find the angry stars
knotted into new constellations;
5)   Eustache de Saint-Pierre wearing the rope
        as though it might prevent him
from falling before he falls for good
and God, huge hands already hanging

open, helpless, curled to find
comfort in their own unreadiness;
and to complete the invisible
    cube sealing them together,
6)   Jean de Fiennes spreading his arms to let
rags that must once have been finery
        fall open to manifest
a nakedness fiercely young again . . .

Yes, they know what is in store, six men
        shambling to the English camp
where the English queen will save them all,
though they do not yet know about that.
        And maybe they are with us,
always with us, lining up—maybe
we deserve a share of what they know
        and don't know . . . Take any six:
1)   the tall man, for instance, in tight jeans
and a ginger turtleneck, the one
        cupping his hands in order
to look straight into the museum—
is he discovering that to be
        bewitched is not to be saved?
2)   Does the black girl —the one behind him
in unforgivable (and unforgiving)
        cerise stretch-pants know we live
as ruins among ruins, rendered lovely
by staring at ourselves in the glass?
3)   One man encased in plastic
has turned around to face the statues,
buttoning his coat against the wind—
        does he guess what he appears
to know: where all is bad it must be
4 + 5)   good to bless the worst? And the two
        who move so much like ourselves—
do they know what we know: that the great
pleasure in life is doing what people say
        you cannot do? At the end
6)   comes a fat woman with a tattoo

on her left wrist—I hear her sighing:
        "God, You have appointed me
from the first day to fall at the feet
of the living and to stand at the head
        of the dying . . ."

                        Do they come
like this to their reprieve? Will there be
at the end a forgiveness ready?
        Rodin himself could not show,
how can *I* tell these six the good news:
"You have been chosen, you will be spared"—
        I am standing first in line.

Cats and dogs out there any minute . . .
and in here, now and forever, death
        of a kind, as if a man
needed a diamond and was given
the moon: desire is a relic here,
        Venus becomes a document;
or to put it still another way,
inches of Vermeer can mortify
        massacres by Delacroix
and acres of subsequent carnage
(only the Dealer Takes All), so that
        even before we get in,
futility bears down on fatigue
in irresponsible foyers where
        a man can know everything
but nothing else. The omnivorous
package waits, and our riches blind us
        to our poverty . . .

                        Bundle up
against the weather and wait your turn;
we are standing where the burial-
        places of our memory
give up their dead. MUSEUM OPEN
SUNDAY UNTIL FIVE. ADMISSION FREE.

On Hearing Your Lover
Is Going to the Baths Tonight

Does it matter? Do you mind?
Here, now, is an opportunity for Mind
over Matter, the one triumph: whatever
    in life we really accept
undergoes a change, the world is not the same—
    a quality is added,
    everything has its shadow.
As for *minding*, now's your chance: what easier
    occasion for opening
letters (not those from you) like so many wounds,
finding literal motives for being left
    in the lurch . . . what *is* a lurch?
Before you start spying for real, consider
    what is wrong here, or who wronged?
    Name one man (you included)
whose venery, given vent, has failed to be
    venereal in bringing
home the old surrealist bacon: tireless
pursuit of the Same New Thing! What do you have
    to complain about? Having
things your own way is not really having them:
    jealousy is out, as Proust
    has taken some pains to prove.
It has nothing to do with love, jealousy,
    it is only passed around
at the same time, like pepper with the melon,
for people who happen not to know better:
    anyone who knows melon
would never touch it. Your fantasy of his
    body doing what it does
    with yours, only doing so
with others . . . is *that* the difficulty? Then

put yourself at ease: two mouths
have never drunk twice from the same chimera.
What he does with you is you; with others, them:
    "he" remains a mystery—
you personify only what you are not,
    and you are not there. Be glad;
that is a world diminished to an often-
cataloged repository of objects,
    possessing no absolute
and final face, no recognitions. There is
    (Keats has the words) no wonder
    but the human face. What is
that face except our body trying to be
    more naked than the body?
Where better than in the dripping faceless dark
for him to discover, and discard, himself,
    returning then, rinsed free . . .
All the terminations belong to others,
    time alone is yours. Alone.

Carrion (continued)

Dear Charles,
                if I may: have there not ensued
between us correspondences enough
to warrant such familiarity?

I know your detestation of Device—
how you hated all contraptions (but rhyme)
and explicitly determined *la vraie*

civilisation n'est pas dans le gaz
ni la vapeur, mais dans la diminution
des traces du péché originel . . . Yet

by mere mechanism has been discovered
a perspective you would have said cut down
the prospects of the sin you called "original,"

though that is a bad dream I cannot share
—after all, you went to some pains to prove
the real is what we can awaken from.

Charles, a means has been found of making time
accelerate within a lens and then
upon a screen, whereby the world can see

"the thing *you* saw that lovely summer day":
carrion, rot incarnate, charnel (all
the words that put death in any body!),

some animal—senseless expression for
what spread, no longer animate, upon
a clump of compost in some vague terrain,

an empty lot which made it plain: the plot
thins. There lay putrescence, an easy or
—who knows?—an eager prey (it would appear

absence of power absolutely corrupts)
to the host of maggots you were the first
poet to apostrophize: vermin, hence verse!

and frenzied creatures with consuming speed
chewed their way through time condensed by light
to change the corpus of mortality

(the whole is always vaguer than its parts)
into an accurate shackle of bones.
Still, not one maggot struck out on its own—

as if destruction had no preference
to show, as if diminishment could come
only at once, en masse, a legion doom!

Blurring the infiltrated eyes and ears,
then filing the mouth to a thoroughfare,
mysteriously they seethed together

before scaling mountainous shoulders and
a belly where, in seconds, who could say
what was ravenous and what ravine? You,

Charles, whose only sensuality
was to be in pain, you would have divined
how the post- must feed on the pre-

and how, in the beautiful process served
according to these engines' evidence,
we are blessed by our deprivations, if

we let ourselves be. Easing what had been
an opus into an operation, look!
the matter lasted, by these lights, at most

a minute, and what kept the worms at one
and the same task, what made their taskmaster,
said the voice-over, out of the microphone,

was a digestive liquor grubs exude
as grubs exert, substantially eye to
eye, so that each assumes it eats the next,

and all these absorbing devotions do in
the dead thing left undone by its own life.
This was revealed by what is called *time-lapse*

photography, which gives our living-room
the languor of an opium parlor—shows
the same blue glow you would have recognized,

Charles, but it was only *television*!
the one expression banned by Eliot
(your surest advocate among the shades

in death's great city) who declared the word
unmete or at least unmetrical for verse.
Say it was gas and steam, then, which tell (or

televise) the truth I *can* share with you,
not to correct but to confirm your joy,
the poetry of casting off life's chains . . .

Watching that carrion consumed, I knew:
what devours us, how paltry it is; but what
we are devoured by—ah, Charles, how great!

At the Monument to Pierre Louÿs

Jardin du Luxembourg

Sage nor Saint nor Soldier—these were not
the sobriquets he fastened onto Fame:
let other men indulge the mummery
endorsed by these obsequious thoroughfares

with such abandon, yard by gravelled yard—
theirs would not be the idols he adored.
What *were* the sacred semblances he chose
to traffic in? And did they cheat his trust?

Inchmeal moss has muddled the design:
a palm? a laurel? or an aureole
as futile as anathemas would be?
The cenotaph *his own estate* bequeathed

(as though forewarned no Popular Demand
would pay a sculptor, specify a plot
and meet the tariff of Perpetual Care)—
the cenotaph! obtrusive as it is,

thwarts all my efforts at decipherment.
Just as well. There is no cause to mind
whatever mutilations have occurred
as though in nothing solider than mud,

to mourn what the successive rain has made
of this "immutable" monstrosity
erected to an undermined career
beginning only when—as History does—

the tale it has to tell attains its end.
Appropriate decay: like "other men"

he lived in search of what he saw as joy,
ecstatic consolations. *There she stands!*

Balancing an urn as effortlessly
as if no more than his very ashes swelled
its brimming load, behind the stele looms
an academic Naiad rather worse

for wear but rising (the intent is clear)
gently from the reeds' enjambment—she
is cold but she is patient, waiting for
the furtive metal of her eyes to fill . . .

Glancing back in haste to catechize
her shoulders where they falter, suddenly
she catches up a hank of molten hair
and wrings it out as if it had become

another green, wet, heavy nenuphar:
she waits for the tune of little drops to fall . . .
Also appropriate: what else remains
of him but *l'odeur de la femme*, page after page?

And even that would soon evaporate
without the fickle traces of three friends
(Valéry desisted, Gide despised,
Debussy meant what he said but managed to die)

—save for such captious camaraderies,
nothing would survive a period taste
but this absurd contraption: brazen Muse
and marble slab on which all syllables

erode but APHRODITE BILITIS—
the rest is . . . silly. Who was Pierre Louÿs?
The real names of the poems in his books,
for all their happy Sapphic hoaxes, are

. . . and Other Poems. Night after night he wrote
as if there were a tide to float him on,
nacre enough to laminate his itch —
who was it called him an oyster inside a pearl?

If once and for all he could make chance into choice,
change what he had to love to what he wanted to . . .
Forever hostage to the chiding animal,
he was elided. In his will was no

peace, as he learned whenever a meal came late
or the nearest pissotière was occupied:
the change never ceases, never being complete.
There *is* a tide in the affairs of men,

but apt to strand them high and dry. You haunt
my frequentations of your great
contemporaries like a thirsty ghost . . .
I read you, *mon semblable, mon Pierre*!

Ithaca: The Palace at Four a.m.

for Katha Pollitt

FIRST WORDS

No god could make up for the ten years lost
(except by ten years found). Nor would I dream
of trying anything so grandiose
my first night home. Was I trying at all?
Hard to say, when it has taken this long
to be in a fitting position . . . Still,

your old responses seemed to be intact
before I even touched you. Wasn't it good?
For me it was: all that I waited for
(and I did wait, you know—those episodes
with silly what's-her-name were meaningless)
ever since we left those invincible walls

smoking behind us, the islands, the sea
between . . . But if you had been satisfied,
would you have left me sleeping behind you?
Not of course that *I* could satisfy you,
but the occasion itself? Surely that
afforded a fulfillment sleep might crown!

Just look around you: not one trace of blood
left on the marble, not a sign there was
anything like a massacre downstairs
only yesterday morning; then dinner—
wasn't that a nice dinner they gave us?
as if they served a banquet every night!

But all of that—or none of it—would do:
the house swept clean of the scum you condoned

229

(I won't say encouraged, but they did hang on!)
and things back where habit said they belonged:
your own husband lying in your own bed . . .
Yet you had to leave it! Without showing

much solicitude for a light sleeper
who might, after all, have been easily
disturbed (straw rustles and an old bed creaks,
you know: I've grown accustomed to keeping
my ears open—wandering will do that),
you seemed to *drift* over to that corner

where you always kept your loom—it's still there!
and with only one clay lamp to see by
set . . . to work? Penelope, I am here.
You don't have to do whatever it was
you told them you were doing anymore—
stop picking at that thing, come back to me!

LAST WORDS

What I "have to do" has nothing to do
with what I have—or with doing, either.
You tell me I have you. Evidently
you can't imagine what it means to live
inside a legend—scratch a Hero and
you're likely to find almost anything!

Having scratched, I found you. Was I surprised?
Once her womb becomes a cave of the winds
which appears to be uninhabited,
there are no surprises for a woman—
she has survived them all. But at the loom
I learned that even you were ignorant,

crafty Ulysses! Weaving taught me: our
makeshifts become our mode until there is
no such thing as *meanwhile*. Not craft but art!

So you see, I must ravel the design
all over again: there is no end in sight.
Ulysses home? You don't come home at all,

wandering will do that, though I say it
who never left. The loom's my odyssey—
dare I call it my Penelopiad?
You think you were asleep just now, don't you,
after those homecoming exertions? But
you were never here at all, my husband:

the sea still has you—I heard you insist
you were No one. No one? How many times
you sighed "Circe" in that light sleep of yours:
she must have had her points, old what's-her-name.
You snored, but sirens sang, and when the moon
silvered our bed you seemed to feel the sun

depositing tiny crystals of salt
all over your old skin. You were away.
That was your weaving—and my wandering.
The suitors are dead, your bow is a prop,
but neither of *us* is present. Let me
give you some peace at this ungodly hour . . .

Be patient—having found or feigned this much,
perhaps the two of us can fool the world
into seeing that famous genre scene:
The King and Queen Restored. It's abstinence
that makes the heart meander: you're at sea,
I worry this web. Lover, welcome home!

Cygnus cygnus to Leda

for Mona Van Duyn

While that charlatan strutted and preened, I watched
   from the bushes: both of you
seemed unconcerned, visibly detached.

No need of a bird's eye view to see, my dear—
   whether you were done yourself,
the tryst was at an end. Now listen . . .

Listening, actually, would have made clear
   just what was up between you
in such preternatural silence—

didn't you suspect *something* in all that ease
   and efficiency—as if
even swans could do it on the wing?

The word *means* "sound," you silly goose, it follows
   from *swan* there must be *singing*!
You might have known from the noiselessness—

you should have guessed: he was a decoy, only
   some god and not one of us!
In our world, no matter how willing

(I *saw* the kind of resistance you displayed)
   girls can no longer "converse
with animal forms of wisdom night

and day"; there must be preparation, doings
   and undoings—otherwise
you get the Seducer you deserve:

a quack! If all it takes is *feathers* to make
      a fine friend somewhat fonder,
   how would you react (rapturously,

am I wrong?) to a strident suitor who comes
      to you not in fancy dress
   but as the Real Thing? Any human

can make History, it's easy as laying
      an egg! Don't you want to be
   more than a god's way of creating

another god? Look into your heart and confess
      the hope (the fear?) of otherness:
   take me and get *out* of history!

Joy, Leda—joy requires more surrender, more
      courage than pain: surrender
   to joy and serve the unknown darkness!

Here in the merciful air that is without
      a shape it chooses to keep,
   some particle of chaos can be yours

beneath the unregarding stars. Lie down now.
      Troy is no progeniture
   worth your having, once its heroes lose

their little immortality. Limbs are no dance!
      Even stones possess a love—
   a love that seeks the ground. Look at me!

It's no affair of mine to save you, Leda,
      but to make you worth saving,
   being lost. It's in you: I can hear

the SWAN. Swan-song. All fates are "worse than death."
      Leda, I offer you all
   except to be human or a god!

Telemachus

After his father's death he married Circe
—Proclus

She could have been my aunt, she looked a lot like those
fragrant ladies who hugged me when they visited:
    friends of my mother's
I learned to call *aunt*—why not Aunt Helen as well
    as all the others?

Of course I knew they were not the same as *real* aunts:
they would laugh and ask the silliest questions, but
    at the mere mention
of what I wanted to do once I was "grown up"
    they paid attention.

This one listened like that. She looked so much . . . taller
than any of them, it was odd I never gave
    much thought to her size;
perhaps because she moved so little. The sunlight
    seemed to hurt her eyes

—she was sitting in the one spot on the terrace
where the canopy produced a corner of shade:
    the afternoon sun
in Sparta is ruthless as Egypt's (she explained)
    in any season—

and she had wrapped a purple scarf around her head,
casting a purple shadow so I couldn't see what
    color her eyes were.
Everything she wore was purple, though, or
    maybe lavender,

even the amethysts in her rings—like purple eggs.
And yet she must have been watching me as she lay

back on the *chaise-longue*
sipping her stinger (sunlight through the awning made
    the drink look all wrong,

as if coals, not ice-cubes, were in the glass), for though
she had never seen me before in her life, or in mine,
    she knew me, she said,
because she had known . . . my father: "you have the same
    mouth, the same shape head,

and the way you blink your eyes is the same . . ." Funny,
just then I noticed *she* never blinked, only stared
    as if she could see
what? What no one else even suspected was there,
    something behind me,

or maybe still to come. "You'll find him, don't worry,
you can't lose a man like that. Of course you can lose
    yourself, and you will:
that's what finding a father means." And she ordered
    the servants to fill

my pack with presents—"souvenirs of the old days,"
she said smiling—among them a silver wine-bowl
    that had been inscribed
For the Wedding of Paris and Helen, except
    those names had been rubbed

out and *Telemachus and Circe* etched instead
(it would be years before that meant a thing). For now,
    there was another
journey: I must return to Ithaca—no use
    arguing with her.

"I've seen it already. I know. Nothing happens—
it never happens, it only is. Your mother,
    your island, even
that immortal witch whom your father bequeathes you,
    all will be given

because like me you will return. Go now. Power
is the ability to lose." And fell silent,
    actually fell
asleep while I was still beside her—a long heap
    of lavender wool,

glossy amethysts and a sort of sour sighing
were what remained of Aunt Helen. I took the bowl
    and all the other
presents down to the harbor and sailed home to wait
    there for my father.

Move Still, Still So

for Sanford Friedman

Now that I am nearly sixty, I venture to do very unconventional things.
                                                                —Lewis Carroll

1925

. . . bothers me, Doctor, more than the rest,
                more than anything
                I've told you so far—
anything, that is, I could tell you.
                You see, I have this
                feeling, actually
a need . . . I don't know what to call it—yes,
                that's right, *tendency*:
                you know what I mean,
you always know, I suppose that's why
                I'm here at all or
                why I keep coming
back to you when nothing ever seems
                to change . . . I have this
                "tendency" to lie
perfectly still when he wants me to
                let him inside me,
                all of a sudden
I turn passive—how I hate that word!
                I mean I don't feel
                anything is wrong,
but it always happens, just before . . .
                I suppose nothing
                private is really
shocking, so long as it remains yours,
                but I wish I knew
                if other women
felt this way. I mean, it seems as if
                once he's in there I'm
                waiting for something.

The stillness bothers me. Why can't I
    accept it? Not what
    he's doing there, but
the stillness: I can't bear it. Why is that?

1895

        And was it my fault
        it rained Gladyses
        and globes? Quite right of Mrs. Grundy,
        sending you to bed
        one whole day before
        your usual time, and since you broke
        the window, making
        you mend it yourself
        with a needle and thread . . . Now, Gladys,
        don't fidget so much,
        listen to what I say;
        I know ways of fixing a restless
        child for photographs:
        I wedge her, standing,
        into the corner of a room, or
        if she's lying down,
        into the angle
        of a sofa. Gladys child, look here
        into the lens, and
        I'll tell you something . . .

All these years, Doctor, and I never
    knew: was I having
    it or wasn't I?
What I thought I was supposed to have
    wasn't what *he* thought
    I should be having,
and to this day I don't think he knows,
    or any man knows—
    do *you* know, Doctor?
Does it matter if you know or not?

How could a man know—
how or even when
a woman has such things for herself.
Men all imagine
it's the same as theirs,
and of course they think there's only one . . .

> . . . No you're not. Boredom
> is something inside
> people, not anything from outside.
> To borrow a word
> from Mrs. Grundy,
> there must be a knot tied in the thread
> before we can sew.
> Your pose is my knot,
> and this camera my way to sew . . .
> Did you ever see
> a needle so huge?
> Of course, having such a thing at home
> is preposterous:
> it is by having
> preposterous possessions that one can
> keep them at arm's length . . .

Before it happens
I don't move, almost not breathing at all,
and I think it's *that*,
the lack of response
he gets discouraged by. He thinks I'm
dead. I wouldn't mind
letting on, Doctor,
but if it happens I just can't speak—
I can't even move.
He thinks it happens
only when I pretend it happens . . .

> Now that I've made friends
> with a real Princess,
> I don't intend ever to speak to

any more children
who haven't titles;
but perhaps you have a title, dear,
and you don't know it.
I'm cantankerous,
but not about that sort of thing—about
cooking and grammar
and dresses and dogs . . .

Sometimes I pretend—to save his pride
　　　　and prevent a row.
　　　　It seems politer,
that way: why be rude about such things?

Now try it a few
minutes like that, child.
Lovely, lovely—one hardly sees why
this little princess
should ever need be
covered up by dreadful crinolines.
Much better that way.
Princess Perdita,
have I told you out her, Gladys?
the one in the Tale
from Shakespeare, who thought
she was a shepherdess, when in fact
she was a real live
princess all the time!

It can happen, and it does, without
　　　　tremendous effort,
　　　　but unless I take
control and make it the way I want,
　　　　it won't work at all . . .
　　　　At a certain point
I have to stop trying to fool him
　　　　and focus all my
　　　　forces on myself.
There must be a feeling that the waves

will come to a crest
—higher waves. Doctor,
sometimes it seems like too much trouble . . .

When the prince saw her—
not doing anything,
just being herself, singing a song
and dancing a bit
at the sheep-shearing,
you know what he told her? Now listen!
What you do, *he said,*
not even guessing
she was a princess, and Perdita
not knowing either,
still betters what is done. When you speak
I'd have you do it ever, when you sing
I'd have you buy and sell so, so give alms,
and for the ordering of your affairs,
to sing them too. When you do dance, I wish you
a wave of the sea, that you might ever do
nothing but that, move still, still so,
and own no other function . . .

Of course it's entirely personal—
there's no way to share
what happens to me,
but I like it that he's there. I always
want to keep my eyes
open, I do try
to make myself feel that much closer
to him, but meanwhile
all I'm conscious of—
the only thing, to tell the truth, is
my own pleasure. There!
That time I said it,
my own pleasure: that is what it is!

And you'll see, Gladys,
that's what photographs

can do, make you a wave of the sea
that you might ever
do nothing but that . . .
So very soon the child-face is gone
forever, sometimes
it is not even
there in children—*hired models are*
plebeian, they have
thick ankles and tend
to be heavy, which I cannot admire.
And of course I must
have little girls, you know
I do not admire naked little boys
in pictures—they seem
to need clothes, always,
whereas one hardly sees why the forms
of little girls should
ever be covered.

I can't make it happen without the right
    imagining. Sometimes
    I can't bring it off
and I cast around in my mind for
    proper images—
    rather improper,
I'm afraid. I may manage to keep
    high and dry by day
    but with the last light
I venture into the water, all
    that white froth fainting
    out into darkness—
as if the world had become one wave . . .

Stockings, even these
lovely ones, seem to me
such a pity when a child like you has
(as is not always
the case) well-shaped calves.
Yes, that's it. I think we might venture

to face Mrs. Grundy
to the extent of
making a fairy's clothes transparent?
I think Mrs. G
might be fairly well
content to find a fairy dressed at all . . .

I know it isn't
supposed to matter,
but whoever said it wasn't so
important for women
must have been a man!

There we are, ready. Now Gladys, dear,
I want you to lie
still, perfectly still.
I'll help you do it, but the impulse
must be your own. Three
minutes of perfect
stillness will do for both you and me . . .

I always feel cheated whenever
it happens to him
and not to me too.
I treasure those glimpses of the waves
and the high white foam.
I am suspended
before they fall. Doctor, what happens
in that one moment
of timeless suspense?
I feel cast up, out of life, held there
and then down, broken
on the rocks, tossed back,
part of the ebb and the flow. Doctor,
would you mind if I
just lay here, quite still
for a moment? Just this one time, still . . .

NO TRAVELLER

Even in Paris

to the Memory of L. Donald Maher, 1921–1966

I

JOUR DE L'AN, 1953
> *Dear Roderick,*
you are repeatedly missed,
and it is a poor, *showy* charity
on your part to leave us for . . . Schenectady:
    I trust your Ma has been made
    properly conscious of the sacrifice!
How long will it be till you can bring yourself
    back to our selfish Paris?
    Until you do, I suppose I had better
keep you filled in—an expression no Frenchman
    would be caught dead (or alive)
    employing. But what else are letters for?
I think the French are afraid of anything
    full or filling: to them
pleine is pregnant (*ergo* French letters, love) . . .
Not "filled in"—I'll keep you *au courant* instead:
    fallow still, and French as well!

Well then, the day after your departure,
one of those dark mornings only Paris knows
    how to drop in December
    like a swine before pearls, I got up
(one must always get up) and in your absence
    determined to dedicate
    myself to seasonable good works:
indeed I found my old *doyenne* stowed away
    just where you said she would be,
    bundled up like a bagful of knitting
in the Rue Jacob pavillion. Quite macabre . . .

"Miss Barney! Dear Miss Barney!"
I shouted through layers of lilac sheets,
lace shawls, peignoir, bonnet, scarves, Lord knows what else,
but she—*l'Amazone*! Miss Boss!
lordliest lesbian in the Faubourg
(that was at least half a century ago
and a whole *cénacle*,
which seems, once more, to have followed her lead
into oblivion), Nathalie Clifford Barney!—
smiling her goat's smile, murmured
in a thrilling baritone that *talking*
was no use: "I am altogether deaf now—
such a comfort. I have found
words much nicer since they make no sound."
I bustled and fussed round her *filthy* bolster
—what was the concierge *doing*?—
and dropped my questionnaire under the lamp
beside her teeth. Armed with that set of choppers
(soaking in what—*sauternes*?)
she could certainly contend with a few
prompted *souvenirs*. No need for me. I fled.

Opportunely, it turned out:
remember those tickets you gave me for
the *concert spirituel* in Sainte Chapelle?
Richard was *lurking* inside:
"Must be the first time in five hundred years,"
he whispered, "the monument is being used
for a music hall: Poulenc!"
Volleys of coughing ensued (December
in Paris: I am sure you still recollect
the likelihood of *la grippe*
in those great stone barns—*ex cathedra* chills!)
but while we waited, a sudden winter sun,
clearly bored with Catholic
festivals—Christmas especially,
which is only for servants—dim, dull, divine,
changed the chapel to glory,
the entire west wall luminous—alive.

All at once, sitting there, bald Richard began
        staring (across me) at this
fat man under the windows, red or blue
as the famished light devoured the famous glass . . .
        He might have had anybody's
        face—absolutely unremarkable,
as though he had been obliged to put up with
        something ready-made until
        more suitable features could be made
to order—and since the proper article
        had never been delivered,
        he had gone about in this blank disguise
the greater part of his life! Richard went on
        peering at . . . what? What appeared
        matter-of-factness at the expense of
matter *and* of fact. Splendor crept over
        our row until it covered
        even Monsieur X with medieval grace—
Rod, you'll never guess. He fell on his knees,
        arms out, as if receiving
        stigmata from stained glass! And then got up
as if nothing had occurred, dusting his pants
        and muttering (Richard heard),
        "A little kneeling is a dangerous thing."
Which served, it would seem, as a sort of password:
        over my red body, our
        Richard (who as you would say does believe
in taking the bull by the udders) began
        whispering questions—in French
        at first (and you know what his French is like—
like worms on the lawn, coming in and out) and
        the fat man answering as if
        the language had sinned and he was assigned
to punish it, then switching (both) to English
        with an evident relief,
        murmuring relentlessly away. But
then the music started—all I made out was:
        ". . . an attempt to escape self
        is likely to be identical with

an attempt to discover it . . ." Whereupon
        the *Stabat Mater* "filled in"
(how else to put it? I was as nearly
bored as enthusiasm would permit), yet the scene,
        instead of being cut short
as it should, went on, Richard *obbligato*,
hissing interrogations in that way he has
        of answering them himself:
"How do you find Paris, from inside, I mean—
wonderfully homogeneous, don't you think?
        Have you met French people here?"
and even (you know Richard) "Is *your* French
adequate to your needs? Might I be of help?"
        I can't tell if Richard is
very forward or just very backward,
but when this person actually *did* reply:
        "The French conceal their virtues
and flaunt all their vices on the surface;
ludicrous, I call it, their lust for dragging
        everything into the light"—
Richard looked as if he had just been slapped.
Or kissed. And just then, nicely framing the scene,
        the sun forsook the windows,
and the whole damned Sainte Chapelle turned to *merde*:
nothing so dead as stained glass lit from inside.
        Richard, *of course*, persisted
with his nonsense about the *unity*
of Paris . . . And lurching past, this person left
        with Richard hanging on his words:
"The French always believe equality
consists in cutting off what sticks out . . ."
                        My dear!
        Now Roderick, according
to Richard, our *anonimo* was none
other than the Fourteenth Way of Looking at
        a Bleak Bard—R claims he knows
the face (incredible!): Why don't you do
a touch of detective work for me . . . Granted
        there was something of the priest

in the man, or perhaps of the eunuch . . .
Who knows? Richness, ripeness, even just a touch
        of rottenness . . . "My poet in Paris!"
    Richard kept harping, "who means more to me
than all your harridans ever could to you . . .
        So I did, in fact, see Shelley
    plain, even in Paris." "Very plain," said I,
which released a salvo of salacity
        about my "Sapphic goose-girls,
    Romaine, Rachilde and Ida Rubenstein! . . ."
This argued with all the eager energy
        whereby he overpowers
    even the people who agree with him!
Do find out for me—just for fun—if this poet
        Richard has such designs on
    is still in Connecticut . . . or is here,
after all? Can it matter, such a *creature's*
        being on hand—even on foot?

    Meanwhile I managed to grope my way
through the disconsolations of a Paris
        twilight, across the river
    and into the *boîte*, sniffling all the way
to the dear Reine Blanche, a menagerie
        without cages, and the night
    closed down as usual. Who cares whom we meet
by day—it's what we do in the dark that's real!
        All I ask is for someone
    to make me fervent, and I'll do his
bedding. Remember?
                    Happy New Year,
                            Ivo

II

Dear Roderick, the New Year has set in—
like an epidemic. The wolves are gone,
but Villon has the winter down *patte bas*!

Christmas *is* a deadly season here,
illustrating the old Parisian rule:
every silver lining is tarnished by clouds.

Life seems so piecemeal: "Oh that, that belongs
to my Litter Period." So much for '52.
Perhaps just sending this, or anything,

to Schenectady will make the pieces fit.
News—not mine, but *the* news, Roderick,
leaves me at a loss for language, clogged

like a bottle of Burgundy held upside down.
Guess what! Paris is being visited
(*graced* is hardly the word) by Crispin himself!

who never once in seventy years detoured
further out of territorial
waters than a weekend in Key West.

Remember Edna's story about Henry James
preferring to stay among the vegetables
when she took him with her to Les Halles—

"precisely because their organs of increase
are not so prominent" . . . Was Europe's meat
too bloody for my poet all these years?

Yet there he sat, the old Comedian,
continuous as an eggshell, right beside
Ivo, and freezing like the rest of us

—only from higher motives, I am sure—
in Sainte Chapelle, contingency resolved
to kingliness. Each time I tried to make

acknowledgments, the Poulenc interfered,
as well as Ivo's scowling all the while,
like a Dying Swan that is very, very cross.

"The kings sit down to music, and the queens"
—to alter Kipling's verse—"stand up to dance,"
by which I mean that Ivo ran away

once I informed him who our neighbor was . . .
Another *fine*, another *fin-de-siècle*
feast or fast with dying dowagers:

the past is always Ivo's choice because
it is drained of fear. I braved the present out,
putting the usual impertinences as

to When and Where and Does the prospect please,
and Will you go on to visit Italy?
("I think not. Italians are only the French

in a good mood.") At least I got replies!
"The tourist's purpose is to be delighted.
Nothing odd or obscure. I have survived

too long on postcards from Paris or Toulon.
At my age, I may say, life melts in the hand,
and I have dined enough with the faithful dead."

Timid yet tenacious, I asked on—
they must have been the questions he could use;
he did not turn away, yet seemed to exude

a gentleness no longer incarnate but somehow
hovering above him in a nimbus, even though
the light in Sainte Chapelle was going dim . . .

Roderick, I was gossiping with a god!
Maybe because I showed I knew as much
without an autograph or a lock of hair,

I was told I might escort him—*steer*, he said—
to the Louvre next day. ("What I want to see
is in the Orangerie: is that the Louvre too?")

In order to make "sense" of the *Nymphéas* . . .
"I have been told one is embraced, they curve
around one in a continuous ecstasy . . .

It seems worth leaving even Hartford for that.
I have always wanted to stand inside the light
which falls at home—falls out, falls down: falls,

that is the point. In Hartford, the light falls,
and what is fallen does not cease to fall.
I'd like to let those water-lilies have

their way with me; I'd like to learn from them:
if Anything could be explained, then Everything
would be explained . . ." There was, of course, a catch!

No one's to know he ever came here—no
first impressions of Paris, photographs
of boulevard encounters, above all

no poems. The whole preposterous episode
is to be wiped out, elided—*never was!*
I made a stab: "And have you come with Mrs. . . . ?"

"No. Journeys taken together lead to hell.
I want to be, this once, a living man
and a posthumous artist. Ideal. Shall we, then?"

Surely this was He-Mannerism at its best,
an invitation being the sincerest form
of flattery; besides, it was a mere *traipse*

squiring the old absquatulator home
to his safe haven in—where else?—the Ritz!
Even incognito our Crispin knows his place.

We talked, or he—dialogue being no more
than a literary fiction taken for a fact
of life—*he* talked, in a timbre bearing words

before him on a salver: "Limelight is bad.
What's best for me is half-light . . . *crépuscule?*
La lumière qui tombe entre deux tabourets:

the profit of French is how readily it submits
to prose. I suppose I am one of those [three rhymes!]
who can tell you at dusk what others deny by day."

By now we had advanced to the Place Vendôme
where the Column bedevils what it can't adorn
and where, at the wicked doorway of the Ritz,

the din of inequity swallowed up my man
as if there were no such still pond as poets!
The night remained. How sad it is to part

from people we've known only a little while!
Hours to pass, to pass through, to pass by . . .
I stopped at the Reine. Ivo of course had flown

that brazen coop which would display till dawn
a nature shocking-pink in tooth and claw . . .
Not much rest tonight. The rest anon.

Well, dear, we reached the *empty* Orangerie
(day-after-Christmas void) and there we stood,
enveloped by the ovals of nenuphars

—yes, rather *like* the islands of Langerhans,
actually: there *is* an anatomical sense
of visceral perspectives. Once inside,

you must admit, a cycle of mustard and mauve
makes it hard to link how much there is *of* it
to how little there is *to* it. Roderick,

do you know what a *temenos* is? A ring of dread,
the invulnerable range the Greeks proposed
around their gods and heroes. That's what I saw:

my poet paralyzed by the perimeter
of a wave without horizon, without shore . . .
He stood stock still, and I think it was awe

he felt at how the visual could turn
visionary. He stayed there a long while
(I, meantime, loaded up on postcards: X

marks where he stood, admonished by Monet.)
"We also ascend dazzling," is all he said,
or all I could make out—is it a quote?

You'd have thought I had *awakened* him
by shouting in his ear; he started up
when I *whispered* was he happy? "Happy here?

—how hideous the happiness one wants,
how beautiful the misery one has! . . .
I think I'll stay a little longer here.

Alone." I left him then, of course—
mine was the backward glance of Orpheus
or of Lot's Wife, the unretarding gaze

that loses the beloved where last seen:
my Sacred Monster loomed, one big black lump
in a circle of besieging light, and Rod,

he was slowly, in a sort of demonic shuffle,
turning, turning round the oval room,
palms out and humming harshly to himself—

it was, I could tell, a ritual exploit
danced by the world's most deliberate dervish—not
whirling but centripetal. Outside

the air was crumbling, there was no more sky—
only that Paris substitute which fills
the calendar till spring. Ivo won't know

what he incanted like a sacred text:
"We also ascend dazzling." All Ivo knows
is Rumanian nursery rhymes and the Almanach

da Gotha, which he keeps in his medicine chest.
Roderick, do you recognize the phrase?
Myself, I think—however insane I may be—

it does console one to have living gods
on whose warm altars one can lay one's wreath,
as I have done—I brought him there, after all.

Dear Roderick, if you have been denied
such aptitudes of worship, I pity you.
But enough about you, dear, let me return

to my distances, my deference: the great
are like high mountains, you must be
away from them to enjoy them properly.

I'd better stop before I've told it all—
some people can tell all before they start;
suppose you try, dear.
                    Happy New Year,
                                RICHARD

III

EPIPHANY
            Today's red letters, Roderick,
        in my new Hermès *carnet*
    are entirely apposite to last night;
the Great Event, on which my various wiles
        converged, has ultimately . . .
    eventuated, and I am at peace,
though as you apprehended, out of pocket:
        one does not dine with a duke
        or even a diva and get off cheap.

It can best be reckoned, my affecting *fête*,
     as a conjugation of
irregular verbs: I disbursed, she gorged,
he dozed, we guzzled, and they—down to the last
     garçon at the Tour d'Argent—
they cleaned up. By now the party has
that incontrovertible inevitability
     always ascribed to the past.
None of it was easy—recall the cast:
the royals, the Count, Romaine resuscitated
     and Zinka semi-extinct . . .
The arduous part had been to get Romaine
out of bed (she never sleeps, but lives and moves
     and has her belongings there)
and into more—or less—than a tuxedo.
Z was wearing some beautiful old Lalique
     that seemed, on her, oddly placed—
like bits of Palestrina rendered by
the dinner orchestra. Of course we set out,
     for Zinka's sake, in French
but I get up hungry from French (not from
the Tour d'Argent: *canard pressé* answers to
     all my unhurried longings) . . .
Besides, as soon as she was satisfied
we had paid sufficient attention to her,
     Zinka lapsed cheerfully
into her *asperges blanches truffées*,
and we were in English, if not at ease. Rod,
     do you remember those *chairs?*
Cushions so thickly covered with buttons
that one feels like a very sensitive bun
     having its raisins put in!
I can't think how "David" (please to observe
the ease with which the Duke's name leaps from my lips)
     contrives to sleep so soundly
on such upholstery. I sat across,
noticing how his hair has turned so much lighter,
     his wrinkles so much darker
in the Nassau sun, that he seems to be

a negative of himself. He gives the feel,
     even the smell, of decay,
of aristocracy *in extremis*,
sinister and trivial and gentle and strange—
     just like an exquisite goat.
Romaine ignored the tiny snores and launched
across the lobster Newburg ("a nice *purée*,"
     the Count had just confided,
"of white kid gloves") into that old routine,
her dissection of Duff Cooper: "the only
     ambassador whose portrait
I was *embarrassed* to paint—it was not
that his *derrière* was so much bigger than mine,
     but that his teeth, when he smiled,
came in three colors: yellow, blue and black!
Excruciating sittings—he *would* smile. And dull . . ."
     Whereat the Duchess chimed in,
abounding in her sense: "*Harold* once said
Duff had been offered thirty thousand pounds
     to bore the Channel Tunnel."
It seemed to bring her back to life—
though it is one thing to be admired because
     you are so attractive, and
quite another to he admired because
you are so attractive still. She really was
     smothered, or at least choked,
in rubies ("four days of a fish diet
and you can wear anything, my dear"), and while
     Romaine's own teeth rattled on
like dice in a box, the Duchess advanced
to Lady Diana . . . "To hear her talk, *as she does*,
     about her escape from France,
you would suppose she had swum the Channel
with her maid between her teeth!" And in the noise
     of sudden silence that fell,
a kind of ghastly horticultural calm,
the Duke appeared to have wakened—to have *heard*:
     "Really, Wallis! there are times
when I fear your taste is . . . elementary."

Roderick, he started up and spoke her name
   with so sharp an emphasis
   that a man at the table nearest ours
whirled round as if someone had been calling roll
   —as if he had been found out!
And you know, I am sure he was the one
Richard *attached* himself to at Sainte Chapelle,
   munching alone now, as if
   on both sides of the Communion Table,
a sort of solitary manducation *de luxe*!
   Of course I asked all around
   if anyone knew who "that gentleman" was,
but to no avail. How much of a lion can he be?
   I may take no exercise
   except jumping to conclusions, but who
wants to believe "my great poet" looks like that—
   an apathetic mushroom
   in gray flannel whom you could no more
read than you could stab a pillow to the heart!
   Zinka, meanwhile, just like all
   deaf people, was provoked because the Count
—so kind!—was repeating Wallis's remark
   which she had happened to hear . . .
The Duchess turned, contrite, to her Duke
and vowed to spend next week in mourning—"except
   for stockings: I haven't worn
   black stockings since I gave up the can-can."
By then Romaine, who enjoys a joke so long
   as the point is obvious,
   had managed to modify her molars
to match the *mousse au mocha* and seemed eager
   to regain what she regarded
   as due dominance of the table by
describing "my first encounter with your papa"
   —this to the Duke of Windsor!—
"at which I do recall a remark made,
one which struck me at the time as notably
   happy, but unhappily
   a remark made by me, and not by His

Majesty." Even the Duke actually laughed
    aloud—a likely signal
  for table-talk to dwindle down to pairs,
which in our circumstances, given our set,
    meant that in every instance
  of utterance, it was only one step
from the incredible to the indispensable.
    As the sole participant
  with perfect hearing, I am empowered
to report one provocative moment when
    the Count, trumpeting into
  Zinka's better ear, announced that he liked
nothing more than lying on his bed an hour
    with his favorite Trollope!
  (but in a circle such as ours, of course,
not much interest was taken, either way) . . .
    Still, I am fond of my *fête*,
  and when you moralize: *où sont les neiges*,
or rather: where is the cracked ice of yesteryear?
    I shall always remember
  not so much the unforgettable group
(one soon forgets the merely unforgettable)
    as that sad, fat diner
  turning with real terror in his face
when David shouted Wallis's name . . . Was he not
    just *there*, like an accident
  looking for somewhere to happen?
                                    Roderick,
if I were you, I shouldn't hold my shutter
    open in Connecticut:
  I think Richard must be right, and the Blue
Guitarist *was* among us. What is the use
    of lying when the truth, well
  distributed, serves the same purpose?
Perhaps he'll attend my next *petit souper*,
    assuming I can persuade
  him to come or Richard to escort him:
hard to determine what the lesser evil is . . .
    Meanwhile Paris must survive

the rest of January and therefore
the punishing presence of the commonplace:
    other people's lives remain
    decorative, to all appearances,
only provided one takes no part in them.
    Enjoy Schenectady, dear,
    and give my love to your Ma, if she can
use it. I see I am running out of news:
    better to dry up than dribble . . .
    Nothing but silence, then, and darkness in
la ville lumière: you deserve better from

                                        Ivo

IV

Roderick Dear, today was to be the last
my poet would spend in Paris — although *spending*
is hardly the verb for what I've hauled him through.

He's always praying life not to give him more
than what it can take back, "my poet" by right
of the cicerone's function, which has proved

a fitful pleasure but a constant joy:
he has that scrap of innocence which keeps
most of us from becoming such a bore,

though in his case there are astonishments:
his modernity seems to me miraculous,
as if he had already attended a party

—say, one of Ivo's ruinous *soirées*—
that has not yet been given. We have gone
to the Luxembourg, where Rilke said he had

buried his best bones; to the Palais-Royal,
counting which cornice had to be Colette's;
and ambled through the Comédie's arcades,

stopping at statues—"which *may* be dignified,
but the absence of which is *always* dignified:
extend to feeling and you have the dignity

of Symbolism." We have seen the Place des Vosges
—"grim, yes, apodictically grim,
but a grimness that has a way of looking pink . . .

Hugo's house? No. Better to think of him
back there on Guernsey. Or Jersey. Was it both?
Easier to endure his claptrap out of fog . . ."

You could see a justice in it, for just then
the sun came out and took a cloud or two
to do some high-class, grand-scale modelling,

Poussin, Puvis, all along the rooftops.
This whole day we scoured the capital,
soaking up the Tuileries, glaring in rows

over the somber well of the Invalides,
after the pleasant Gallic fashion. Paris is
"beyond measure interesting." The point is,

he is never disappointed, though outraged
deeply enough to satisfy my own
resentment of these people and their past;

perambulating the quays, not long before
I took him to the Aerogare, he gave
the last of his Lutetian homilies,

the consequence of his holding off so long:
"I can't help it. What is more I don't
want to help it. I've reached a time of life

when nothing helps now; for me the word *France*
evokes a notion of courtesy, of the correct
pitch between persons, whereas the word *French*

means only a sullen concierge and disputes
in shops, alarmed pedestrians and rude
bus-drivers. All my life the word *France*

has meant unity and justice, while this week
I have learned to listen, in the word *French*,
for the nuances of division, nepotism, shame . . .

Now I have seen the Louvre, where the word *France*
glorifies the idea of conscientious work,
art and organization, finished craft;

but among art dealers I find the word *French*
evokes the mystique of improvisation, no more
than a paltry and urbane experience . . .

I have seen Notre Dame, and the word *France*
means a people standing above pettinooo;
I have bought newspapers, and the word *French*

suggests a citizen never free from scandal—
and if he has done vile things, I am not
solaced by learning he quite meant to do them . . ."

We had reached the best of the bookstalls, the one
where you can find all the old Symbolistes;
I pointed out the complete *Mercure de France*,

year after yellow year. He opened one to find
—1897—the Bazalgette translation
of *Leaves of Grass*: "*Nous autres, nous montons*

éclatants et énormes, comme le soleil!
He quite intoned the words, as if the light
of January and the sudden wrack of cloud

that darkened the whole Seine were adequate
illumination: "Yes, but if the light
in your body be darkness, how great is darkness?"

The river moved, and we moved too—the books
in their iron boxes seemed to move with us,
literature from stall to stall the same,

most of the wretched tomes the color of mud,
of the sluggish river. He didn't seem to mind
the weather or the smudged, identical dross;

"The future of the past is never sure.
This must be the one place in the world
where a man can realize what he writes

is a river too. It is continuous,
no burden on the memory, but a way
—made up of all ways—of reaching the sea."

Rod, I shall never pass those dusty bins
and the hags who guard them (themselves guarded by
a shivering mongrel in a shabby quilt

eager to snap, the instant you reach in
for an uncut first of *Les Nourritures terrestres*)
without seeing him still above the river

—the river of books and the winter-weary Seine,
apparently quite content to let them both
run by him—to be *overrun* by what he sees . . .

He says the body forgets nothing, and reveres
things that do not return—for him no moment
is wholly lost: all past experience

is potentially present for him, and this one
visit can withstand an entire life!
He even responds to what seems singular:

three white swans paddling past the Louvre,
a copy of Pierre Louÿs's *Astarte*
(I got it for Ivo) that had once belonged

to Duse, according to the paraphed *dédicace*.
Everything "once belonged." All ownership
is a weakness which passes perception, as I learned:

abruptly he turned back to the *boîte* and bought
—without a cavil at the cost—that one
Whitman-honored volume of the *Mercure*

and stood with it at the top of the river stairs
like a rueful Père Noël, extending the book
and a fistful of hundred-franc notes as well!

to every passer-by, muttering his phrase,
"lancer ce livre comme un bateau," until
one boy stopped, snatched the money, plunged

unquestioningly down the slippery steps
(where every clochard in Paris must have pissed)
to the river itself, and leaning on a ring

set in the embankment launched the book
as if it were a Hindu barge—the waves
took it, open, floating, sinking . . . Whereupon

we drifted loose, neither of us speaking again
once my poet pronounced himself content—
"a ceremony bought is a ceremony still"

—walking single-file up the Rue des Saints-Pères
to the comparative safety of a *café-crème*.
Of course, once we left the river, I recalled

that what he had murmured in the Orangerie
was what he had found, in French, along the Seine.
I looked it up as soon as he had gone,

and I think I understand, now, why he stood
that way, revolving among the *Nymphéas*:
"How quick the sunrise would kill me," Whitman said,

"if I could not now and always send
sunrise out of me." It was the play
of surfaces that held him, infinite,

centerless, unstructured: only ecstasy,
an airless moment when he might not send
the water-lilies back. "Speech is the twin

of my vision . . . unequal to measure itself."
A moment there, he trembled on the brink
of what Sir Thomas Browne so grandly calls

"ingression into the divine shadow." But then
my old wizard—Wallace this time, not Walt—
summoned up his forces, mustered his magic,

and managed to meet Monet's with that same strength
he has survived by at home, where certainly
he differs from all poets since Eden who

in search of the invisible have obscured
the visible. Not surprising that his last
tourist touch should be to *see* something:

"Objects, other lives, inveterately appeal—
call to me, whether I answer them or not.
Would it be a nuisance to stop by

the bird-market behind the Hôtel-Dieu?
Toucans and tanagers, birds-of-paradise—
even time, perhaps, for a blue macaw . . .

nightingales are splendid creatures, if
only I had a bush that might afford
the right retreat . . ." Ivo had been warned

and with his latest *objet de vitrine*
posted to meet us at the Café de Flore.
Once I deliver my poet to the air

we can resume our halfway-decent lives.
Closing in, the day dies out in one's arms
at this hour, stretching its final light

in what would seem a final agony,
too proud to make more of a commotion
than that one patch of purple to the left,

and up there, all that leaking peach.
You've seen cats die like that, haven't you?
stiffening into darkness without a sound . . .

Later my poet joined us at the Flore
where people listen to each other's alibis,
in what will be a *monologue des morts*:

once he leaves, we shall not hear of him,
only read his new book, his latest, his last.
It has been a week, Rod. Who would have thought

there was so much to learn about the moderns?
He is, or conceals, a very ancient myth,
and tending him is the arduous pursuit

of Ariel. From which only lust and tenderness
bring relief: a bird in the bush is worth
a feather in your cap. *Love,*
                                    PAPAGENO

V

Roderick Dear, it is the last infirmity
        of illustrious clichés
    to be "deeply serious": I risk it
for the truth—truth is what I can't help thinking,
        and obliges me to ask
    what are poets for?
                    Last night, Richard brought

his to our table—the stout fellow observed
     by the half-light of stained glass
  and the full glare of Money's Tower, one
and the same corpulent anonymity,
     all introductions to whom
  were carefully fudged and camouflaged
by the heartiest kind of manly greetings—
     I prefer kissing people,
  handshakes are abhorrent, though I grant you:
desire distracts. No danger there—or here;
     the old gentleman had come
  fresh from the bird-market, which was to be
his final impression of Paris. Not bad.
     Only shyness made him seem
  a touch insolent. Intrinsically
his voice was elegiac, and I can't say
     that he had the vanity
  of the true artist: a serious reason
against his being one. He was stuffed so full
     of his avian *trouvailles*—
  "Wings have been plucked from birds to make angels
of men, and claws from birds to make them devils"—
     there was no talking *to* him.
  Listening was odd enough, caviare
to the general, tripe to the few, something
     for everyone. He kept on
  about what he had evidently drunk
too much of to keep to himself: "Just consider
     the neglected incidence
  of love-cries, the human phenomenon
hardly examined by any novelist,
     yet ranging as birdcalls do
  from whispers to the screech of hysteria,
always sounding alien to the emitter
     invaded and possessed by
  some astral spirit with wild ideas
of its own . . . The most mesmeric music I know,
     though literature is silent
  on the subject. It is the woefullest

ill of old age to be certain that one shall
     never hear a new version . . .
  Venturing along the rows of cages,
I heard them summoning me once again, birds
     or women—cadence itself
  at a certain pitch of intensity
becoming a form of substance . . ."
                       Roderick,
     I may embroider somewhat—
  this is not all he textually said,
but what an enemy might be paid to quote
     from his words. I embellish,
  and you may detect a certain garlic
of derision in the salad I toss you
     (if your taste-buds have blossomed)
—I could not endure another moment
of our complicitous little ritual:
     not Richard's adulation
nor the presumptive poet's eruption.
His phoenix played the incendiary with
     all too manifest a faith
  in its own ashes. If you ask me, Rod,
the question of identity is still open.
     I grant you, he kept us all
allured (and aloof), shining on us yet
hiding his light, like some great variable
     yet constant moon, *Somebody*!
But there is no bore like a brilliant bore,
and I believe Richard lost his way looking
     for a genius who might fuse
life and art—*I* had abounding proof
that such a prodigy was not to be found—
     the formula still unknown.
  Richard, of course, with his love of poets
second only to his love of vulgarity
     would revel in the humbug—
one more fly in the amber of homage.
Well, all of us long to have our Great Men—or,
     if we have something in us

of a woman, we do like that something
to be a Great Lady. If we do not have
    Great Men or Ladies either,
    we invent them. Myself I shall return
to my helpless monsters, nourishing for them
    a passion of finality . . .
    Before I frequented my dear grand freaks
I ached and tried to turn away from the old—
    I feared how bored they must be,
    how listless and dispirited. I judge
differently now: they are reduced to *mere
existence*, and do not mind!
    Meanwhile I am sure R is writing too—
soon you will have other evidence by which
    to determine . . . Remember,
    Hölderlin was a madman who refused
to believe he was Hölderlin . . . Here we do
    everything but anything,
    and I abandon Richard to his fate,
wishing him luck! . . . God created luck because
    He did not know what to do
    otherwise with those of us who cannot
make something out of ourselves.

Love ever,

Ivo

Love Which Alters

During the summer months of 1912
Reynaldo had been reading "our romance,"
for so he came to reckon it (at first
you love no longer, then long afterwards
you manage not to love), in paragraphs
and pages as it would be parcelled out:

fansticks, each fantastically carved
yet each a thing apart . . . For the life of him
he could not see how all of it would come
together, how each scene was set to shift
the next until the whole thing folded up,
collapsed by one mauve thread all through . . .

"You cannot see it for the life of you—
it won't be yours. _I_ see it now, I know
the way it goes, the way it comes to me:
the freedom of the rosebush is the rose."
So much for authorship! Reynaldo read
what he was given, mystified, intent,

until on All Saints' Day—November first—
he was summoned. Clearly something had occurred.
"Bunchibils, I need your help—your ear,
just yours —you know what Madeleine is like
in arguments: as if you were dreaming the dream
where you appear in public quite undressed!

And Emmanuel is worse: he knows so much,
and what he knows is so abstruse, he finds
an answer absolutely out of the question

in terms of mere talk. Bunchibils, I need—
I need your bedside manner of the mind.
One word, Reynaldo: *what shall I call my book?*

It has become a book this time, I think,
and any number of names has come to light,
each replacing the next. Help me choose one.
How does it sound—*Stalactites of the Past?*
. . . *of Melted Days?* Is there a music in it—
Stalactites of Melted Days? Or how about

Reflections, wait, *Images—What Is Seen
in the Patina . . . Mirrors of the Dream?
Belated Days?* Oh, I have others. Listen:
A Traveller in the Past—it must have that
at work inside it somewhere: I have nailed
my colors to *The Past.* What do you think

of this: *The Past Prorogued?* Oh yes you do—
when a case has been suspended or postponed
the court is said to be *prorogued.* You hear
the root of questioning in it, I like that:
interrogate—prorogue—I don't see why
people can't look things up, I always do.

All right then, what do you make of *The Past
Delayed . . . The Past Belated . . . The Past Erased?
A Visit to the Past?* Myself, I keep
coming back to *Reflections . . . Dreaming Glass*,
on the order of "looking glass" . . . And still
The Days' Stalactite haunts me—Bunchibils,

are you listening? Of course I care,
it makes a difference, even if it is
only a tempest in my chamberpot,
as you so elegantly say. It matters to me
what stalactites are, and if they drip
down to their form or build up from the floor:

there must be something to intimate a pursuit
of the past: a visitor, a traveller . . .
I give you one week to winnow out a name.
Make it something like . . . like Christianity—
Good News, not good advice! Until you come
up with something, I shall be down with it,

with palpitations (if you know what they are).
This incapacity I feel to own
or to own up to memories is more
like a disease. Mine elude me still;
I cannot really make them mine except
at rare moments, in odd flashes. Perhaps

your method, Bunchibils, of taking them
to bed with you, is best. Perhaps what I want
I have already, here in what you've read.
Fine things are all the finer for being—awhile—
forgotten. We shall brood, the two of us,
and breathe, Bunchibils! We need to breathe . . ."

Then on November seventh, as if there were
no doubt, no hesitation—as if in fact
alternatives had never been proposed,
the title appeared in a letter to Grasset:
"I want the whole experiment to be called
In Search of Lost Time. What you will bring out

next year is only an investiture, the roof
of the cave in which my deposits form themselves,
crystal by crystal. I enclose the proofs,
but only for the first two hundred sheets,
I need the rest to work on still—there are,
you will see, all sorts of changes to be made."

Concerning K

Not one breath. Even the flags had . . . flagged.
Decades of usurpation and fatigue
foreground these polaroids—the postcards lie—
and every street in Prague appears to lead
to a blackened sepulchre. Nowhere to go,

unless one is in the Market for Fleas. Why not?
The Festival was over, they had crowned
and drowned in Tokay poetry's Clown Prince,
Don Giovanni had (again) been foiled,
and the charter flight was bumped another day.

Mitteleuropa was up for sale, piecemeal;
picking desultorily through the booths,
you and the person we both call X fell out:
"—infinitely desirable—" "—Bohemian dreck—"
over the daub you photographed "for me" . . .

Boredom, according to Walter Benjamin,
is a brood-hen on the egg of experience:
a rustle in the leaves will drive her off.
Not one sound. Tenantless the leaves
hung from every willow, every oak.

At least those booths were cooler than the street.
So that was where you found it, in the dark
(as what was not, in the rabid city—gnostic,
rabbinical, patristic, kabbalistic): *dark*
was the distempering of discovery!

Painted in darkness, out of darkness too,
and dubiously meant, on muddy duck,

for a martyred Saint manacled to a stump,
the carcass oddly cavernous for being
so gaunt, more oddly luminous for being

so terribly hard to make out . . . But you did
—if not with X—make out (forgive me!) Saint
Sebastian . . . (Who else? What other throes could be
so eagerly submissive, so thrilling, so lewd?)
And the model! Could anyone else have stood

even a moment for what your letter calls
"a morbid appetite for arrows"? The moral is:
Don't pose as a Saint or you may become one . . .
Not one of the Happy Many, who suffer so far
and then collapse, exhausted, over and out;

just the opposite—the more a Saint suffers,
the fiercer the energy summoned to endure
This Saint, or the human violence that masks
his sanctity in martyrdom's masquerade,
is beyond mere pain. He needs no doctrine,

only opportunities. Here is a good one:
the soul unties its shoes, pulls off its socks
and stands revealed. Still life is still life,
and ears apart—apart from what? Part bat!—
the body you identified (and *coveted?*)

is geometrically impossible, the parts
greater than the whole. Which you wanted to buy?
Own? Haul back to . . . me, I guess. For once,
X and reason prevailed. Imagine possession—
forever to face such darkness, and such light!

The self, divine in each of us, is not
to be fully entered into. Manifest here,
or there, whereof these polaroids report
enough. I know about as much of Prague
as he—your precious, phantasmatic Saint—

knew of Amerika. Photographs transform
space into time, any image will do,
and does: leathery oils whose lesson is clear
(disdain for the world is not love of God)
and whose identity is plain as day:

Kafka writes in his diary for 1912
The painter Ascher has asked me to pose
for a Saint Sebastian. I am to pose nude.
Let it rot in Prague where you found the thing.
X spots the mark. You must resume your life.

Oracles

to the Memory of Vera Lachmann, 1905–1985

Not here. I must be out of the wind,
   under something—otherwise
I cannot light these insipid weeds
   alleged to be cigarettes.
Even they are forbidden, of course,
   but it is too late to mind
or at least, at my age, to matter . . .
   Yes, here: this will do. *In time*,
they say: *time heals*—though what can that mean
   to men your age? What have you
to heal? Myself, I cannot afford
   waiting much longer to heal,
always a matter of waiting, no?
   When it comes to *doing time*
here is the place: Greece knows how to wait.
   Meanwhile, as you young men say
(and mean well by it, though you will learn
   that no moment *replaces*),
I have made what my physician calls
   a massive recovery—
I suppose he is telling the truth:
   the only men you can ask
honesty from are the men you pay
   to get it from. I have paid . . .
Enough to let me smoke a little,
   if I really have recovered.
Not much of an exploit, once they set
   a machine inside your heart:
after all, what is the heart itself
   when you come to think of it
but a mortal machine? In my case
   somewhat less reliable

than most machines, somewhat more
   mortal. In *any* case, though,
all a heart has is the *eminent*
   dignity of a machine,
like so many Swiss inventions—banks
   and boredom and . . . chocolate.
And since that emplacement (I am spared
   the details), my condition
—that is what I have, a *condition*—
   is serious, but neither
fatal nor severe; it is merely
   something that I remember
on certain occasions, like a poem
   (what we say about ourselves
is always poetry). It would be
   offering ignominy
to the gods, perhaps, to live happy
   and well to the end: the gods
exist because men are ill, and as
   Anatole France used to say,
the gods' impotence is infinite . . .
   Best to grow old like the rest
in a *mingled* manner, consonant
   with an ordinary fate.
I have been happy and well this spring—
   too happy, I fear, to be
really well. Understand me: I have
   glorious days, and conclude
that a degree of physical pain
   renders happiness perfect.
The best thing to be said for old age
   —of course we do not always
or even often say the best thing—
   is that it is the one means
discovered to this day for living
   a long time.
            . . . I should have thought
such intuitions wasted on you:
   we never believe others'

experience, and only inchmeal
    will you be won over by
your own. Think of all the boys who died
    young as you—too young to have
learned their own wisdom. Though their own minds
    were active as phosphorus,
they died in whispers they did not hear . . .
    So I am taken aback
or perhaps it is forward—at least
    I am stirred up, seeing
you fellows return so readily
    for another dose of these
mischievous commonplaces of mine,
    just when I had decided
that to be heard out as an old bore
    is *the* ineluctable
consequence of one's declining years.
    (Boredom too has its prestige—
which the reason knows nothing about.)
    But then you are after—or
into, that is what you inquiring
    Americans say nowadays—
you are into something specific?
    Never mind the *properties*;
I shall tell you what I know, even if
    today you find me looking
rather frail and untrustworthy in
    a far too suggestive and
actually Japanese dressing-gown . . .
    Dislike of modernity
and of outdatedness are in fact
    identical; hence my . . . garb.
Of course it is a disguise; there is
    little likelihood of "truth"
whenever feelings of pleasure have
    any say in the matter.
Proof of pleasure is pleasure itself—
    nothing more. I cannot take
my time gracefully, but I take it:

flesh was never intended,
  as Nikisch once said of *Pelléas*,
  to be a success. The most
I can hope for is to age like wine,
  not ferment like vinegar.
You follow me? You are back again,
  so I suppose you must . . .
Ours is a comfortable doom, here:
  just as someone said *un ours*
et c'est la paix, so it is with me:
  un mécanisme et la santé
s'est retrouvée. Or very nearly.
  (You understand what I have said?
French is spoken in every language,
  even on this old island
where the dialect sounds like water
  draining out of a bathtub!)

Very well then, however ill: here
  I lay, tastefully buried
in my texts—my pretexts—quite content
  to be dusted off only
during seizures of necrophilia,
  dozing till you dug me out
—excavated me, that is the word—
  from this classical soil,
all too honorifically lodged
  in this Harmless Institute
for Hopeless Scholars, groggy by night
  and gaga by day. You know
my colleagues? You have looked us over,
  examined the . . . specimens?
Except for myself—whom I regard
  as a *foregone conclusion*—
there is in some sense no single woman
  on this island—only wives.
Quite possibly they were women once
  and have deteriorated . . .
I dine with them sometimes—to improve

the moral tone—theirs or mine,
who knows? They have done up each "guest room"
in the place to resemble
the cell of a rather pansy monk—
Marimekko drapery
and *tofu*—no, *futon* on the floor . . .
Modern man wants to sleep close
to the ground, like animals: we
furnish ourselves with matting,
do away with the bed, and thereby
annul the human threshold
between waking and dreaming. We dream,
of course, on our sleek pallets
—even scholars-in-retirement dream—
but who knows how such decor,
queer as it is, affects us? Between
"it came to me in a dream"
and "I dreamed" lie ages of the world,
but which is truer: spirits-
who-send-dreams or an-ego-that-dreams?
We are not awake because
we have done away with the dream, but
only when we have swallowed
the dream once more, and digested it . . .

As for our Scholars themselves—
you know, Goethe says a celibate group
can create the greatest works,
but an old bachelor will seldom
produce anything sensible.
Equally true of old widowers.
They would be glad to renounce
all Kant and Spinoza to possess
the memoirs of Aspasia . . .
Most of them have been rendered deaf by
hearing the birds sing in Greek
(as they do, but not to the exclusion
of all other languages):

deaf men, but alas quite the reverse
    of dumb; courteous though, and
of course they can be altogether
    engaging—with just a hint
of the usual halitosis—
    to outsiders.

                    . . . No duties. None.
We *do* nothing here, month after month
    —it is nothing, to offer
one lecture each summer to young men
    like yourselves, you *listeners*!
Words are the opium of the West—
    syllables seduce the world,
and history does not merely touch
    language, it takes place *in it*;
the day will come when we each have turned
    into a dictionary:
the substance of things hoped for—our faith!
    Till then we give our lectures.
Even this year, mine went off quite well—
    just one pause when I forgot
what I was going to say next and
    suddenly heard my watch *tick*
tick tick until I realized: *that*
    is my heart! A fine moment.
All the moments are fine now, all days
    simple. As if in a trance . . . -
Perhaps it is not me but some other
    woman, one who likes passing
absurdity under your nostrils
    like a wine connoisseur
extolling old brandy—another
    woman in an unpossessed
place, the future of her memories,
    sitting by this silent sea.
When you believe *I am I* and *she*
    is she, you are unconscious;

when you believe *I am she* and *she*
  is I, you are cognizant . . .
One more of my formulas.

                                Young man,
  I know what you are thinking;
you are thinking I must be a witch
  or at least a wise-woman,
something of a sibyl, but I warn you:
  be cautious here, lest shallow
call to shallow. This is modern Greece!
  Have you not learned what that means?
We are wide awake, and this island,
  once the place of prophecy,
is the site of a Scholars' Retreat
  which combines the infantile
and the degenerate—or perhaps
  it is merely innocence
and inevitability? No,
  you must not be fooled by such
dissimulations. My gown hangs round
  what is left of my body
like classical draperies . . .
                                Hellas!
  To most people, classicism
means *work in class*, and as my mother
  who knew—knew intimately—
Professor Wilamowitz-Moellendorff
  used to say (though not to him):
an hour is enough of anything . . .

  You see, we are all alike,
we Eminent Germans—not so much
  the pupils as the victims
of history. Perhaps that is why
  we write as we do: because
the expression of history in things
  is precisely that of past
torment . . . We Germans are the people

unable to tell a lie
without believing it ourselves. And
    by now you must have observed
our horror of adults with no degrees,
    or at least with no titles . . .
Eminent Germans always seem to be
    swimming deep underwater—
only Nietzsche, that lonely dolphin,
    plays on the sparkling surface . . .
Here, at least, we drown in Aegean
    radiance! Is that why you
—even you fellows—come here to lie
    on these beaches, these black stones,
like so many lizards in the sun?
    No wonder you take me for
some kind of Circe . . .

                        As I explained,
    I have no magic powers.
I am something of a prisoner
    myself, for all liberties
taken, for all licenses given:
    I cannot go up or down—
that is natural. I must abide
    by the level of things, not
venture very high (no danger there)
    or very deep . . . But until
you have attained, or been attained by,
    my years, you cannot conceive
how much depends on mere surfaces . . .
    Why "mere"? Say *sheer* surfaces,
steep as these Cycladic palisades—
    that is where the meanings hide.
In the gods' life, what we understand
    is the moment they lie *hid*:
if I tell you this place is holier
    than others, I only mean
more holiness has run out of it.
    Appearances are apparitions!
What would a god be without weaving

appearances round himself,
or Aphrodite without a cloud
to protect her? Imagine
a goddess *worse for wear*! Meanings hide
in surfaces, that much I know.
Where else could they go?

Truly, I have
lied so much about my age
I forget how old I really am . . .
I think I look sixty-five,
I *admit* to eighty, and some days
when the wrong wind manages
to make its way around the corner
of the *taverna* terrace
I know I feel a hundred and ten!
We become, gradually,
as old as we look, and by the time
we look and have the same age,
it will be all over . . . I can wait.
We are made out of nothing,
Valéry is right, but what we are
made of keeps showing through . . .

All
is nothing, but afterwards: after
everything has been endured.
Till then, everything is something
other than what it is . . .
You are not likely to make much of
what I have just said to you . . .
But then, you are not likely
to be here . . . What is *likely*?
It is an irony, it is even
a paradox you should be
asking for these reminiscences,
these webs I have been spinning
so long—God forbid you might call them
ideas! *Those* my colleagues have,

and from my colleagues I have learned: all
    fabrication of ideas
is evasion of a story . . . But
    for all my stories—have I
even told you one? Have I begun?
    —and my storytelling, too:
I am not like what I have professed
    in those learned articles
of mine, footnoted so flagrantly
    (the test of a vocation,
after all, is how much you can love
    the drudgery it involves).
I am a woman of learning, not
    wisdom. I have been granted
the liberty of those who have ceased
    to circulate, and it is
remarkable how . . . true to itself
    life becomes, how *transparent*,
once one is no longer part of it . . .

    No, *I am no oracle*,
though there are certain observations
    I have come to share, certain
intuitions you might call *mantic*
    (if you wished—like my colleague
counting up aorist variants
    in the closet next to mine—
to keep them from taking any part
    in your memory). For me,
the world is a living animal—
    not an immutable form,
but waxing and waning—not to be
    coerced or calculated,
but something unforeseen that we learn
    by initiation, not
by experiment, a vital force . . .
    The world is subject only
to choice, not to solution—it is
    a *figure*; one I observe—

if it matters what I do . . .
          I have
    Gibbonian apprehensions:
it seems to me that an extinction
    of all art is prefigured
in our growing incapacity
    to represent history—
historical events. To us the past
    always appears as destroyed
by catastrophes. Perhaps it is,
    perhaps that is our tradition.
Adequately to hate tradition
    one must have it in oneself . . .

For sure my fears are not Pythian:
    I have not suffered the one
fate that really is "more dire than death"—
    beyond death, cancelling death·
the loss of my own identity . . .
    No doubt you can tell—it is
what I cannot bear to relinquish . . .

There you are, at last we come
—*finalmente mia*—to a chapter
    of the story, I should say
stories, theirs as well as mine, this time . . .
    A little anthropology
is a dangerous thing: when *I* came
    to the end of the story
brought to light here—the shrine, the priestess,
    the responses of the god—
having followed the last residues
    of the law's millennium,
I gave up any claim I might have
    to *oracular wisdom* . . .
Call it a failure of nerve—call it
    anything. What was *practiced*
on this island, and on others too,
    was not prophecy, it was

deliverance. That is what I learned:
    Sacred Games in which the lost
god was recovered, by a change from
    sorrow to joy, from darkness
and sights of inexplicable terror
    to light: the discovery
of a god reborn. You can see why
    there were worshippers before
there were gods—the ritual always
    precedes the divinity . . .
It is why the Oracle had been,
    so long, a woman: you are
a man, or become one, only by
    ceasing to be a woman . . .
Even Jesus gave up his mother—
    he too was a man, of sorts . . .
Till the third century, responses
    came out of a woman's mouth,
out of her body: answers given
    at once, without reflection
and without interruption. She was
    entheos: a god was in her.
And if she answered "wrong," that was
    because she answered at all—
real answers are not something outside
    the question. Age after age,
the world around these islands *believed*
    and was prepared to believe,
purifying, offering, waiting . . .
    Have we any conception
of the demand on her? Of the weight?
    At Patara, she would be
chained inside the temple after dark
    so the god could get at her,
enter her—his medium, his lips . . .
    (It was the first witticism
I ever made in English without
    translating: for the priestess
to be entered was to be entranced—

entrance was entrancement . . .) So.
And when there was no more such speaking—
    when "oracle" was the same
patronizing disparagement as
    "testicles," your tiny heads—
then the voices fell silent or turned
    fickle, even menacing.
Pausanias tells of one Pythia
    beguiled to attempt her trance,
even though the omens were adverse—
    her words could not be made out:
hoarse noises, as if her throat was filled
    by "recalcitrant spirits"—
screaming as she fled from the altar,
    whereupon everyone fled,
even her attendants, and found her
    apparently recovered,
yet within a few days she perished .
    It is a form of proof that
everything believed—and nothing else—
    exists. You ask me about
a change—I see you have heard something
    of Pythian *replacements*—
boys for virgins . . . All of it began,
    perhaps, with that death. A sort
of admonition to try elsewhere . . .
    You know, I believe events
occur in series—nothing happens,
    then several things happen
in quick succession, as though life
    had been gathering up strength
over a long time for an effort . . .
    Unofficial oracles
—by rights a contradiction in terms—
    were first heard of in such times:
esoteric cults, séances held
    in sacred places, sometimes,
but hesitantly: what was the use
    of a temple, people asked:

a temple is the place where men weep
  together. Now there would be
no weeping, but pleasure and the god's voice—
  the god's voice would be pleasure.
An oracle was consulted "at home,"
  by citizens at their ease,
and among these there would be a man
  known as the *pelistikê*
who tried to incarnate the god's voice
  in *katochoi*, mediums . . .
This done by fair means or foul—*fair* meant
  smearing the eyes with nightshade,
and *foul* meant sexual possession.
  The modes tended to become
identical: whether you immersed
  your *katochos*—largely yours,
by now, because you had paid for him—
  in brimstone and sea-water,
or joined the jabbering creature in
  a parodic communion,
your fingers driven about the flesh
  with such heat that in your haste
to have the divine message, they seemed
  to smolder and burst into flame—
ceased to make much of a difference . . .
  The most suitable of such
partners were supposed to be persons
  "young and simple"—mainly boys:
Minucius Felix jeers and calls them
  Prophets without a Temple,
vates absquet templo . . . I have found
  recipes for casting them
into the proper trance state—it seems
  to have been *de rigueur*
to invite the god by erotic
  excitement. Reluctantly
at first, the god came more readily
  once the habit had been formed
of entering the same vessel . . . We know

of one boy, Aesidius,
who had only to stare intently
  into scented coals: at once
he fell into a trance, as well as
  your arms, and out of him came—
as he stirred, witlessly murmuring
  under your touch, oracles,
reliable ones, in the highest
  inspirational manner.
Of course you heard in the words he spoke
  only what was already
in you, but to know what was in you
  you needed the words spoken,
and for this the motions of "passion"
  were indispensable. So
you could regard these boys as trophies
  of action, as instruments
of knowledge. That was not their function.
  Their function was to revolt
—being adolescents—against themselves
  and thus to release a god.
The cues of induction could be learned—
  anything at all distinct
from daily life, whatever was odd
  would suffice: bathing in smoke
or dressing in "magical" chitons.
  Moreover, as you may guess,
manifest profits were to be made—
  although provisionally:
it appears that when these children grew
  accustomed to such methods,
when they came to *enjoy* the treatment
  received at their masters' . . . hands—
they no longer resisted the pneuma
  sufficiently to obtain
worthwhile responses. If there was
  no pain, no tension, there was
no sacred word. You cannot step twice

—if I may put it this way—
into the same stream of consciousness . . .

Such matters should be left to
women: we are so much more equal
    to them than men. Consider,
for instance, the female animal,
    her fear of copulation:
to her it must bring nothing but pain:
    merely listen to the cats—
pleasure is a late acquisition.
    When you watch the animals
spellbound in their intercourse, you see
    how the females undergo
love in bondage, objects of violence . . .
    Women know this still, even
now, and a memory of the old
    injury persists.
                    Of course
I learned more than I . . . I learned too much:
    the special knowledge I gained—
what in religion is often called,
    by the blind, revelation—
has defeated me. I cannot bear
    to remember what I know.
And perhaps I am wrong, knowing it:
    perhaps the boys were . . . useful,
after all. Does pleasure presuppose
    in those whom it has chosen
a limitless readiness to throw
    oneself away? It is past
women in their wisdom—it is past
    grown men in their arrogance.
You must be very religious indeed
    to change your religion . . .
These women who served the shrine for life,
    who bathed and drank from sacred
vessels and by chewing the laurel

held intercourse with the god—
even those boys, not that much younger
than yourselves, I imagine,
whored out to the offhand appetites
of the spiritually dim,
seem to have learned what I . . .
                    No,
not what I have lost sight of:
I am not blind. Nor did I fail
to learn. I learned. I did not fail
to understand, and understanding
has not failed me. I simply
—simply!—did not *practice* what I learned.
I just learned . . .
                    Without the world's
assistance we cannot see two things:
our face and our life in time.
To know the first, we must have mirrors;
to see the second, clocks.
Once possessed of these, we inhabit
a world bereft of the gods.
Can you understand me? It is why
I have abandoned pursuit
of what I once so merrily, once
so mercilessly studied.
Gentlemen, I am opaque; I know
everything I must do, while
those boys, for example, had only
to let themselves be devoured.
I am not worthy . . . And my colleagues,
controverting each other
into fame, are not worthy of me!
Listen to them: an abstract
and purely individual tact
becomes no more than . . . lying:
how we dupe each other over meals,
where silence is the rule, since
taboos on talking shop and distaste

for talking to each other
are in reality the same thing . . .

So you find me here, alone,
one of those intellectuals who are
   the last foe of the bourgeois
and the last bourgeois—an exile from
   my own world and an alien
in theirs . . . waiting for the flood! Ever
   since we were said to "rise,"
we bourgeois have waited for the flood . . .
   Now here you are, and although
you are not quite what I call the flood,
   I am glad you flushed me out,
enchanted you returned for a new . . . spell.
   It is wonderful to live
with spirits of the great—with the dead—
   but one must meet the living
to secure a sense of one's own worth. Nor
   would I give the impression
of asceticism—that is an aspect
   I am eager to avoid,
being under the strictest orders
   from that physician of mine
to laugh at least twice a week. I wish
   my dentist were more of a help . . .
But you are not to think of me as
   a tragic figure, should you
think of me at all. I shall remain
   here until all the voices
cease, and dust has filled the path of Greece . . .
   What . . . extrication it is,
living without anticipating,
   dying quite regularly:
I sometimes think I should like to have
   the rest of my insides out
—taken right out—and machines put in
   for the lot. It would be best

not to know what such things as the lungs,
    the spleen and the gall-bladder
might be, if one were willing to press
    a human creature against
oneself with any fervor at all . . .
    You, I suppose, are willing,
are you not? And you will marry, too—
    young men marry, even if
they are obliged to discover wives
    at the top of a bookcase . . .
Men appear to find their wives
    in strange places . . . Adam
found his in himself; many find theirs
    in other people's beds, and
my father's friend, Professor Mommsen,
    found his in his cook!
                              No,
I see . . . It is not marrying, but
    burning that is your fate. So.
And that is why you asked . . . Why you came
    here, and why you came to me!
I have no heart, as I told you, but
    my brains are in the right place:
my mind works best when it is almost
    too late. I shall tell you, then,
how it was with the boy . . .
                              On the night
    you decide on Aesidius,
you will be taken without warning
    in the dark, bathed, anointed
by other holy boys, you will drink
    water brought from Lethe's spring,
and you will forget who you are. Then
    you will study a secret
image and be robed in white linen
    bound with the sacred fillets—
only then, the omens favoring,
    will you be conducted down
the ladder into a dark place where

the boy Aesidius will
receive from you—his body from yours—
the divine message, swiftly
articulated. Merely put your
hand under his arm: the god
that is in him will pass between you
though of course this cannot be
comprehended by either of you . . .
The consequence of certain
anomalies is to emphasize
what is normal: so you may
learn if what we have called normal is
reality . . . or torpor.
Your pleasure may leave *you*, but he will
keep it, solidify it,
enrich it: he will transform the time
of a minor occasion
which you have managed to share into
realizations whereby
you will be enlightened, as temples
are gilded: and who can say—
perhaps such anointing will endure . . .
Then you will drink
from Mnemosyne's spring, in order
to remember afterwards
what has been revealed . . .

                                 What has been . . . I
have said enough. You should be
leaving before I tell everything—
Moses, you know, probably
said to himself: *must stop before I
tell everything*, that is why
there are only Ten Commandments.
                                      No,
I can get back by myself
perfectly well. Thank you for coming—
I shall not, in leave-taking,
tell you, as English-speaking people

often tell *me*, to "relax,"
to "take it easy." Such formulas
   are borrowed from the language
of the nursing home, not from active
   life. Just . . . *wiedersehen*. Our talk
has enlivened me a little, even
   talk of my own derision
and discouragement: knowing one has
   no body left to speak of,
one cannot entertain the god, *ripe*
   for the tripod, so to speak,
not when one is shrivelled to seed. No
   restraint is more annoying
to a woman than being left to
   her own discretion. Mine waits
for me. Goodbye, my dear fellows, come
   back tomorrow, and perhaps
I shall get on a little with
   my chronicle of vanishings.
Burckhardt locates the psychic sources
   of learning, of scholarship,
in "our unfulfilled longing for what
   has vanished"—let me say it
for you as well as he does, *unsere*
   unerfüllte sehnsucht nach
dem Untergegangen . . . So. You follow me,
   yes?
            We have been fortunate.
I really have enjoyed your visit—
   you must know: with you I seem
to hear myself speak as a stranger
   —without recognizing myself.
Only after you are gone shall I
   discover that it was . . . I.
Being alone is so important:
   you have to keep finding new
tactics for doing it—otherwise
   you feel at home so quickly,

which is to say you are quite lost.
                              —No,
    I shall not say any more:
my purpose henceforth will be to set
    words side by side in silence
and watch—watch the words.
                              Goodbye, go now,
    leave me. Go. Goodbye, goodbye . . .

LIKE MOST
REVELATIONS

Occupations

for David Alexander

Of course we're still using the old stationery—who can find paper these days?—but as you see, the lettering outside has already been changed, and to all intents and purposes this is now the Galerie Millon (I was Mathilde Millon before the late M. Bernheim married me). And l believe the Reichs-marschall will find that nothing shown him is on the list of Proscribed Artists. May I call your attention to these—no, not the very recent things: anything begun since 1942 I find a bit too stiff (no doubt the rigidity of an intimated end), but a choice among the later canvases, my dear Reichs-marschall . . . After all, the man is well into his seventies, and we may call anything done in the last decade a late work, wouldn't you say? Though the gallery has represented Bonnard since . . . oh goodness, since before my mar-riage, these paintings have just reached us. The old fellow keeps them ever so long in his studio, down there at Le Cannet, endlessly reworking what I feel to be the lessons he has learned—you see, here? and over here, particularly— from his friend Matisse.

8 January '42
Le Cannet

Dear Matisse, I have sad news:
Marthe has died—of what she called
her "immortal disease" . . . First the lungs
were attacked, then the digestive tract,
yet she managed to survive each new onset
for all the pain she must have been suffering,
until at last, just six days ago,
the heart gave out. We laid her to rest
in the graveyard I can see
from upstairs at Le Bosquet:
a comfort to me,
knowing she is there . . .

I think you recall
the strange delusion:
unclean! Marthe unclean!—which kept
her so many hours immersed
in the bath. We had made it a joke
between us—very nearly a joke,
enough of one for me to paint her there,
how many times? A modern Naiad, or as
Monet would have said, a nenuphar!
Our little ceremony for Marthe
brought back the time, can it be
twenty years? when Vuillard and I
and old Clemenceau
laid Monet to rest . . .
So much of life
is buried already!

Just consider this delightful view of a mimosa tree from the studio window,
for example: it was begun in 1939, along with other momentous enterprises,
if I may say so, and not finished (though what works by this painter can ever
be called finished?)—not released, then, until only a few weeks ago, when the
old fellow himself had the canvas sent to me directly. We may sell it along
with these others—thank goodness he is exempt from the Doctrinal Tests,
though like Matisse and Dufy not considered "meritorious" . . .

All the same I still believe
in reality, the way
Cézanne believed in it—I believe
in repetition, that is, and I am
at work on some new views of the Bay . . . They must
be new, because every day I see different
things, or I see things differently:
the sky, the fields, the water beyond,
it all keeps changing, you could
drown in the differences.
Yet that is just what
keeps us alive, no?
Despite our bad skies,
how the spring responds!

Daily on my walks, some new
species of flower appears —
as if each one were having its turn!
this morning the first almond blossoms,
like proclamations attached to the bare trees
(a kind of bravery, I can't help thinking)
and soon the mimosas will begin
to set yellow pennants in the woods,
as if it was a signal!
Of course everything begins
on the ground and moves
up, but I see things
best against the light . . .

*I can let you have such work in lots, at a most attractive rate for the whole
group here in the gallery . . . Amusing, by the way, that barely perceptible
woman's face down there on the left, yes, at the very bottom, almost drowned
out by the light. She is looking up the stairs toward the painter, not out
the window at all, where the mimosa suffuses the whole picture with gold,
filling the window so that it has something of the appearance of stained
glass . . .*

the horizon lies
much lower in my landscapes
than it ever did before . . .
You know, at our age, we tend — except
for P, of course, who is hardly one of us —
to be more interested in objects than in
the construction of the universe.
These encroachments, these occupations —
by disease, by sorrow, by
the Germans — come in great waves,
you know what I mean:
that thing old Rodin
always used to say,
about how it takes
an exceptional array
of circumstances to grant
a man seventy years of life and

the luck to keep doing what he loves.
Oh, the waves come, they keep coming over us,
and though we may be nearly drowned, they leave us
    just where we were, and we know that if
    they are strong, we are even stronger,
        for they pass, and we remain . . .
        "Old Rodin": what insolence,
          my calling him that!
          we're both much older
              than he lived to be,
              pontificating
in front of the Gates of Hell
    —remember those afternoons
in the Rue de Varennes, lecturing
overdressed women in his garden . . .
Did you ever believe we would be that old?

*Such a pleasure, my dear Reichsmarschall, indeed a privilege, to be able to
offer these canvases for actual purchase. Only last May, you know—we were
obliged to destroy—in the courtyard of the Louvre!—some five hundred
pictures by Masson, Léger, poor old Kisling, even Picasso, really horrors—
all canvases entirely unfit for sale. The fire went on all day, and the smoke
covered the sky, even the next morning . . .*

                    27 February
                    Dear Matisse,

It is not easy, keeping abreast
of events, nor have I any great
    longing to know what may be
    happening in the world, I
        almost said the real
        world. Don't believe that.
              A few days ago
              I learned about Joss—
not how he died, just his death.
All that *l'Éclaireur de Nice*
reports is that he had been "ailing" . . .
Over forty years since Bernheim-Jeune
took me on, you must have come to the gallery

soon after—about nineteen hundred and nine?
What a long time Joss did the one thing!
Most people are not conscious enough
to exult in monotony,
but perhaps God is—perhaps
God says each morning
to the moon: "Encore!"
I know that is what
Joss would say to me
whenever a show came down.
And today, inside black borders,
Mathilde Bernheim writes to say she is
asking "his" painters to testify—
you must have had the same letter—to what Joss
has accomplished for "Independent French Art."
She thinks this will save her family
from the persecutions . . . I was glad
to write, as you must have been,
and Dufy, Rouault, Derain . . .
But to tell the truth
none of this will do
the least bit of good.

*I am so happy to know that this lot is passing to such appreciative hands,
and eyes, of course. Is it not charming, the woman at her toilette, seen as if
by accident through the doorway? Wonderful, that in these dark times
the painter could find so much light to celebrate, such depths to plumb so
brilliantly!*

Dear Matisse, you know
as well as I: the Germans
acknowledge a single name
among "French" painters. Our conquerors
recognize only our conqueror,
if I may put it that way—perhaps you see
Monsieur Picasso as no such thing, Matisse,
but I have textual evidence
as to how that Spaniard has seen me.
"I like him best, your Bonnard,"

he once wrote Joss (who of course
passed on this good news),
"when he is not thinking
of being a painter,
when his canvases
are full of literature"
—this is really what he said—
"rotten with anecdotes." Did that suffice?
Not for our Pablo. Kahnweiler was
kind enough to send the latest bulletin,
and I am compelled to copy it out here
for your edification—one way
to exorcise the curse of the thing,
or so I hope: "What he does
is not painting—he never
goes beyond his own
sensibility.
He doesn't know how
to choose. Take his sky—
first he paints blue, more or less
the way it looks. Then he looks
a while longer and sees mauve in it,
so he adds a touch or two of mauve,
just to be sure. Then he assumes there may be
a little pink there too—why not add some pink?
If he looks long enough he'll wind up
adding a little yellow, instead
of deciding what color
the sky really ought to be.
Is that painting? No,
that's taking advice
from Nature, asking
her to supply you
with information: Bonnard
obeys Nature! another
decadent, the end of an old idea . . ."
There you have the words, my dear Matisse,
of a fellow artist, a practitioner
of the *métier* we have shared, all of us

for how many years? Is this the man
I can ask to speak to Herr Abetz
  on behalf of Joss Bernheim—
  and of Mathilde Bernheim?
    If you can do it,
    I leave it to you.

Very well, we shall send the entire shipment to your private car at the gare de
l'Est. Two cars? All the better! And the bill to the Einsatzstab Rosenberg.
No, no, all these have come to us from the artist himself—not one from
other dealers. Graf Metternich was at some pains to stipulate: the stock of
Seligmann, Wildenstein, Loeb, e tutti quanti *must be transferred to the*
Embassy as a security for eventual peace negotiations. I understand perfectly.

        . . . After yesterday
      I belong, once more,
  to the human race—a trial
  member, but a member still,
all because they have decided to
operate: the surgeon has bestowed
civil status, even a country, on me:
my country is The Hospital, and I am
  Dr. A's patient in Room 14,
  on whom Dr. B will operate.
    The corridor where I walk
    and wait and write this to you
      is my realm; no one
      dreams of disputing
        the territory.
        I see other men,
    and women too, who have been
    operated on, brought back
  on their gurneys, the surgeons, interns
and nurses clustering around them
like white flies. Through their doors I can hear the groans
these patients make, even in their sleep, the same
  groans I shall make, when it is my turn.
  The nurses know me, and I know them:
    one comes for "temperature,"

one for "blood," and another
with "pills." The pill nurse
is pretty, the rest
are young. When I walk
past their glassed-in booth
I always hear them talking
about us, their patients. Theirs.
And for the first time in a long while
I find humanity better than
I had supposed. Now I can more easily
regard my own death, which no longer divides
me from the world. It is possible,
nothing more. It becomes a simple
statistic. In rooms off this
corridor, a percentage
of patients must die,
and this percentage
is what they attempt
to reduce. Each nurse
in this wing will regard my
death as her failure—the one
who looks like Danielle Darrieux's
daughter says that after each "deceased"
she won't sleep for a week. My death no longer
exposes me to the living. That is why
I have made my will so easily
and told my notary where to find
the pictures I had hidden
so long. I have forgotten
nothing, for it seems
only fair to meet
with an attentive
precision the same
precision they devote to
my file, from which no X-ray,
blood-analysis, or fever-chart
is missing. I too want to present
the anesthesiologist with a man
according to the rules. But once you obey

the rules, there is nothing left to do
but wait. I wait. And I look for what
    it could mean, this death of mine
    that seems so near. I admit
        I will be nothing
        (otherwise death is
                not death, and even
                one's thoughts about it
        are just playing with words). And
        without my body, what is
    left of me? No reading the paper,
    no talk with the doctor making rounds.
No action of any kind. But do I make
these actions I assume I am making now?
    It is my newspaper, printed in
    an edition of thousands, that puts
        pressure on me to read it;
        the doctor comes when he feels
            like coming, evades
            my questions, departs:
                there is my freedom.
                Which is nothing but
        my uncertainty about
        what is going to happen
    next. Of course, that is my freedom, but
    having been introduced into this
vast machinery, I am not even sure
such uncertainty as to my fate is part
    and parcel of my life—my death is
    not enough to dispel it. No doubt
        I am the total of my
        memories and nothing else,
            that huge collection
            gathered by my life
                and dispersed by my
                death. But so many
        of these memories—I see
        now they don't belong to me . . .
What did I do that was mine? I went

to the parish school, served out my term
in the infantry—and I was not alone.
In each photograph I belong to a group,
and someone must draw a little cross
over my head if I am to be
identified. Dear Matisse,
nothing is there. What remains
is the almond tree
I was working on
the morning I came
to the hospital.
Pray God it will be there still
if I am allowed to go home . . .

*Of course we have carefully weeded out all the identifiable portraits: in the
Bonnard lot there were a number of studies of my late husband and his fam-
ily, his friends. They were obliged to join the others in three requisitioned
rooms in the Louvre, where, as you know, they were slashed to ribbons by mem-
bers of the Einsatzstab themselves—a regrettable procedure, but apparently
a necessary one. You know, my dear Reichsmarschall, we French have an old
poem which I always like to recite in times like these:*

I claim the right to act as if
the War were an old dog sitting
at the lovely feet of our France . . .

Poem Beginning with a Line by Isadora Duncan

The third time I resisted D'Annunzio
      was years after the War,
and to dilapidations in My Life
      every limb testifies
since the escapes (elementary enough)
      of those Houdini days!
I find it pitiful to contemplate
      our mutual conceit
on those absurd occasions, now we know
      all that has intervened.
Yet what *do* we know, really? I say "all"
      as if I had been schooled
in catastrophe, when Triumph was my mode.
      His too, apparently . . .

Raising his eyelids as though he were
      removing his trousers,
the poet stood in my Paris *loge d'artiste*,
      towering under me,
the *chaise-longue* crammed with his chrysanthemums
      —"lion blooms," he called them,
"*Ecco i leoni*"—and licked his lips as if
      they were someone else's.
That was my first evasion: "They smell—" I said,
      "they smell like drowned sailors."
Whereupon virtue was intact: Italians are
      grimly conventional—
so much easier to shock than to persuade.
      The next time, my escape

was dicier, for in his own domain . . .
      I was dancing in Rome,

and what occurred, or failed to, at the hotel
    was not, as I recall,
the outcome of odious comparisons merely,
    but of actions: the sheets
were thrown back, and Gabriele showed
    a sincere if brackish
enthusiasm for my thighs—"columns more
    melodious by night
than Memnon's temple at dawn"—and just then
    Deucie, my Doberman,

leaped on the bed, wild in my defense
    or was it my defeat?—
another jealous bitch like the Marchesa Casati!
    But could a dog deter
that lover at that point? It was my own
    screams of "Deucie, down!"
which shrivelled my assailant to his doom
    as only memory can,
Deucie—Duse: mine as much as his,
    the disgrace awakened,
in a sacred name consigned to comedy,
    the fiasco of farce—
laughter has no erectile tendencies:
    Deucie and I were saved . . .

In Nice, too, that *third* time (counting was
    a crucial part of it)
even desire, for him, was out of the question
    without the distractions
of vanity. And love impossible. He would be
    entitled only to
lies and funny business, and so I fell
    or would have fallen yet
again, if it had not been for the odd crystals,
    powders, grains, the uncut
gems and a thousand gorgeous trifles poured
    for the sake of "aura,"

some burnt, some merely glowing like embers
    around us where we lounged

in that silly mummy-case of an apartment—
    another hour there and I
should have died in the odor of Orient
    as some are said to die
in the odor of sanctity. Did *I* say as much?
    I must have—the remark
made his eyebrows play like summer lightning
    up around his hairline
(bald as an egg, but he has a hairline still).
    Checkmate! I've learned it means
Shah mat: the king is dead. Such artifice
    was bound to spring a leak.
Out cold, bequeathing me a carcass quite
    uninhabitable . . .

My resistances, as I have called them, were
    no more than submissions
to Animal, Vegetable, Mineral Realms—
    flower, dog, druggery.
I wonder how to escape, were he to press
    new designs that must be
obscene to be believed? Trust inertia
    over the intellect
I cannot muster . . . At least it makes a tale,
    a sort of haphazard
Scheherazade. And if we were never amazed,
    there would be no stories
to tell about us. Believe in the mystery
    of Woman: it gives her one.

A Lost Art

Vienna, 1805

There is no ceremony to stand on,
just walk in! No call to be dismayed:
it is not chaos you see in my shop,
but the leavings of creation; nothing
can do you any harm, and nothing is
so far along that you'll do harm to *it* . . .

Suppose you sit—just put that on the floor—
over here . . . Never mind, I can fix it:
legs are the least of my difficulties,
there! Welcome to the land of the missing,
where little is past recall. Or repair.
This? Oh, this is my *first* capybara,

I persuaded a chamberlain I know
at the Palace—whom you may know as well,
he's been up there for years, for *dynasties*:
Herr Pufendorf?—to let me have it back,
once I had pledged myself to substitute
a more convincing representative.

No, no, the eyes are set too high, and *green*!
a libel on the living article . . .
I keep it here, fallacious as it is,
to remind me, in a cautionary way,
that I can do (and have done) better work.
I have long since eclipsed such things, rising

from capybara to *homo capax*:
honest progress. A pity you cannot
confirm my boast; a word to Pufendorf,

not so long since, would have afforded you
the sight of my *magnum opus*, displayed
in the Imperial Museum—kept out

for years, just standing there in . . . state,
I have been told, in spite of protests from
the poor man's family. Not Pufendorf—
he has no family, to my knowledge!
"Poor man" refers to our black Angelo
Solyman, who was to be seen entire,

naked from head to heels, and all between,
the upshot of my labor and my skill . . .
It would have been no trick at all to do
a costumed figure, just the face and hands
set off by the white court dress, the gold braid,
the medals he invariably wore;

quite another matter to show the man's . . .
manhood, as my commission specified;
why, just to gain possession of the corpse
was a crime! Or would have been, if I'd
been caught: stolen at birth, stolen at death—
a slave's fate, for all the honors bestowed.

Then came the wife's compunction—she had been
widowed by a Flemish general and
married to Solyman in secret rite,
though in Saint Stephen's Cathedral. Yet
not even the Cardinal-Archbishop
could baffle the Emperor's plan. And I?

I did as I was ordered, did my best:
I allude to the *new* Emperor, of course,
not our late Joseph, who abhorred the sight
of stuffed animals of any species
(the entire Imperial family
suffered from this . . . susceptibility,

until Francis—in so many respects
the converse of his uncle). Now Francis,
Solyman safely dead, commanded me
to prepare, preserve and present him
as a perfect specimen *in all respects*.
He meant, of course, *in one*: I was to find

a way of representing what is held
to be the special virtue of black men,
although, however . . . outstanding in life,
our man's endowments were, most likely, dimmed
by being dead, revived in part and stuffed!
Moreover he had died quite civilly—

no evidence from the gibbet would grant
a hint of eventual scope to my art
nor any sculptor's manual of scale
suggest a means of reckoning how much
I might have to contend with. And I could
hardly ask the wronged widow for details!

An old cookery book delivered me:
by gently passing oil of cloves, it said,
over the affected body parts . . . Well,
even in the coldest larder, it seems,
an ox's member could be coaxed to life
or at least to life's dimensions, for a while.

And so it came about that Solyman—
born a prince in Pangusitlong, raised
a slave by robbers in Messina, sold
to one General Lobkowitz, by whom
he was bequeathed to Prince von Liechtenstein
who freed and later pensioned him for life—

a Mason, moreover, in Mozart's Lodge
(where both attended assiduously!)
who spoke German, Italian, English, French,
an excellent player of faro and chess,

observed in Frankfurt by the adolescent
Goethe at the Emperor's election—

this very Solyman you might have seen
for yourself in all his mortifying
splendor in the Museum, though of course
what I had studied to produce was more
of a demonstration piece—much visited
by our ladies, and some gentlemen too!—

than any emblem of human headway
in what civilization we may have—
something by way of a memorandum,
actually. No, I never visited:
I did the work, it is gone. Why torment
myself further? I know what I achieved.

I am told that after the bombardment
(though before Bonaparte entered the town)
the thing—my masterpiece!—was stolen
from its case by old Countess Zacharoff
and later vanished in the deplorable
looting of the Zacharoff residence . . .

For Robert Phelps, Dead at Sixty-six

The Times reports six years in Elyria,
    browbeaten suburb of your childhood
before my own had begun in Shaker Heights,
    the brighter side of Cleveland's tracks . . .

years I never took into account, nonplussed
    by your habit of addressing me
— or any other man you regarded as
    worthy of the gaudy attention

to bookish leanings and upstanding looks
    you were gaily ready to bestow—
as "my dear boy," "my son" and "my child," although
    you were clearly the one to be raised

— or lowered— to the permanently askew
    level of our promiscuities;
it became entertainment, "telling Robert"
    last night's scurrilous episode

and watching your vicarious blush appear,
    followed by the squeal of gratified
incredulity which greeted each disgrace . . .
    Oneself is always an abstraction—

le concret, ce sont les autres. To which end
    you listened more intently, waiting
like some credulous minotaur in his cave
    for Theseus to arrive, whereupon

you became Ariadne, eager to oblige.
    What can we relish if we recoil

from vulgarity? Not your problem, was it?
    Masterpieces you called "strenuous,"

and were satisfied—or so you asserted—
    with patching up Colette, endless
apprenticeships to other men's disclosures,
    Jouhandeau, Wescott, Cocteau—not "works"

but the launching-pad that sends the rocket up;
    how gleefully you would disparage
or dismiss the monuments I so envied,
    standing emulously in their shade . . .

What *you* wanted—it amounted to addiction—
    was life recounted without design,
without that tyranny—just "the real thing strange":
    letters, diaries, secrets written down,

and not having to dilute or deprave them—
    better one small bold astronomer
than any number of big decorous stars!
    Even silence can be indiscreet,

and not everything we make up is a lie.
    About a thousand book reviews
made you too familiar to care much for Fame—
    what you liked was how others were moved,

strangers. Your own maneuvers you confined to
    the background—more room there than up front
where the young struggle and sweat for their applause
    —lovely, though, those intervals of flesh

under hot lights! Such was your *gran rifiuto*:
    I wonder if the delicacy
of your domesticities (that son unseen,
    that wife dedicated to her art)

made your love for men the mirror type
    of mine, you the critical voyeur
resisting "production," I proliferating
    among nameless bodies, finding soon

how many were dying who never used to . . .
    Granted: you would not write. Then your hand
began to shake so, you could not write. It was
    Parkinson's, as we would discover,

but was it not at first a failure of your will?
    Those years you passed off as "successes,"
triumphant manipulations of decor;
    I recall seasons when you devised

"literaries"—a noun, *voyons*—for our latest
    Mme. Verdurin. Besides the fun,
she paid far better than mere authorship, since
    the rich, my dear, are always with us.

I sat at those tables with you, glib, grinning,
    ungainly, so greedy for limelight
on my terms and abashed by your forbearance,
    those evenings of unavailing skill.

Silence = Death, according to the slogan
    broadcast for AIDS. Yours was another
silence, as you said with an absurd chuckle;
    a guy can't go on living all the time.

At least it was not the plague, not *our* plague, only
    Parkinson's, only cancer. You smiled,
invoking plausible pretexts—embarrassed
    (such was your humility) to die

among the victims, to benefit even
    erroneously from emotion
reserved for the unwarrantable dead.
    Forty years out of Cleveland, we live

and die in the same Village now, Robert dear,
    and Shaker Heights seems quite as good
a place to have gone from as your Elyria.
    It was the wrong family member

you summoned up: you are the man I should be
    if I had not been the child I was;
not son, not father either, but—I know it now—
    the lost brother found, *Vale frater.*

Like Most Revelations

after Morris Louis

It is the movement that incites the form,
discovered as a downward rapture—yes,
it is the movement that delights the form,
sustained by its own velocity. And yet

it is the movement that delays the form
while darkness slows and encumbers; in fact
it is the movement that betrays the form,
baffled in such toils of ease, until

it is the movement that deceives the form,
beguiling our attention—we supposed
it is the movement that achieves the form.
Were we mistaken? What does it matter if

it is the movement that negates the form?
Even though we give (give up) ourselves
to this mortal process of continuing,
it is the movement that creates the form.

Writing Off

All participation in art is based on the existence of others.   —Hebbel

"In a field I am," our latest laureate
          divulges, "the absence of field,"
content, if not resolved, to be missing
          in action, missing in passion—
forsaking as a form of *being there*!

To live on nothing is one theorem
          which Thoreau would have understood;
and not only to live on it, to let
          Nothing do our living for us . . .
It is the converse claim I wish to lodge,

a premise that we are because we make
          some sign of presence, all
that is signified by the marvellous
          post-juridical compound
self-evident. The claim is likely

to be clamorous, uncivil, often
          sacrilegious in its effects
(hence the tendency to label it
          at minimum a misdemeanor,
more likely a mania). I refer

to the patently incorrigible
          yen to inscribe our handiwork,
or rather the play of our hands, upon
          whatever amplitude is bare
enough to enable our disclosure.

As a rule the billboards are not put up
          to put up with our marauding,

and it is a tribute to the discretion
        of our poet's heretical
heroism that he scores identity

by cancelling the evidence of it,
        withdrawing himself from the scene.
Most of us are not like that. We require
        a signature; KILROY WAS HERE
we scratch on the fresh paint, and sigh

with authorial satisfaction. Now
        behold the field from which Mark Strand
proclaims himself absent: here is a wall
        and at its base a ruined car
filled with spray-cans that strew the ground as well,

and every inch of wall and car and ground
        is covered, cancelled, *encrusted*
with the spirit-writing known as graffito,
        cursive abuse, cacography
which by its very glut becomes glamor,

a collaborative chaos of uncials,
        illegible and thus elect.
According to Erdmann (*Arabische Schriftkunst
        als Ornamente*, Bonn, 1910)
"Writing is one form of art in general

whose aesthetic aspect is often so
        hypertrophied as to neglect
its chief purpose as communication . . .
        Horror vacui is of great
influence in the arrangement of signs."

Erdmann is right. The walls cannot be read
        as anything but palimpsest,
elemental commands made vacuous
        by the subsequent autograph
of those who obeyed them. Writing alone

appears to count, a thousand words worth no
            picture, "graphic," as we observe:
the quenched car is so tangled in a scurf
            of scribbles (the moving finger
having writ) that waves seem to have broken

over the ravaged and obviously tireless
            machine in opalescent foam,
a sea of troubles unopposed, unended . . .
            Bonnard, who could never leave off
retouching his canvases, would envy

these scaling laminations, pellicles
            of self-assertion which has turned
anonymous by superfetation. Here
            perhaps our laureate is met,
for these scriveners have made something

occasioned only when no one member
            conspicuously functions
in the field—repressed *and* represented
            by unspecifiable rinds
and flakes. (How many times we must peruse

these depths before the deepest impulse floats
            to the surface and is legible:
the inenarrable FUCK which appears
            only after the eye has long
frequented more decorous instances!)

Theirs is a polypoid scheme—a structure
            of self-immolating moilers
(like the pyramids and the cathedrals)
            wreaked upon the carapace of
what pyramids and cathedrals we have . . .

But for all the luscious integument,
            a variorum of texture
any post-impressionist might covet,

is it meant to be seen? The wall,
the filthy field, the gutted car engorged

with the spray-cans which have given their all
　　　　　are unknown to view, closeted
from the eagerest archaeologist
　　　　　of our cities' decline and fall.
Only a fluke snapshot insists: *this was,*

and my words, irresolute witness to
　　　　　such performance. I used to think
graffiti meant nothing but insolence,
　　　　　the mean and meager vandalism
which was all *ressentiment* could muster,

yet the wasted splendor of an empty
　　　　　lot in East Los Angeles
redefines the state of the art. how much
　　　　　of the world's making was never
intended for human eyes! Luxor, Lascaux,

sacred places where we learn we can change
　　　　　our faith without changing gods (and
vice versa) . . . To which I add the image
　　　　　of an unvisitable shrine
where obscure artisans have succeeded

in transcending the five destinies
　　　　　by which we claim to be guided:
mind body nation language home. This is
　　　　　how we learn, by just such unseen
art, to approach the divine. Next slide please.

For James Boatwright, 1937–88

Behold the depths to which we are undone!
A life divided, but only between despised
chores and disparaged cheer—is that a life,
or headlong delay

hanging out till Events enliven the heart?
Enliven? Erase!—then scrawl to lethargy:
the Moving Finger eventually writes off
the hand that needs you.

Gamely you ignored the Greek who maintained
that what he called leisure (*schole*) and school
(what you called labor—found laborious)
were somehow the same;

your classes you valued only for the hours
enfranchised with the once and future young—
the sole lesson learned from such "professing"
was how much longer

youth endures than those who are young assume.
By thirty—you were thirty when we met—
you guessed the closely guarded secret known
to most of the world:

we are not happy, but at least we have
pleasures. Whereof the nightly exercise
—no salt-free regimen, no seaweed baths—
kept you coming back

for more. You had become one of those men
stricken by their maturity as if by

an incurable disease. And then there was
no *as if*, only

the long downward months of which you spent
every moment dying, nothing left
over for the evasions which had been
your lingua franca

(talk is the opium of the healthy).
What the same Greek wrote you heeded now:
the more I am alone the more I am
mythological.

As Keats, who understood, observed,
"until we are sick we understand not."
In time, the vacuum had perfected itself—
teaching? a chaos

of clear ideas; travel? you travelled
about as well as a basket of raspberries;
and love? the arduous pursuit of those
who would not allow

capture or even catching up . . . Was love,
Jim, ever more than a hand poked through
the shower-curtain—a blurred touch easily
rinsed away, laughed off?

Perhaps. For you it was another way
of learning how to stand the loneliness
produced by culture, or by culture's dreams.
So can dreams come *false*,

old friend, for there has been too much
shaving of the cedar-wood round the lead—
the lead itself powdered away at last,
the pencil pointless.

You went with a sigh of relief—to me a sign
that any past we might hope to reclaim
spreads like an oil slick, wide behind us,
and the oncoming

years of retrieval diminish even now
until our name becomes, to memory,
a synonym for weaknesses endured,
or worse still, adored.

For David Kalstone, 1932–86

What became of him after the cremation? . . . Below David's windows, Maxine took a small vial from her purse and emptied it into the Grand Canal . . . Into the tidal river just east of Stonington I emptied the white gravel of our friend . . . A last teaspoonful had been saved to mix with earth.   —James Merrill

My own stake in his story had been pulled up
    years before such benignly recounted
elemental emptyings, comminglings; and
    wisdom asserts it is delusional
folly to dwell on the past. Well past sixty,
    I know little more about wisdom now
than we did at thirty, but lots more about
    folly, and of course I tell what I know—
the mind makes itself by making rules; the facts
    insist on exceptions . . . Fact: his ferry

crossed the bright Lagoon a dozen years ago
    leaving Palazzo Barbaro behind
with all the drastic ease of "Life" in Venice—
    a more exuberant mundanity
than he was born to in McKeesport, achieved
    in Lowell House tutorials or had
thrust upon him (easy mark!) by Manhattan:
    "living Beyond Reproach is well and good,
Richard, but it would be nicer if the place
    were just a few blocks closer to the Park!"

I met his boat in Padua, where we gave
    one another the warm shoulder (buggers
can be choosers), both of us electrified
    to be so literally Out To Lunch,
as our correspondence of the seventies
    (relinquished from "the files" by his estate)
makes evident we were, gaiety welling
    thin and fast . . . I instance this encounter
—far from our last, though the last to reward
    contested attachment with an image

worthy of his powers—for the symbolic
 rection of the thing: just where I dreaded
drenching (or drowning!), immersion anyway
 in the littoral drift, I would see him
with one tactful butterfly-kick scoot across
 our social shallows to the next tide-pool.
This spawned a certain unmerited scorn
 (had I not longed to escape the very
marination he so madly plunged into?)
 and it is only justice to invoke,

for tonic fun of my funerary picture,
 the spectacle of David emerging
out of the fiery Venetian furnace,
 blinking, sun-blind, in his genial mood
of acquiescent panic. As Jane Austen says,
 "a mind lively and at ease can do
with seeing nothing, and can see nothing
 that does not answer." Witness my friend
traversing the lagoon to make I-contact . . .

 Which deeps have now been further dimmed
by a vial of surreptitious cinders
 poured from a gondola by prudent friends
to join the Dreck of Ages; more recent swill
 discolors the ashes off Stonington;
and dark as the Styx, from my vantage, is the Charles
 where decades ago in Cambridge we first
discoursed upon the Theory of Desire—how
 evaded, how endured—happily trudging
to the grave of Henry James (DK leading,
 blinking hard against the light that failed

to blind him only because he was half-blind
 already)—the sun off the river fierce
on an afternoon of transcendental snow,
 obeisance to that great garrulous Shade
the one sure thing our tentative hearts could share.
 So much rope we accorded each other,

the reverence of certain figurations,
    certain forms by fond artifice achieved:
Balanchine and Bishop and the creator of
    Merton Densher. "Denture, David? Didn't James

for once bite off less than he could chew?" "My dear,"
    he rounded, "I'm glad you said that to *me*"—
art was always an unpersuadable justice
    done to the world, and contemplation
of poems indeed the temple undestroyed.
    . . . Dear discerning critic, now that all change
has been put past you, now that even *your* eyes
    could find, as in a glass clearly, the Forms
of Loss, I wonder—can we be reconciled
    to affections that started with a stone
and ended at sea, all the makings we most

    valued apparently *insoluble?*
Winnowing those letters of mine you kept (Why?
    Can I have corresponded *to* the man
who wrote them and *with* the one who read them first?)
    it seems to me I missed an easy clue
by ignoring a mutual friend's remark:
    "the True, the Passionate Kalstone comes out
at the Bechstein . . ." That, and one much harder hint
    found in a letter of *yours* from Venice:

"Everything lovelier than it would become,
    Nothing so lovely as it once had been . . ."
But I suppose what divided us *for real*
    was the pursuit of happiness (founded
on forgetting—only wisdom, poor wisdom,
    relies on memory), or what we took
for happiness, erotic hallucination
    which makes the strangest bedfellows of all.
Who could have thought that irregular line-up
    of communicants at the altar-rail

of sex, in which we took our place, would one day
    possess the power to destroy itself?
Perhaps nobody in creation but our old
    deracinated prestidigitator
whose props you so relished in the Palazzo
    until the plague unhoused you even there —
his the imagination of disaster,
    his the genius for following it out . . .
The task has always been what The Master called
    the wear and tear of discrimination

day by day, and ever since you played on us
    that vanishing-trick called dying,
I am left with the consequence of silence —
    it must always be silence *of a sort*,
of course, never zero silence: those last days
    of your undisclosed disease, your silence
made the one intolerable answer . . . Now
    that I live, like most of us, in a world
which has ceased to exist, it will have to be
    your silence I harp on, look to, learn from . . .

What with repeating and forgetting, is it not
    a marvel there can be meanings at all?
Your silence is a sentence I parse, even
    by remembering your loss. Losing,
I realize: meaning consists in trying
    to mean something: there is no other way.
My mind like another Isis gathers up
    your divided ashes, I watch your boat
cross back to Venice and go from less to less,
    vanish into the dark . . . I see you go.

Homage

I

We pay what tribute we can—of course it is you
who has paid, or who pays now: woe unto you
when all men shall speak well of you (Luke 6:26).

Dear Mr. Howard, I had heard you were coming over.
At present I am living in the country. A dark place
has one advantage: the only possible thing

to be seen, if offered, is a light. *I cannot tell*
precisely when I shall be back in Paris, but
as soon as this is clear I shall write again

and propose an appointment. Thirty years ago . . .
Whatever the weather, your publisher explained,
you would be gardening, or else *au golf,*

whereupon I saw you far out at sea
(I knew you had no car, but perhaps a yawl,
like Mallarmé—what *gulf* in Issy-sur-Marne,

where the fish can't be seen for the weeds?)
until my French recovered. *Meanwhile I look*
forward to meeting you. Much too wet

an April to have missed you on the links—
too wet for flowers, though the ferns rejoice:
with fronds like that, who needs anemones?

II

One writes, in the end—was it not why you wrote
to me: mere civility from Seine-et-Marne?—
not to say something but Not to say something.

Such was the lesson learned (at least rehearsed)
waiting for Beckett: the missing links between
inscription and erasure, a secret not

an illusion. And still we pester you as I
decades back had done. It is difficult
to get rid of people once you have given them

too much pleasure—particularly those
who are convinced that they possess a key
and will not rest until they have arranged

whatever you wrote into one big lock;
to whom *your* Proust had scornfully remarked:
a work with theories in it is much the same

as a present with the price-tag on it still.
No ideas but in nothing, then,
for my part of the tribute. Happiness

—I guessed as much in 1958—
is no laughing matter. That would be
the other thing. Or would be everything.

To the Tenth Muse
A Recommendation

    Individual
no longer, but goddess, gimmick, grace, indeed you have been
divided among our needs until all that remains is myth,
    the name we give to

    whatever exists
specifically because it has language for its cause.
Sappho! we descant, and pursuing merely a fond
    ideology,

    our encompassments
of your career and character, however skilled,
however illuminating, like all definitions
    wither their object.

    How much is certain?
Your father's name, your mother's, and that you had three brothers.
Perhaps you married Cercolas, a rich man from Andros—you tell us
    you had a daughter,

    whose name was Cleis.
And at least to the ensuing Greek poets you were a Lesbian
in more than a geographical sense. That is enough
    for my purpose here

    (one more *use* of you),
which is to curry favor for the candidate *listed below*.
(Most institutions—and you are inveterately said to have
    presided over

    an academy—
request from the sponsor "a brief review of the applicant's major

strengths and weaknesses as a potential graduate student
    and an assessment,

    where possible, of
her stability, motivation and aptness for working with others."
Forgive if you can the absurd phraseology: these are
    the forms we use now,

    they mean no more than
a touch of the hand, the gesture attempting to remove
the garland which has become a nuisance to the wearer.)
    Ma'am, this is the case:

    Lynda Schraufnagel
who died last January of lymphocytomatosis
would tolerate my classroom in order to show cause
    for later parlays

    chez moi concerning
the unsuccessful poems she had managed to produce
and the ones to be attempted now that those were behind her,
    shocking recitals

    of what to me seemed
an inordinate life if it was to be imputed
to the decorous catechumen watching me from my sofa.
    I mourn her, although

    it is difficult
to justify my grief (for if mourning needs no excuse
the way we live—and die—now, it still has to elbow out
    stiff competition):

    during those sessions
I had not been, or had not succeeded in becoming, despite
the intimate hours we pored together over her verses,
    an intimate friend.

Whatever it was
I happened to "know" about Lynda she had confided to poems,
and only the poems to me (the nuance won't have escaped you
    —you of all people).

    Angular, graceful,
her manic glee in assuming the mask of a scornful dyke
deceived me about her age—I thought she was a *girl*!
    She was forty-one

    when she died, just now,
but a coltish ease in each movement reinforced the style
of adolescent insouciance I attributed to her grins . . .
    I would discover

    she had been married,
yes, but he was a transvestite; she had greedily abused
every substance in the book, *yes, but she was no reader*;
    the nuns had taught her

    to bear the ennui
of almost any routine she would be faced with, *yes, but
now she knew how eagerly she had welcomed victimization.*
    No matter what chore—

    bank-teller, waitress,
student-teacher, even the tedium of my assignments—
could be sucked into her secret knowledge: *women are dupes!
They let men have them*

    *to avoid having
themselves.* And that's where you come in, Ma'am, taking up
the slack to have your say, your way, now that Lynda
    is beyond my help

    (which she put up with)
or any assistance from decorous sources (which she despised).
I don't mean to darken counsel (who could advise Sappho!)
    but if, in your lost

inimitable
manner of speaking, you were to resume where we left off,
you might explain that sexual attraction makes the strangest
      bedfellows of all,

      that to surrender
oneself for anything but desire is to destroy that part
of oneself which from the first enabled (or compelled)
      one to surrender.

      So much of her life
seemed a longing to *get lost*. Perhaps you could,
in death, convince her about finding. Genius alone
      can afford to vex

      itself as she did
without suffering injury. She suffered. I make
no such claim for Lynda Schraufnagel the poet, the woman.
      Merely I observed

      in her (and with her
in myself) that our deepest desire aims at transformation.
Now that she is past changing here, with us, Ma'am,
      I leave it to you.

TRAPPINGS

Dorothea Tanning's *Cousins*

synthetic fur over cotton stuffing, wood base, 60 x 25 x 21 inches, 1970

She came to him in dreams, as he to her
in waking. And that was how they would meet,
ever wrong from the start, however right
                    for the act, melting
together yet somehow sadly apart,
orifices certainly unmatched to
protuberances, although affording
                    opportunity,
it appeared, in the oddest places; no
completion but the striving, the struggle,
the melancholy abandonment of his
                    strain, her stratagem:
eventually, then, it came down to
this immense tedium, another name
for all our tenderness, solicitude.
                    Ready and waiting,
but the hope forlorn, the motive foregone:
she tyrannically submissive to
his compliant despotism, he yielding
                    over and underneath
to her surrender—her victory his
peculiar triumph. As if they neither
expected nor could resist, when it came,
                    renunciation!
Their embrace, or—better—their lenient
enacting of what Milton himself calls
intimate impulse, has reached that
                    pitch of expertise

when the thing seen becomes the unseen thing.
With enemies like themselves (all *cousins*
"descended from a common ancestor"),
                              what lovers need friends?

Nikolaus Mardruz to Ferdinand, Count of Tyrol, 1565

My Lord recalls Ferrara? How walls
rise out of water yet appear to recede
   identically
   into it, as if
built in both directions: soaring and sinking . . .
   Such mirroring was my first dismay—
                my next, having crossed
                the moat, was making
   out that, for all its grandeur, the great
pile, observed close to, is close to a ruin!
   (Even My Lord's most
   unstinting dowry
may not restore these wasted precincts to what
   their deteriorating state demands.)
                Queasy it made me,
                glancing first down there
   at swans in the moat apparently
feeding on their own doubled image, then up
   at the citadel,
   so high—or so deep,
and *everywhere* those carved effigies of
   men and women, monsters among them
                crowding the ramparts
                and seeming at home
   in the dingy water that somehow
held them up as if for our surveillance—ours?
   anyone's who looked!
   All that pretension
of marble display, the whole improbable
   menagerie with but one purpose:
                having to be seen.
                Such was the matter

of Ferrara, and such the manner,
when at last we met, of the Duke in greeting
My Lordship's Envoy:
life in fallen stone!

Several hours were to elapse, in the keeping
of his lackeys, before the Envoy
of My Lord the Count
of Tyrol might see
or even be seen to by His Grace
the Duke of Ferrara, though from such neglect
no *deliberate*
slight need be inferred:
now that I have had an opportunity
—have had, indeed, the obligation—
to fix on His Grace
that perlustration
or power of scrutiny for which
(I believe) My Lord holds his Envoy's service
in some favor still,
I see that the Duke,
by his own lights or perhaps, more properly
said, by his own *tenebrosity*,
could offer some excuse
for such cunctation . . .
Appraising a set of cameos
just brought from Cairo by a Jew in his trust,
His Grace had been rapt
in connoisseurship,
that study which alone can distract him
from his wonted courtesy; he was
affability
itself, once his mind
could be deflected from mere *objects*.

At last I presented (with those documents
which in some detail
describe and define
the duties of both signators) the portrait

of your daughter the Countess,
                    observing the while
                    his countenance. No
        fault was found with our contract, of which
each article had been so correctly framed
        (if I may say so)
        as to ascertain
a pre-nuptial alliance which must persuade
        and please the most punctilious (and
                    impecunious)
                    of future husbands.
        Principally, or (if I may be
allowed the amendment) perhaps Ducally,
        His Grace acknowledged
        himself *beguiled* by
Cranach's portrait of our young Countess, praising
        the design, the hues, the glaze—the frame!
                    and appeared averse,
                    for a while, even
        to letting the panel leave his hands!
Examining those same hands, I was convinced
        that no matter what
        the result of our
(at this point, promising) negotiations,
        your daughter's likeness must now remain
                    "for good," as we say,
                    among Ferrara's
        treasures, already one more trophy
in His Grace's multifarious *holdings*,
        like those marble busts
        lining the drawbridge,
like those weed-stained statues grinning up at us
        from the still moat, and—inside as well
                    as out—those grotesque
                    figures and faces
        fastened to the walls. So be it!

                                    Real
bother (after all, one painting, for Cranach

—*and* My Lord—need be
no great forfeiture)
commenced only when the Duke himself led me
out of the audience-chamber and
laboriously
(he is no longer
a young man) to a secret penthouse
high on the battlements where he can indulge
those despotic tastes
he denominates,
half smiling over the heartless words,
"*the relative consolations of semblance.*"
"Sir, suppose you draw
that curtain," smiling
in earnest now, and so I sought—
but what appeared a piece of drapery proved
a painted deceit!
My embarrassment
afforded a cue for audible laughter,
and only then His Grace, visibly
relishing his trick,
turned the thing around,
whereupon appeared, on the reverse,
the late Duchess of Ferrara to the life!
Instanter the Duke
praised the portrait
so readily provided by one Pandolf—
a monk by some profane article
attached to the court,
hence answerable
for taking likenesses *as required*
in but a day's diligence, so it was claimed . . .
Myself I find it
but a mountebank's
proficiency—another chicane, like that
illusive curtain, a waxwork sort
of nature called forth:
cold legerdemain!
Though *extranea* such as the hares

(copulating!), the doves and a full-blown rose
   were showily limned,
   I could not discern
aught to be loved in that countenance itself,
     likely to rival, much less to excel
            the life illumined
            in Cranach's image
     of *our* Countess, which His Grace had set
beside the dead woman's presentment . . . And took,
    so evident was
    the supremacy,
no further pains to assert Fra Pandolf's skill.
     One last hard look, whereupon the Duke
           resumed his discourse
           in an altered tone,
     now some unintelligible rant
of *stooping*—His Grace chooses "never to stoop"
    when he makes reproof . . .
    My Lord will take this
as but a figure: not only is the Duke
    no longer young, his body is so
           queerly misshapen
          that even to *speak*
     of "not stooping" seems absurdity:
the creature *is* stooped, whether by cruel or
    impartial cause—say
    Time or the Tempter—
I shall not venture to hypothecate. Cause
     or no cause, it would appear he marked
          some motive for his
          "reproof," a mortal
    chastisement in fact inflicted on
his poor Duchess, *put away* (I take it so)
    for smiling—at whom?
    Brother Pandolf? or
some visitor to court during the sitting?
     —too generally, if I construe
          the Duke's clue rightly,
          to survive the terms

of his . . . severe protocol. My Lord,
at the time it was delivered to me thus,
   the admonition
   if indeed it was
any such thing, seemed no more of a menace
     than the rest of his rodomontade;
            item, he pointed,
              as we toiled downstairs,
    to that bronze *Neptune* by our old Claus
(there must be at least six of them cluttering
   the Summer Palace
   at Innsbruck), claiming
it was "cast in bronze for me." Nonsense, of course.

   But upon reflection, I suppose
           we had better take
           the old reprobate
at his unspeakable word . . . Why, even
assuming his boasts should be as plausible
   as his avarice,
   no "cause" for dismay:
once ensconced here as the Duchess, your daughter
   need no more apprehend the Duke's
          murderous temper
            than his matchless taste.
    For I have devised a means whereby
the dowry so flagrantly pursued by our
   insolvent Duke ("no
   just pretense of mine
be disallowed" indeed!), instead of being
     paid as he pleads in one globose sum,
          should drip into his
          coffers by degrees—
    say, one fifth each year—then after five
such years, the dowry itself to be doubled,
   always assuming
   that Her Grace enjoys
her usual smiling health. The years are her
     ally in such an arbitrament,

and with confidence
My Lord can assure
the new Duchess (assuming her Duke
abides by these stipulations and his own
propensity for
accumulating
"semblances") the long devotion (so long as
he lasts) of her last Duke . . . Or more likely,
if I guess aright
your daughter's intent,
of that young lordling I might make so
bold as to designate her next Duke, as well . . .

Ever determined in
My Lordship's service,
I remain his Envoy
to Ferrara as to the world.
NIKOLAUS MARDRUZ

Mrs. Eden in Town for the Day

Sorry I'm late. I had to drive *way* out of my
    way to pick up coyote piss—
for the garden. We use about a quart a month:
    it really does deter the deer.

This man I know at the zoo keeps it for me, for
    a group of us, actually:
all gardeners. He happens to *be* a keeper—
    of coyotes, hyenas, wolves,

whatever—and he keeps coyote piss as well
    (under refrigeration, of course),
sells it right there at the zoo. I hate the long drive,
    but I love having no more deer

in the garden. Expensive, too, or should I say
    dear, but it's definitely not
a competitive item—where else can you get
    coyote piss that's full strength,

not reconstituted from crystals or some kind
    of concentrate? It has to be
fresh—from the wild—or the damn deer just ignore it.
    I wonder how such merchandise

would be collected? Tom says there's something
    they call a Texas Catheter,
really not much more than a perforated
    condom attached to a bottle . . .

Have you ever seen such goings-on at a *zoo*?
    Well neither have I—but of course

I wasn't looking . . . Who would be, unless you *knew* . . .
    However he gets hold of it,

it works! Today our keeper told me *human hair*
    has the same effect, on most deer—
we could try that. Think how much cheaper, for one thing:
    a year's sweepings from Tom's barber

would cost less than a week's gasoline! Even so,
    people's hair . . . Better the other:
I wonder which animals would keep off if we tried
    our own instead of coyotes'?

moose   dik-dik   gazelle   caribou   hartebeest   gnu

Homage to Antonio Canaletto

Venice spent what Venice earned. —Robert Browning

The operas for which he made designs
in his father's shop
had consequences;
        he never got over the Bibienas'
                        groundless perspectives,
                        and until he died
        such vistas would haunt him: however close
to veritable
palaces he came,
        their porticoes and balustrades composed
                        a proscenium
                        of hysteria.
        But who could count on theaters for pay?
Workmen were always
threatening to quit,
        impresarios "embarrassed," castrati
                        and sopranos in
                        reciprocal fits—
        what could a talent do but "solemnly
excommunicate
the stage" (his own words)
        and set up shop in Rome? A year later
                        he was home again,
                        Roman lessons learned:
        certifiable views of City Life
mattered a good deal
more than the *Scena*
        all'angolo. Unvarying Venice
                        mattered most of all,
                        the abiding dream:
        little canals (what else?) colonized by
perfunctory dolls.

First a sketch was made
    (recorded by the *maestro* on the spot),
        then redrawn by him
        more decorously
    indoors, where the *product* could be prepared:
the sky painted in,
sometimes even clouds,
    across the canvas acres, inch by inch,
        and then the contours
        of buildings incised
    into that sky-skin to provide guidance
for eventual
roofs and cornices,
    hemicircles marking an arch, a dome
        (all this done of course
        by apprentices).
    At times he was obsessively precise
and in exquisite
detail would devise
    the reigning Doge's coat of arms to fill
        a space smaller than
        a baby's thumbnail
    on the ducal barge; but more likely
San Marco would glow
or gloom as it had
    generations ago. Venice might change,
        stories be added,
        campaniles fall,
    but master-drawings in the studio
perdured his pattern
Serenissima
    years on end, a topographical hoax,
        though one sure to work
        as long as *he* worked:
    Grand Tourists continued to pay dear for
proof that they had been
duly discerning
    guests of the carnival Republic by
        acquiring views from

Canaletto's hand.
"His merit lyes in painting things which fall
immediately
under his ogle,"
McSwiny wrote to England. Why not go
to England as well
as to Rome? Respite
from the routine of Venetian *vedute*
lured him a moment
that endured ten years:
armed with letters to the Noble Lords, he
proved (what could he prove?)
a disappointment
to potential patrons who claimed they saw
deterioration
in his dirty Thames,
and rumors even started he was not
"the veritable
virtuoso, no
Canalet at all, but an impostor!"
— easily foiled by
his cool reportage:
a *View of Whitehall* scrupulous enough
to rout all skeptics.
He stayed on, well paid
but never (as aristocrats assumed)
to paint their houses,
their horses, their dogs . . .
Nature he loathed, and next to nature, sport.
Having provided
plausible prospects
of Warwick Castle, Cambridge, Eton, Bath!
he was heard to sigh,
as longed-for Venice
loomed upon his homing horizon, how
glad he was, never
to have to portray
another tree. Another thirteen years'
practice made perfect

sense; he persisted.
    Hester Thrale (become Piozzi) bought,
                    long after his death,
                    "seven Canalets,
        to which his myriad imitators seem
hardly more than a
camera obscura
        in the window of a London parlour" . . .
                    Remembered, required!
                    in attestation:
        "Your own Canalettos will have given
a better idea
of the gondola
        than I can convey," a friend of Byron
                    wrote to Hallam,
                    and a few years on,
        for Théophile Gautier (and not for us?)
Venice had become
"*avec ses palais,
    ses gondoles, la ville de Canaletto!*"
                    On a last drawing
                    (made inside Saint Mark's)
        this busy little man, so early prized
for reproducing
whatever might fall
        under his eye, proudly informs us: "Done
                    without spectacles.
                    A. Canaletto."

Family Values I

After Fuseli, *Milton Dictating* Paradise Lost *to His Daughters*, 1797

He was an early riser, four o'clock
manè, even after sight was lost.
He had a man to read to him: the first
language he heard was the Hebrew Bible,
at half-past four. Then he contemplated.
At seven his man came to him again,
reading still, and writing for him, until
dinner; now as much writing as reading.
Of his three daughters, it was Deborah,
the youngest, who could read to him as well,
Italian, French and Latin, also Greek.
After dinner he would walk some three hours:
he always had a garden where he lived,
and there his exercise was walking till
he went to bed, often-times about nine . . .

ANNE   Deborah will serve, will also *serve*,
        bearing his *mild yoke* till even she
        suffers from what our father likes to call,
        when either of us ventures to complain
        of lassitude in eye or hand—or mind!—
        a bestial and sublunary burning;
        then it is my turn. Mary will not come
        when we are called, I know not how it is
        with her—she manages to stay apart,
        and it is always I who must relieve
        my sister where she stands, taking the words
        from him, terrible words out of the air
        as they come, unceasing, to us. I sit,

sewing the while, until our Deborah
fails, and when the silence falls, I begin.

DEBORAH   *Come girls, it is time: I want to be milked!*
such is his humor, so he summons us
—he *would* be cheerful, even in gout-fits—
but no frolic for me, the *faery pen*
he favors over Anne and Mary, far
the better scriveners (nothing he cares
for letters he cannot see, theirs or mine):
Wake to be the word that is your name,
Deborah, bearer of glad tidings, born
through death and known to me by darkness, wake,
utter a song . . . This to my thirteen years.
What does it mean that he will call me his
Cordelia, heart of hearts? Am I the more his
without a mother, and are these sisters
—merely for knowing her—Regan, Goneril?

MARY   There is so much to be hidden, so much
hiding goes along . . . But who calls it such,
a merely surreptitious exploit, when
we know he cannot see what we would hide?
I will not come to this. Let my sisters
wear the red slippers even as they take
down the words of Eve. It shall not be
seen by *my* hand that she rhymes with *deceive.*
Father is cheerful, his sight not so much
lost as retired, "withdrawn into myself,"
he says, "where it sharpens rather than dulls
the edge of my mind." Acuminated thus,
let Anne and Deborah scriven him out,
for I will have no part of *secret things,*
the scandal of the story. I shall wait
and wipe no tears—neither from his blind eyes
nor from my own that see my sisters go
their ways. Deborah looks very like
her father. I am on the distaff side.
What difference can it make or matter?

There is another wife to tend him now,
to wipe the tears forever from his eyes.
I watch them all from my unsuspected
corner in the dark (did I not say there was
hiding done—even Father hides something—
though we do not share the things we shroud:
Anne darning her rags, Deborah at the desk,
catching each word upon her cunning quill,
forbidden scarlet on their pretty feet,
and Father like some prelate in his chair,
luminous as a gargoyle, and as blind . . .

     . . . All the time of writing his Paradise
Lost, *his vein began at the equinox*
each autumn, leaving off at the vernal,
or thereabouts—it was generally May—
pale as the candle that he studied by.
And this for a lustrum at least of his
doing, two years before the king came in,
finishing about three years after
the famous Restoration. Much visited
by the learned, more than he did desire,
and by the gout as well, autumn and spring,
but with this he was blithesome, and would sing.
His widow has his portrait, very like,
which ought to be engraved, the images
before his Works doing him no honor.

Family Values II

After Delacroix, *Milton Dictating* Paradise Lost *to His Daughters*, 1827

MILTON TO LEONARD PHILARAS, ATHENIAN
(FROM THE LATIN):

> . . . *While yet a little sight remained, when late*
> *I lay in bed and turned to either side,*
> *there used to shine a copious glittering*
> > *light from my shut eyes.*
> *Then, as my sight grew less from day to day,*
> *such colors as there were decayed; and now,*
> *as if that lucency had grown extinct,*
> > *it is mere blackness,*
> *or a blackness dashed and woven in*
> *with ashes wont to pour forth of themselves.*
> *Yet such a shadow, still before me now*
> > *by night as by day,*
> *seems always nearer to a whitish thing,*
> *behaving so that when the eye should roll,*
> *there is admitted, as through a chink, some*
> > *charity of light.*

ANNE   It is our Mary picked them, fresh an hour
       ago, and from the garden where you walk
       each evening—where you know the ways. Oh no,
       not here, not now! When is she here with us?
       Mary goes, leaving a summer sweetness,
       and leaves us to *our* ways (you know them too)—
       shall we be on them now? Father, you turn
       aside, indifferent to where I sit
       attending on the words you have prepared.

Giant your hand upon the tablecloth
appears to read its pattern stitch by stitch
thrusting your nails into the Turkey cloth
as if (with blossoms dropping on the wool)
the odor of those roses could be seized
between your thumb and fingers: Touch and Scent
becoming Sight. So what you were you are;
though blind, you see! The spirit afterward,
but first the touch. Your last words, Father,
stand just as you spoke them: ". . . *Eternal Spring.*
Not that fair field of Enna . . ?" What comes now?

DEBORAH Ready in arms I hold the lute, knowing
you will have music when the words resist
coming, and coming even, Music Ho!
The poem, you told us, is "like music":
A man must have an ear for it. And some
have none at all. Father, I know you hear
me playing, and when you suddenly speak
the lines our Anne will write, I know you hear
their music too, though music not the same:
I watch you say the lines, holding the lute's
belly against my own, its crooked neck
over my shoulder, and watching I wait
for the silence, for that other music
of yours to cease. Then, Father, I begin!
Sometimes, playing, I hear you whisper words
to the strings as they move, and I wonder:
are they already there, such words, or do
my fingers draw them from you with the strings?
Does my music make your music, Father?
It is a dim taper, this mind of mine,
and much needs trimming! Which daughter knows,
also serving, what is done best for you:
Anne scrivening? Myself ready with the lute?
Mary, perhaps, who never writes a line,
never plays a note, but leaves beside you
flowers you can only guess, and goes?
O Sound and Scent of Darkness, who is here?

And so, good sir, whatever ray of hope
your famous Greek physicians shed on me,
all the same, as in a case incurable
                I compose myself,
since as a wise man warns us, many days
of darkness are destined for all, and mine,
amid sweet voices, easier to bear
                than that deathly one.
What keeps me from resting in the belief
that eyesight lies not in my eyes alone
but, for all purposes of earthly life,
                in God's providence?
In truth, while only He looks out for me,
leading me forth as with His hand alone,
I shall have given willingly my eyes
                their long holiday.

Family Values III

After Romney, *Milton and His Two Daughters*, 1794

I leave the garden, as a woman must
leave gardens—*under Father's orders leave
undeplored cities as well, leave behind*
                    whatever places
fathers and husbands, brothers even, say
must be left when there is another life
to be led somewhere, anywhere, *a life
                    not hers, another's*:
that life calls her, therefore she will come in
from the garden, for example, being called
by her father who looks up, *Our Father
                    who cannot see me
but divines I am here*: to me he turns
the crannies that now, with him, pass for eyes,
even as my sisters scribe and sew and
                    give no sign they know
we share the very room: Anne will not look
up from her work, and Deborah looks up
only to watch Father (*watching for me—
                    what a game we play!
like maypole colors on a broken shaft,
wound over and under: a braid of girls,
and I, the loose ribbon always*). All days
                    loose, although not free:
mine the garden tendance, summer days
(*Martha not Mary should have been my name*)
I keep the briars from the paths he walks,
                    and without a cane
Father *in the cool of the evening* moves
among my roses which the darkness brings

to sweetness, never losing his way.—Look,
                    how the light rises
from Deborah's book, *Father's book as well*,
as if the very verses she takes down
caught fire from her neck and hair, inflaming
                    Annie's profile too
at the touch of that apricot shoulder,
and leaving Father's face a silver mask . . .
I come upon them in the partial dark
                    (I mean, the shadows
serve what is happening, *partial* that way)
and make my outsider's discovery:
this moment has no message, no intent
                    till I descry it!
There has to be a witness to the scene
"to speak of secret things that came to pass
when Beldam Nature in her cradle was,"
                    so Father has said,
or *Bedlam in her crypt*, as I would say . . .
Only because I see my sisters hiding
are they hidden too from the sightless seer
                    who is our father;
only because I enter on this scene
is it a scene composed at all. Just so
God watches us, and makes a meaning
                    for the innocent
as for the guilty. Sisters, which are *we*,
who lead such lives? I like my saying *lead*,
as if our lives, all three, were but some brute
                    within a halter,
to be conducted so. That time I tried
to write for him, as Deborah now writes,
Father's words moved forward *out of silence*
                    and out of darkness
as if to a mark where I sat by him,
so clear I could not write for him again,
despite the times he calls for me to do:
                    "gathered like a scum
and settled to itself, such life shall be

in eternal and restless change, self-fed
and self-consumed" . . . Such life, yes: a woman's.
               There is no garden
untended, no scene unseen. I know that
now, coming in so still and suddenly:
so much for theologics, mine at least!
              I have read to him
the terrible charges of *ambition,*
contention, corruption, even worse things,
articles of abuse from great doctors,
                  vilifications
of his every word: "pseudo-Quaker!
semi-Arian! Arminian! Mortalist!
Anabaptist! anti-Sabbatarian! Divorcer
              and polygamist!"
He did not wince, but brushed the words away
like plaguey flies, and only smiled to say,
"People have a general sense of losing
             Paradise but not
an equal gust for the regaining it."
I wonder what a *Mortalist* can be,
if Father minds so little the misprized
              acrimination:
how glad he is to begin each day's task
with the other girls, mortal certainly
as he himself, though cherished beyond life:
           "the different sex,
in most resembling unlikeness, and most
unlike resemblance, cannot but please best
in aptitude of that variety
            and be pleased as well . . ."
Soon it will be time for his evening walk.
Leaving the girls to wonder, Father will
come to the door where he must know I am,
             as he knows the time
for walking. He will touch me on his way
and murmur *duty's done*. My raked gravel
yields to his certain steps. The path is clear.
           Father, duty's done.

The Job Interview
with André Breton, 1957

The question, Monsieur Gracq advised, had best
be asked, and answered, in the Old Lion's den:
would I, duly scrutinized, be allowed
                    to translate *Nadja*?

Factors in my favor: I did speak French
—the one parlance necessarily shared—
and my links to certain Proscribed Figures
                    were, to him, unknown.

Bravely enough, therefore, I proceeded
through the Place Blanche and up the Rue Fontaine,
though in my heart (or in some other place)
                    I knew the danger:

Breton's legendary loathing of queers . . .
Ever since Jacques Vaché had overdosed
on opium in a Nantes hotel, naked
                    with another man,

Surrealism's pope had unchurched men
of my kind, condemned our "perverted race"
to a paltry outer darkness, claiming
                    he could sense, could *smell*

an intolerable presence . . . Fee fo fum.
Climbing his stairs, I wondered if I gave
off the emanations of turpitude:
                    would he detect me

by the scent of my "disgusting practice"?
Was I entitled to conceal from him

—indeed *could* I conceal the taint which made
　　　　　whatever talent

I might have merely an interference,
an imposture? A scuffle of slippers,
and the author of *Nadja* let me in
　　　　　past the museum

of surreal objects, himself another
museum of sorts, who had shown epigones
how to read, how to live, and how to love.
　　　　　Some epigones.

Others had failed—rejections, suicides;
of which no hint discolored our encounter,
affable to a fault. Perhaps the three
　　　　　decades since Nadja

had revealed to the world her Accidents
of Sublimity had blunted Breton's
erotic stipulations: and I was so
　　　　　pusillanimous

as to keep my *tendencies* to myself,
where they fluttered helplessly enough:
of course I knew in my heart that the one
　　　　　surrealist act

—O coward heart! would be to challenge this
champion of liberation, this foe of all
society's constraints, but I could do
　　　　　nothing of the kind,

nor need I have. O reason not the need:
I left the Master of the Same New Things
with every warrant of his trust in me
　　　　　as his translator

(*Traditorre—tradutore!* in fact,
if not in French), and forty years have passed
since that traduced encounter. Where are we?
Nadja in English

is still in print, and people still hate queers.
I allay that heart of mine with the words
Breton wrote to Simone, first of his wives
(and a Jew like me):

criticism will be love, or will not be.

For Mona Van Duyn, Going On

As for me, I lost all sense of human possibility

Blacking out, we say; but it was more like
ablution in the Country of the Blue,
that region of "altogether elsewhere,"
    possibly sacred . . .
Arriving hungry after airborne hours
for a Poetry Festival, I had
fainted among my fellow bards, offstage.
    Out of the blue, then,
came (before I could recognize your face)
your voice, incredulous squeal that oddly
mixed with carpet-figures and the fragrance
    of Spray-O-Vac Rose:

"Richard, *you* passed out!" The accusation
was evident: any *évanouissement*
to be sanctioned here was really your thing,
    and my spill or spell
on the floor—though I had no notion of
its drama at the time: leave that to you!—
was probably a version of that same
    "drive for attention"
to which, Mother said, I was always prone
(surely the *mot juste* now). In any case,
I knew I had no such viable contacts
    with the Other Side,

no likely means of recuperating
messages left indecipherable
unless I put myself to Mona's School:
    where else grapple with
such hard-won experience, no sooner gained
than gainsaid by means of your so-envied

rhetorical conversion-hysteria?
    Such was the lesson
of your lyceum—no wonder you laid claim
or likely connoisseurship at the least
to these episodes of "fallings from us" . . .
    In a life given

to any of these obliterations,
to debility, danger and despair,
let it come down! as the Second Murderer
    famously remarks;
make no attempt to spare anyone grief,
but Go For It, fail without fail, settle
down at the center of the worst and wait
    there for whatever
news we never hoped or hated to hear
half so much, dispatches you especially
listened for and lovingly retrieved: not
    to know anything,

but only to be looking for something,
renouncing the possession of wisdom
in favor of the power to observe.
    Most of us, Mona,
spoil our poems (our lives) because we have
ideas—not ideas but approved topics
that can be carried around intact. Oh
    watch me faint once more,
and this time make a true recovery:
acceptance of the vast erroneous
community of pain to which we all
    belong. No ideas

but in nothing! No failures but those proved!
To become poets, *to become* human,
never *to be*, for as soon as we "are"
    we are no longer
human perhaps, nor even poets . . . Once
I had come to, I obeyed Van Duyn's Law:

we only are by virtue of (it *is*
   a virtue, I guess)
our continual tendency not to be . . .
You scraped me off the floor, and we performed
our poems in a state of perfect health—
   until the next time.

Lee Krasner: *Porcelain,* a Collage

oil and paper on panel, 30 x 48 inches, 1955

Take it down Tear it up Turn it over Make
    it new out of old makings:
exert what that venerable scatterbrain
    in Weimar once called the Power
of Pulling Yourself Together whereby
    the master is first revealed.
Exposed is more like it: shown for what you are.

Porcelain! If a watched pot never boils, what
    happens to a pulverized one?
These are not heroic fragments, nothing here
    inherently shapely! No
identifiable vessel remains: you
    picked up the pieces all
over the place and laid them down again

according to your own ragged politics
    of reaching and retracting, no
better than breathing really, putting mere drips,
    untimely ripp'd, not so much
where you saw they belonged, but how you surrendered
    to their various discomfort:
an open mind must be open at both ends!

The wrong papers, the wretched old canvases
    discovered to be no more
than rehearsals for much new catastrophe:
    this purple patch, that sliver
of viridian woven into the web

of accommodating earth,
our only planet not named for some god . . .

Then glued these scraps, these scrapings, these scrupulous
approximations to some
consistent field of accidents all that year, once
your wild partner in chrom-
atic fantasy had spilled himself out of
life like a puddle of paint:
these exist only because they have been made to —

compelled, this time, to sort together without
alienation, which means
they are a final vision. No, semi-final,
since the whole soul is never
one, save in ecstasy and not merely when,
as Yeats declared, it has been
rent. Another twenty years had to be lived

before there were Krasner collages again,
entire paintings ripped to shreds
to let the white light through. But that was when
you were dying, as you knew.
Meanwhile, there were other allowances
to be made, other makings
allowed. You decided once again to paint.

A Sibyl of 1979

The river lay white that afternoon, the highway too—
  apparently frozen to a standstill.
Muriel Rukeyser hobbled to her high window,
  standing beside me, both of us looking
down at the big meat-trucks parked on West Street, empty now
  but not as they would be after dark, men
furtively climbing in and out, walking away fast.

"Do you ever go to the trucks, Richard—go inside?"
  her voice close to my ear, low, determined.
The question, its very tone, took me by surprise: so
  she knew what that meant, *going to the trucks*—
even in the dead of winter, the cherished, feckless
  secret of many who still persisted . . .
And even if she did know, the question surprising:

were we on those terms? What terms? "Dangerous, isn't it—"
  the voice persistent as she took my arm
"doing . . . what you do, inside there?" Staring down at them,
  I told her I never went to the trucks.
"I'm glad. That's not a judgment, only relief. Only
  my own cowardice, really . . . Dear Richard,
I asked you here because I want to give you something

you may be able to use. I can't. When they sent me
  home from the hospital, after my stroke,
it was right here, this computer-thing: supposed to be
  helpful because it changes what you write
so easily, so easily restores what you change . . .
  I tried it awhile, but it doesn't work
for me: I don't need to change things so much any more,

not the way you do, my cautious friend. I'm past changing."
   About the trucks nothing more was said, and
I took the virtually virgin computer home
   and plugged it in. Nothing occurred, until
a few days later, my fingers "wandering idly"
   (just as in Sir Arthur's *Lost Chord!*) over
the unresponsive keys, these sentences appeared, words

she had abandoned, "past changing" now: *No thought wakens*
   without waking others . . . There is one proof
of ability, only one: doing it! . . . The more
   you love yourself, the more you are your own
worst enemy . . . Seers don't need to be observers . . . We keep
   learning—involuntarily, even—
and finally we learn to die. Muriel learned, and died,

but reading her words the screen retained —sortilege? poems?
   I faltered: time was, if you lost even
a tenth part of the Sibyl's leaves, you too would be lost . . .
   Was now the time when if you kept even
a tenth part you were saved, as a frightened man is saved
   by words? *You will not be deprived because*
your dreams did not come true, but because you never dreamed.

The Sibyl, Petronius reports, could not die, only
   wither away until she was so small
she survived in a leather bottle, pleading for death.
   Muriel's bottle was her own body;
I bring her words up on that pale, superseded screen
   where they glow like omens, benefactions:
Everything you really possess was given to you.

A post-script, seventeen years afterwards. The gift
   I bring would be quite as bewildering
to you as that computer: what would you make, Muriel,
   of a CD claiming to reproduce
(on the right contraption) *The Song of the Sibyl*—words
   the very ones Aeneas might have heard,
music from as late as the Tenth Century? . . . My offering.

The Manatee

New Smyrna Beach, Florida

She never took much credit for "The Moose"
  —"it all just happened that way"—
and sent our questions packing as abuse

of her privacy; Elizabeth Bishop would say
  enough had been said, would smile,
and class, we knew, was over for the day.

We longed to ask her, "Why, why do we feel
  this sweet sensation of joy?"
an ecstasy attributed to all

of us on that bus of hers . . . Was that the only
  appropriate response when
some great big (harmless) lummox "happened" by?

Had it been joy for Robert Frost (a man
  more likely to feel alarm
than unaccountable delight upon

being looked over by an Alien Form)
  that time Whatever-it-was
appeared to him "as a great buck" and swam

providentially out of sight across
  the pond? Would either poet
make common cause with odd affects like those

of Witold Gombrowicz (who, I admit,
   is an apocalyptic
sort of witness)? In June, 1958,

G was walking down a eucalyptus-
   lined avenue when a cow
sauntered out from behind a tree. "I stopped,

and we looked each other in the eyes; so
   tense was the moment I lost
my bearings *as a man*—that is, you know,

as a member of our race. It was the first
   time, apparently, I was
experiencing the shame of a Man come face

to face with an Animal. What then ensues
   is obvious: one becomes
an Animal also, and uneasy, as

if Nature, on all sides, were watching." Shame!
   Fear! Joy!—reactions vary
strongly when we meet The Other, it seems,

but given such discrepant histories,
   I realized that our great
human hope, watching the manatee rise

or emanate—no other verb could state
   so well the means of its ap-
parition: a *manatee* must *emanate*—

out of its New Age of jeopardized sleep
   in the slime of Turnbull Bay,
is to greet The Other (whatever gap

grins between us) as Another—let's say,
   members of a cast one is
proud to share the Comedy with today.

Les Travaux d'Alexandre

for Dominique de Menil

bronze, 23 inches, 1967

My dear Magritte, I'm glad to be in touch
again and, in the nature of the thing,
quite literally, bumping into one
of your last works, eighth in the disputed
succession of those "sculptures" you had seen
only in wax, never the finished bronze—
though you did make a finicky design
for this heroic object (one of five
to which as ever an unlikely name
seems to have been fastened from the start).

By all accounts such naming was a group
affair: you and your cronies and Georgette
would think up proper titles, so to speak,
once creation was put paid, a done thing,
hence ever to be known by that device . . .
When all his conquering was over and
Asia in his grasp, the hero wept:
his past deleted by his present put
his future beyond him. You called this work
Alexander's Labors, of course! What else?

Moreover, dear master, colliding with
this culminal object, I summon up
the apposite sense of what's past, passing,
or coming to pass (as your fancy name
for it, for once, makes ultimately plain):
held fast within the octopine embrace
of a burly root, confined there surely

since sapling days, a most efficient ax
is clearly captive of the very tree
it has, just now, reduced to a mere stump.

Your paradox so inveterately
enacted—back to front or night by day,
every antithesis which brings about
the extermination of time—what's that
but the task of any art? You made it
more sudden, more seditious maybe, but
is it not the same, this quattrocento
panel by Benozzo Gozzoli, say,
his *Dance of Salome*, where on the right,
gown eddying from her completed turn,

the girl demands what, in a sinister
niche, the glamorous executioner
prepares to . . . execute, though far upstage
Salome (again! the same gold folds, but
docile here) presents her scarlet mother with
the head she still must ask for on the right.
"The same," but more fiercely epitomized
in your harsh emblem. Maybe that's the cost
of our modernity: the death of time
instanter! and we have misread the signs—

what if *this* is time's real life: the salvered
head in her mother's lap which Salome
implores unsevered from the living saint . . .
What if *only* a rootbound ax can fell
the tree that has overgrown it in time—
not in our silly sequence, our *and then* . . .
but in that Other Time, my dear Magritte,
the time you told by one wonder after
the next, till the hero's labors were done
and wonders had to cease. Wherefore these tears.

Among the Missing

Know me? I am the ghost of Gansevoort Pier.
  Out of the Trucks, beside the garbage scow
  where rotten pilings form a sort of prow,
I loom, your practiced shadow, waiting here

for celebrants who cease to come my way,
  though mine are limbs as versatile as theirs
  and eyes as vagrant. Odd that no one cares
to ogle me now where I, as ever, lay

myself out, all my assets and then some,
  weather permitting. Is my voice so faint?
  Can't you hear me over the river's complaint?
Too dark to see me? Have you all become

ghosts? What earthly good is that? I want
  incarnate lovers hungry for my parts,
  longing hands and long-since-lonely hearts!
It is your living bodies I must haunt,

and while the Hudson hauls its burdens past,
  having no hosts to welcome or repel
  disclosures of the kind I do so well,
I with the other ghosts am laid at last.

Our Spring Trip

Dear Mrs. Masters, Hi from the Fifth-Grade Class
of Park School! We're still here in New York City
                    at the Taft Hotel,
you could have guessed that from the picture printed
on this stationery—I inked in x's
        to show you our rooms,
which are actually on the same floor as
the Terminal Tower Observation Deck
                        in Cleveland, Ohio,
which we visited on our *Fourth*-Grade Spring Trip,
but nowhere near so high as some skyscrapers
        in New York City:
we've been up to the *top* of the Empire State
and the Chrysler Buildings, which are really tall!
                        But there's another
reason for writing besides wanting to say
Hi—we're having a problem Miss Husband thought
        you might help us with,
once we get back to school . . . yesterday we went
to the Dinosaur Hall of the Natural
                        History Museum
for our Class Project—as you know, the Fifth Grade
is constructing this life-size Diplodocus
        out of chicken wire
and some stuff Miss Husband calls papier-mâché,
but no diagram we have shows how the tail
                        balances the head
to keep our big guy upright—we need to see
how the backbone of a real Diplodocus
        manages to bear
so much weight: did you know that some Dinosaurs

(like the Brontosaurus) are so huge they have
                    a whole other brain
at the base of their spine, just to move their tail?
Another thing: each time Arthur Englander
        came anywhere near
our Diplodocus, it would collapse because
of not balancing right. This went on until
                    David Stashower
got so mad at Arthur that he flew at him
and gave his left shoulder a really good bite
        so he would keep away . . .
That was when you called the All-School Assembly
to explain about the biting: biting's no good . . .
                    Even so, Arthur
decided not to come on this year's Spring Trip.
Well, we took a Subway train to the Museum
        from the Taft Hotel,
in fact that was our very first excursion,
but the noise, once we were on the platform,
                    was so loud one girl,
Nancy Akers, cried (she always was chicken)
when someone told her that terrible roaring
        the Expresses made
was Tyrannosaurus Rex himself, and she
believed it! — then we went to the Great Hall where
                    we were surrounded
by Dinosaurs, all the kinds we had studied:
some were not much bigger than a chicken, but
        some were humongous!
One was just a skeleton wired together,
so it was easy to see how we could make
                    our Diplodocus
balance by putting a swivel in its neck.
All the other Dinosaurs were stuffed, I guess,
        with motors and lights
inside: when they moved, *their* heads balanced their tails!
There was even a Pterodactyl flying
                    back and forth above

our heads, probably on some kind of a track.
But even though Miss Husband tried explaining
      (for the hundredth time)
how the Dinosaurs had all been extinct for
millions of years, not one person in the class
                        believed what she said:
the idea of a million years is so *stupid*,
anyway—a typical grown-up reason . . .
      You know the Klein twins,
the biggest brains in the whole Fifth Grade (a lot
bigger, probably, than *both* brains combined in
                        that Brontosaurus)—
well, they had a question for Miss Husband: what
if the Dinosaurs' being extinct so long
      was just a smoke screen
for their being Somewhere Else, a long ways away?
And Lucy Wensley made an awful pun on
                        stinky and *extinct* . . .
Actually, Mrs. Masters, we've already
figured it out, about death: the Dinosaurs
      may be extinct, but
they're not dead! It's a different thing, you dig?
When Duncan Chu's Lhasa jumped out the window,
                        or when Miss Husband's
parents were killed together in a car crash,
we understood that—that *was* being dead; gone:
      no body around.
Isn't that what dying has to mean—not being
here? The Dinosaurs are with us all the time,
                        anything but dead—
we keep having them! Later, at the "Diner-
Saurus," the Museum restaurant, there was
      chicken-breast for lunch
stamped out in the shape of a Triceratops!
Strange how everything has to taste like chicken:
                        whether it's rabbit
or rattlesnake, it's always "just like chicken" . . .
Anyway, Dinosaurs are alive as long
      as we think they are,

not like Duncan's dog. And that's just the problem.
By next week, though, we'll be back in Sandusky,
                          and while we're putting
the swivel into our Diplodocus's neck,
you could explain to us about Time—about
     those millions of years,
and Dinosaur-chicken in the Diner, and
chicken-size Dinosaurs in the Great Hall, and
                         where they really are.

Henri Fantin-Latour:
Un Coin de table, 1873

All those men have gone. Over a year
since they left the table where you have arranged
   matters, assortment of properties
that set the "natural" stage of *natures mortes*,
   the apparatus of your practiced
art, or at the very least the articles
   of your everlasting apprenticeship:

   the consuetudinal cup and glass,
the former drained to show your skill, the latter
   filled, for the same purpose, with wine from
a pitcher that has perdured here eighteen months
   (though turned, now, to face the other way);
a cruet which is well rehearsed, a compote
   covertly upstaged by that silver bowl . . . .

   You have shifted the rhododendrons
from the right (where they supplanted old Mérat
   who would not share a purposed *Hommage*
à Baudelaire with beasts of such behavior
   as the poets who stare in separate
lethargies past each other on the left:
   Rimbaud, Verlaine, abominable pair!)

   to the foreground, lavish corollas
standing in for laureates of shameful life
   and for enshrined (and shaggy) lions
blameless in their oblivion ever since —
   now we name them only from the list
drawn up by the orderly Mlle. Dubourg,
   whom you would marry in a few more years.

It was to maintain the new ménage
that you sold, in England, eight hundred portraits
    of flowers! while sending to the Salon
voluted *fantaisies* that have duly turned
    to more hectares of blackened leather
than all the Wagnerites in Paris could buy.
    You kept your shameful secret (so you thought)

    of those remunerative roses,
hollyhocks, pansies, peonies, whatever
    she brought in from the garden each day,
and went on portraying *ces messieurs* in all
    their grave coats, their cretacious collars,
their gold watch fobs and their contemptuous stares:
    Around the Piano, In a Batignolles

    Studio—and all the while you knew
what you dared to acknowledge only in oils:
    these perennials and the power
to paint air around them which was all you had,
    all you needed. At the retrospective
of '06, *tout-Paris* was fluttered to find
    such flowers never seen in France before.

    No lions here, no Rhinemaidens,
just an empty table, its white cloth still creased,
    these months, as if fresh from the mangle,
the patient props and, wholly unjustified
    by any important theme or scheme,
not even a pot to grow in, these branches
    of rhododendron . . . This life . . . This art . . .

At Sixty-five

The tragedy, Colette said, is that one
does *not* age. Everyone else does, of course
(as Marcel was so shocked to discover),
and upon one's mask odd disfigurements
are imposed; but that garrulous presence
we sometimes call the self, sometimes deny

it exists at all despite its carping
monologue, is the same as when we stole
the pears, spied on mother in the bath, ran
away from home. What has altered is what
Kant called Categories: the shape of *time*
changes altogether! Days, weeks, months,

and especially years are reassigned.
Famous for her timing, a Broadway wit
told me her "method": asked to do something,
anything, she would acquiesce *next year*—
"I'll commit suicide, provided it's
next year." But after sixty-five, next year

is now. Hours? there are none, only a few
reckless postponements before *it is time* . . .
When was it you "last" saw Jimmy—last spring?
last winter? That scribbled arbiter
your calendar reveals—betrays—the date:
over a year ago. Come again? No

time like the present, endlessly deferred.
Which makes a difference: once upon a time
there was only time (. . . *as the day is long*)
between the wanting self and what it wants.

Wanting still, you have no dimension where
fulfillment or frustration can occur.

Of course you have, but you must cease waiting
upon it: simply turn around and look
back. Like Orpheus, like Mrs. Lot, you
will be petrified—astonished—to learn
memory is endless, life very long,
and you—you are immortal after all.

TALKING CURES

Close Encounters of Another Kind

A dim haunt known as The High Dive
was the scene of my first rapt exposure to
the drawling vowels and the dismissive smile
by which you delivered to outer darkness
  an already blacked-out companion
still decorative enough, despite the toll
of drugs and dirty dancing, to elicit
what seemed, at first, like an indulgent kiss-off:
  No, don't wake him: let lying dogs sleep.

Horrified and charmed by such abuse
(once the point sank in), I knew enough to steer
clear of such tactics as the Freezing Shoulder
and (your words) a Sociable Stab-in-the-Front . . .
  But now you were . . . here! That laugh of yours
could not be missed, even in a triplex flat
(I had my oxymorons down) where gay men
gorgeously dressed (and even gowned) made movement
  —there must have been a hundred of us!—

difficult but quite a lot of fun.
I think the place had belonged to Doris Duke
in the thirties when The Drive meant Riverside,
or was it Barbara Hutton's hideaway
  back then? now come (or coming) to this:
my first *thé dansant*, and with a novice's
nervousness I had to take a piss! I sought
(and found) the proper cubicle for comfort
  till I flicked on the light, whereupon

Bingo! right there on top of the tank
appeared a pair of minuscule dragons locked

in coital combat, motionless and *hissing*!
Had I had a foreskin then, it would have shrunk
        to string. As it was, what I did have
retracted; I zipped up and quickly withdrew
to join the decorously appareled crew
(though some were already making out,
        quite unimpeded by their raiment,

        in postures all too reminiscent
of the grappling creatures I so cravenly
left behind)—and found myself now face to face
with you, James Merrill, Terror of the Revels,
        waiting your turn with marked containment.
"Two . . . two lizards in there," I stammered, "fucking
on the toilet tank. They're not moving, but I didn't . . .
I couldn't . . . I don't know how they got there or
        why they're doing that, but you shouldn't . . ."

        And as you glided past me into
the powder-room with the imperturbable
amenity of Talleyrand, you murmured
in the languid accents distinctly recalled
        from that earlier encounter and
reverberating ever since down shared decades
when I would hear them with eager delight, yes,
but always with a touch of fear: *Well of course,
        dear: iguana see, iguana do . . .*

Knowing When to Stop
October, 1939

. . . Destroy the dogs, Highness?
Where did you ever get such an idea?
That's not our British way. It sounds more like
some primitive practice than anything
   appropriate to
the death of a modern public figure.
You know the kind of thing I mean: Siegfried
or Sardanapalus—the perished hero
   laid out on a pyre
surrounded by his wives, his dogs, his things,
all to be done away with, given to
the flames along with his defeated flesh.
   Who could imagine
anything like that in London today?
Your Highness will never experience
such barbarism here in Primrose Hill,
   on that I give you
my word of honor as an English vet
—than which, I venture to say, there can be,
in such a case, no firmer guarantee:
   we don't do such things!

Of course we don't, dear Dr. Gravesend, not
any longer. But may I remind you
even so (speaking as a foreigner)
   such things have been done.
And having done things, just the once, becomes
a ruinous reason for doing them
again, even after so long
   an interruption.
Perhaps the notion you did away with
the dogs is a primitive atavism

of mine. You see, for us Professor Freud
        was our patriarch,
a kind of tribal hero, gone although
never truly absent. It was because . . .
Did you know—how could you know?—it was I
        who gave him the chows,
first Jofi, then Lün. For Jews in his day,
such creatures were not, as they are for us,
(for me, at least) erotic household gods—
        vermin more likely,
I had to laugh when my old friend would say:
"Dogs love their friends and bite their enemies,
quite unlike people, who are incapable
        of pure love and hate
in their object relations." They were his
companions to the end, almost the end . . .
You probably know what happened then,
        if you were sent for . . .

No, Princess. I knew (it was all I knew)
that nothing could keep the Professor from
his visits to the quarantine kennels
        here at Ladbrook Grove.
He crossed London every week to see Lün—
played with her, talked to her for an hour.
I myself had done the operation
        (ovarian cysts)
on Jofi, so I could see for myself
how moved he was by her sympathy
during his own surgery: "as if she
        fathomed everything,"
he kept saying, "One wonders when one will
get used to it. But of course one cannot
easily recover from seven years
        of intimacy . . ."

Oh, the Professor and those "ones" of his!
All the same, "one" brought Jofi to Paris
—it can't have been an easy maneuver—

and on to London
where you operated on her cysts,
and "one" saw Lün through quarantine as well,
and then they were with "one" for good, or so
                    we thought, till the days
of the last operations when putrid
secondary infections ate a hole
in the Professor's cheek. The smell of which
                    drove away the chows.

Now that's . . . I must confess I am surprised
to hear his dogs forsook the Professor.
No one mentioned that when I was sent for—
                    not to destroy them,
Princess—to take them back to Ladbrook Grove.
We found a home for Lün; Jofi's still here,
you may see her whenever you please, though
                    she's too old to be
placed with strangers now. I can't help thinking
how peculiar it is, the Professor
being abandoned, rejected by his
                    own dogs at the end . . .

That was how he knew it must be the end.
When the dogs no longer came to his bed
but stood beside the door—not cowering yet
                    not allowing him
to touch them—the Professor no longer
refused sedation: "Now it is nothing
but torture, and makes no sense any more.
                    Remember our pact."
So Dr. Schur gave him the morphine then,
and later that night our Professor died.
Surely you can understand my seeing
                    something heroic
in the whole occasion, perhaps something
primitive, as you say, something even
barbaric about consenting to death
                    when love is denied,

yet something befitting these times when
so much is taken away, so much lost . . .
You know, I don't believe I feel much need
      to visit Jofi . . .
Better to leave the poor old girl in peace —
she's had a dog's life. That's one difference
between us and them, Doctor: stench or no
      stench, I hope I'd have
sufficient piety if not "pure love
and hate in object relations" to kiss
      my master farewell.

Colossal

For close to a thousand years, if you can trust
a patchy Island Chronicle, the harbor
at Rhodes was strewn with huge pieces of bronze;
some, of course, were submerged and are still
there, imperceptibly disintegrating;
you can make them out—is that a shoulder?
perhaps a knee—in certain seasons of the sea,

but most of the seventy-cubit Colossus
(the god Apollo who once guided us well)
lay where it had fallen on stone embankments,
on the beach, on half-sunken ships, their wreckage
a reminder that the statue had been cast
from abandoned armor and bronze weapons
of Macedonians whose siege had failed.

Almost certainly the Chronicle was wrong
or for some advantage of its own had lied
about the arrangement of the Lighthouse God
whose legs bestrid the . . . harbor, offering all
entering vessels an hour-long scrutiny
of the Apollonian scrotum—no doubt
a feature of that Rhodian anchorage.

Now, after a millennium, Apollo
was Ares once more: all the bronze collected
by "Saracen" merchants, shipped to Trebizond
and melted down (again!) for cannon. Not all—
one portion was kept out of the crucibles
by Anna Dalassené, a Byzantine
lady of whom it was frequently observed:

"those cold words 'mine' or 'yours' were never uttered."
It was she who claimed a brazen yard-long chunk
which had first been a spear and was then recast
as the god's phallus. Why the noble Anna
sought and kept the thing is unknown. It vanished
into the Women's Quarters and has been seen
by no man since. So much for the Chronicle.

Success

Her dealer, who handled successful artists,
        was a successful dealer,
and his Christmas party, too, was a success:

we all knew it was, for weren't we all there?
        And the successful artist
being handled in her eighth decade knew it

too, although she was so old, and had been so
        unsuccessful for so long
that she seemed to pay no mind to anyone.

She sat quite still, her rosy scalp glistening
        through her rather thin white hair,
and gave no sign of hearing, or ignoring,

any of our successful conversations.
        Above the chair she sat in
(like a furnished bone) loomed the decorative

focus of the long room which had been handled
        by a successful designer
of skeletal interiors: a Roman male,

oversize, and barely under overweight,
        every muscle equally
successful—classically nude but not

in the least naked as any man would be.
        And as the talk continued,
Alice Neel leaned back and looked up into

the forking limbs above her head, a pure
       pelvic arch indeed denuded
of the usual embellishment, so that

all that met the eye was a shadowed empty
       socket, the mere embouchure
where once unstinting paraphernalia

must have lodged. "Very fragile things, penises,"
       she mused, and for a moment
no one there succeeded in saying a word.

THE MASTERS ON
THE MOVIES

Now, Voyager (1942)

Henry James in 1885, the same year he publishes (serially) *The Bostonians*

Poor old Boston! Better still, or worse, poor Back Bay!
    Inevitably synonymous with
every cramp and curb and suffocating check
        the flesh is heir to,
    heir*ess* in this instance—Charlotte Vale,
        indentured to a gorgon Ma,

and doomed to be undone by lonely lovelessness:
    happily, here, the *gorgon* turns to stone,
her ugly duckling being metamorphosed
        (medical magic
    and the mystic manipulations
        of modiste and parlor-maid)

to a wandering Wanton of the Caribbean,
    returning as a swan and odorous
with erotic reminiscence to take up
        charitable works
    in cheerless Boston, for which she has
        no likely capacity . . .

The thing is dim to me: Charlotte and her married lover—
    what they did and what they should *not* have done;
chiefly there glows for me the figure of
        a Changed Woman who
    understands when she is spoken to,
        a peculiarity

I prize, as I find it more and more rare. For the rest,
   on the mild midnight of our actual
screen, I see a phosphorescence, not a flame:
         mostly abuse of
   voluminous dialogue, absence
      of all the other phases

of presentation, so that *line* and *point* are replaced
      by a vast formless featherbediness,
   billows in which one sinks and is lost. And all
         so unrewarding:
      it takes us our whole life to learn how
      to live at all, and having learned

we die. I make out Charlotte is flexible, as Walt
      enjoins, with all his enviable
   talent for simplifying . . . Be it so!
         Even if, my dear,
      we don't reach the sun, we shall at least
      have been up in a balloon.

Lost Horizon (1937)

Joseph Conrad in 1907, the year *The Secret Agent* was published

         Do not be deceived:
   the best of such *songeries* are but trash.
   I hate them, one and all—ineptitudes
   which constitute surely the lowest form
   of amusement, affording nothing more
in the way of *art*
      than a flickering distraction to dolts
   condemned to sit in darkness, mental life
   utterly suspended, watching patterns
   of pretence gibber and squeak before them.
         A sharp-witted child

can make mere shadowgraphs in pantomime
(Borys has devised a wonderful wolf!)
do more for us than these delusive shades
disporting in an overheated hall . . .
Yet hold! I *have* seen
one movement of a "movie" which has made
sight into Vision, all the blind soul craves:
that moment when a creature who enacts
the Eternal Feminine—Margo? Bargo?
                    Garbo, it must be!—
becomes before your eyes a ruined hag
once she quits the sacred haunts (lost indeed!)
of a hardly Himalayan Tibet . . .
Instantaneous and incredible
that human matter
could accomplish such disintegration
without passing through long-lasting pangs
of inconceivable agony. Here
was warrant of the long and loathsome dreams
                    dreamed in the instant
of waking, a whole past life lived with dire
intensity in one last pulse. Yet such
mirages—sudden! slow!—can serve us
only in the incomprehensible
alliance of their
irreconcilable antagonisms,
compelling us to admit what we always
dreaded and denied, that ages of pain
can be lived between two blinks of an eye:
                    the horizon found!

Woman of the Year (1942), The First Hepburn–Tracy Film

George Meredith in 1891, the year *The Amazing Marriage* was published

The shambles, the charnel, the wrinkle—none
   of these to be encountered
where the sleekest of amazon daughters
   reigns in *superior health*,

and will reign for some three decades, speaking
   in sentences like scissors,
walking as if born to armor (Woman's gait)
   in a heartbreaker's dozen

of tourneys-to-come, playing opposite
   (opposing) a masculine
adversary—grizzled chin and chiseled grin—
   consternated to be turned,

by the very carapace he employs
   as defense, into a lump
of no account. Soon *she* will learn to live
   out of or inside herself

(it comes to much the same), deprecating
   principle for mere success,
visibly undisturbed by the prospect
   of intellectual value

inseparable from bodily strife!
   Here's an artful pother to rouse
excitement at the several stages
   of their story: catechize

the sacred Laws of the Great Game, lay
   open Secrets of the Hearth . . .

So may the peplum of even the most
   classical goddess be clipped.

Tongue to speak and contend *versus* body
   laid out for probing. Moral:
slack beds make slick battlefields. Since they err,
   imagine they are human.

King Kong (1933)

Rudyard Kipling in 1894, the year he publishes *The Jungle Book*

   Once upon a time a Saxon scop
heard of or saw (in those days men commonly saw
      what they wrote about) the ruins of
an old Roman city, half buried and falling
      to pieces in the jungle somewhere
in the south of England. And the tale he made
      of his weird discovery—we too
can almost see the band of hunters or raiders
      scrambling through bushes, picking the thorns
out of their legs, standing stock-still in the presence
      of that mysterious dead city—
his saga was my paragon for "The Cold Lairs"
      overrun by a Monkey People.

   Well, I had hoped for something like that,
nothing like the shaky travesty I was shown:
      Denham lost on an "island" where he finds
natives offering Kong their annual maiden . . .
      How could he fail to ask himself: What
happens to those girls? What does the ape do with them?
      Surely Miss Wray herself was aware
of the terrible and transcendental—*sublime*,
      as Burke would have it—experience
of being loved by Kong. Could it be lost on *her*,

being preferred by a god to all
those consensual black beauties—does it not
    signify the White Woman's Burden?

    Even old friend Haggard, he of *She*,
who shares with me the Empire's enemies—would *he*
    so moralize a huckster's conquest?
I scorn the evasion, relieved these failing eyes
    could make out no more than a white rag
fluttering in a black fist. Nor can I believe
    New York was the end, especially
that business (*sic*) of the Dark God's death, falling
    off a skyscraper! For *can* Kong *die*?
'Twas in the jungle that we lost our Simian Lord,
    shambling past some indiscriminate
dinosaurs to true Doom: identity and time
    ever defenseless against Desire.

Queen Christina (1933)

Willa Cather in 1934, when a second film version of *A Lost Lady* was set in Chicago, and
Barbara Stanwyck given an affair with an aviator

    Increasingly, conclusively, I am
    confirmed in my unalterable choice
    (surely it *was* a choice, I do not make
    chance decisions) never again to allow
anything of mine   anything I *write*
    to be taken away from me and turned
    into "material" I have *not* written:
    a play, an opera or (God help us!)
    a *screenplay*, as Hollywood proclaims it.

    The ultimate wisdom of my resolve
    was impressed upon me only tonight,
    when a ludicrous account of one more

Roman conversion had me giggling and
horrified: I am   and ever shall be
    emulous of the young queen's embracing
    a practice so much in accord with her
    aspirations (and her accomplishments!),
    but the film elided all such matters—

    Descartes' friendship, Pascal's dedication
    of the just-invented adding-machine
    to "Madame la Reine," and above all her
    political *astuce* in establishing
her cousin Charles on   the throne of Sweden.
    Only Garbo's features were convincing,
    and a certain waywardness which I am
    tempted to take on faith, despite the terms
    of that trumpery *romance*. What stuff!

    I suppose it is feckless to look for
    anything more from the movies. My own
    imaginative knowledge is of loss,
    the consequent action of what I write
is of loss as well;   necessarily
    whatever celebration I can make
    of my experience will be of loss.
    Call it poverty who will. There had been
    a grain of truth in one moment—the scene

    where Garbo (absurd to call that lovely
    creature traipsing about in velvet boots
    Christina) tries to memorize the room,
    running her hands (unforgettable hands!)
over the mantelpiece   and around the walls.
    But even Garbo is not worth my words . . .
    Leaving the "film palace," I could see
    my own breath in the air—numb October
    in mournful retreat—and a sickle moon.

Keeping

Among the friends my mother found it mete,
in her disparagement, to call "kept men";
John H——, like certain secrets, was *best kept*,
till even his unseamed integument
began to verify the poet's verse:
"we are the eyelids of defeated caves."
The time was past all keeping. Johnny aged,
—enough to get himself what Mother called

a "real job" (Mother never guessed how much
work it took to keep a kept man's life unreal);
he got the best, of course: no longer kept
but keeping—keeping watch over the hoard
of Palazzo Guggenheim, guarded or
maybe given away by Marini's horse
and rider erect on the Grand Canal.

Peggy meanwhile was elsewhere. Having now
a Fafner of her own to mind the art
(how much had she ever minded?) she could
leave town with a clear conscience—to buy more.
Johnny's tale abides, dilemma of
a dedicated chatelain: "My *dear*,
you've no idea what Venetians are,
even visiting types—the temporary

Venetians: thieving magpies, all of them!
Whatever's not nailed down is . . . gone,
and whatever *is* gets pried loose—gone too,
God knows where! I can't imagine *selling*
the objects they contrive to steal—maybe
they just keep them: *ricordi di Venezia.*

What I do know is that every week,
especially when the Biennale's on,

the dong of Marini's horse or the dick
of his happy rider would *disappear*,
broken off for some vile or virtuous
trophy—the one, the other, or the pair!—
to deck what mantelpiece I dare not think . . .
I asked the sculptor to *do something* (he's
from Naples, they know about looting there)
and look what he came up with: these!

which bring to mind my last protector's sleek
hood-mascot on his Rolls, a crystal *chien
phallique*, conveniently removable
—it was Lalique, after all—when cruising
rough neighborhoods, as we were wont to do,
or parking in Parisian *terrains vagues*.
Same principle. Devised, upon request,
for our equestrian *envie de bitte*:

I screw them in to have the Full Effect
(if *she*'s in residence, or Alfred Barr
drops in), *un*screw them when I'm here alone
—I know the drill, although I'm not so sure
which is likelier to befit the horse
and which the horseman . . . Peggy always says,
'Who would notice?' Well, I would, for one,
but that's the difference between life and art."

Portrait in Pastel of the Volunteer Friedrich-August Klaatsch, 1813

from the catalog of a German private collection

Little is known about this young Volunteer
depicted in the intricate uniform
of the King's Own Hussars, Second Regiment,
        aside from his dates
of birth (he is fifteen here: Juliet's age)
and death (he will be thirty: Shelley's). Schomberg,
Prussia's leading military historian
        (of course, Schomberg leads—
what else is there for a Prussian military
historian to do, following the Peace
of Tilsit? Anything but follow!), Schomberg
        judges from the height
of the upturned black lamb collar that the boy
must have held the officer's rank of Cornet,
and adds that such gold-braided fur-lined jackets
        were normally worn
over the left shoulder except in winter,
which (to the leading historian) suggests
our soldier's likeness was taken in winter . . .
        From the catalog
we learn that Klaatsch has lived half his life. *Aye,
in the catalog ye go for men*. What if
you were to rest your hand right *there*, barring
        the gun-metal-gray,
slightly faded sheet with your own living flesh?
Make sure your fingers afford no aperture,
but mask the countenance beneath them so as
        to conceal those eyes
which even at this remove you find it hard

to meet directly with your own, allowing
yourself by this one gesture to concentrate
                all your attention
on the other parts of the face, on the mouth
specifically. Suppose you try that now,
lay your hand there (a risky action *in life*,
                likely to be met
with a drawn saber and an angry challenge
—though barked in a boy's broken timbre, too loud
for control, the reaction a little too
                instantaneous,
revealing that you are not the first to make
such a move upon his person): his reply
to any contact more familiar than some
                obligatory
passage of arms between comrades might do you
real damage. No touching, just looking: call it
a kind of military reconnaissance.
                Observe, for instance,
the way his hair has been left fashionably
undressed, *à la* Bonaparte, intimating
(surely the right word) our hero has just come
                in out of the rain,
or engaged perhaps in some more strenuous
maneuver on a no-less fraught battlefield,
that alternative no-man's-land, the bed . . .
                Inconceivable!
No lover's hand has preceded your fingers
so eager to smooth those cowlicks or caress
that uneventful skin, those impervious ears:
                Narcissus mirrors
your desire with a certain distaste, a certain
contempt—his response will be like those matches
which light only a while after being struck:
                momentarily
they have forgotten what to do . . . Say you have
masked the eyes, then—escaped the accusation
shining in those agates that a decade hence
                none of this endures,

nothing survives of the boy except . . . a man
(which survival is the worst breach of faith
in all your idolatry). This being art,
        not life, do this much:
cover the eyes. The Cornet's other features
offer what his eyes withhold, and you resort,
having parried that icy reproof, to those
        inviolable
lips in their exemplary conformation;
falling upon them, you may well discover
in the ready pastel flesh, unharassed by
        that arraigning stare,
the alluring contumely that Heinrich Kleist
was first to honor in his Prince of Homburg,
and Rilke in that fading daguerreotype
        of his young father—
the pure sensuality which must depend
on never being known to its possessor,
unsmiling acquiescence which is the whole
        seduction of Mars.

Hanging the Artist

We just can't!—
I trust you realize, Morimura-*san*,
what a powerful and possibly
traumatic impression these pictures of yours are apt
to make on our Houston art-lovers . . . Perhaps
the word is unfamiliar to you—
no, not art-lover, *traumatic*. I must say it is
truly impressive how much English you *have*
managed to learn . . . Of course there will be
some words you haven't had the chance to master, words like
traumatic—it means "deeply painful
psychologically." But what *I* mean
is that for our audience, which to this day believes
the camera can't lie, photographs like yours . . .
No, of course, how *could* there be any
photographs like yours . . . *except* yours? I'm speaking purely
hypothetically, if you know what that means.
Oh, what the hell . . . Your work may cause pain
as well as pleasure. I've tried, as you'll see, to arrange
the show to avoid the unfortunate kind
of misunderstandings that arise
in cases like yours—no, that's not what I mean: there *are*
no cases like yours, really, but provincial
museum-goers (and Houston is
provincial, there can be no doubt about that), even
if they are art-lovers, tend to be repelled
by images that seem to question
or repudiate—you follow me?—the status quo
of gender. It seems to upset people when
standard notions of male and female
are so disoriented—if I may use such a word—
that they are completely fooled, at least at first

glance, and first glance is all most Texans
will spare for what they don't have to pay for . . . Now
    you have posed and photographed yourself
        with such versimilitude, damn,
so accurately as classic heroines of the screen
        in fabled predicaments—oh dear, let's say
        in dramatic moments familiar
to us all—not only recognizable but
        convincing, that I thought we'd best start with you
            as Kate Hepburn in *Dragon Seed*—
no one could resent something as high-minded and as . . .
        Oriental as the scene you've chosen where
            Peony says, "Come into the garden.
Wan Lung, bring a reed and a bowl of hot water, for
        I am with child." And then we move on
            to the scene in *Of Human Bondage*
where your Bette Davis screams at your Leslie Howard
        (wonderful, how you do them both), "You pity
            me? Well, I pity you, you *cripple!*"
After that, I think your images can make their own
        way in any order you like—Marlene
            and her marvellous coq feathers,
Vivien Leigh in the gown made of green plush portieres,
        Liza Minnelli on that chair in *Cabaret*,
            down to your hallucinatory
(don't bother) version of Marilyn trying in vain
        to gain control over that little white dress.
            I know you sent us *two* Marilyns,
but Morimura-*san*, we *couldn't* show that first one:
        the dress was up to her waist, the girl
            was naked, I mean *you* were naked,
and right in the middle of that big black bush of hair
        was a prominent penis (I know you know
            what *those* words mean). Morimura-*san*,
believe me, the fact that it wasn't a *real* penis
        makes no difference whatever. The Houston
            Contemporary Art Museum
will not show Marilyn Monroe with a penis, now
        Get. That. Straight. How the rest of the show is hung

is open to change. Let me repeat,
I welcome you and your wonderful art to Houston,
though I must remind you that there is a point
of pro-vo-ca-tion beyond which
tradition, and our trustees, will not be moved. I hope
you've understood my English. *Sayonara.*

Elementary Principles at Seventy-two

When we consider the stars
(what else can we do with them?) and even
recognize among them *sidereal*

father-figures (it was our
consideration that arranged them so),
they will always outshine us, for we change.

When we behold the water
(which cannot be held, for it keeps turning
into itself), that is how we would move—

but water overruns us.
And when we aspire to be clad in fire
(for who would not put on such apparel?)

the flames only pass us by—
it is a way they have of passing through.
But earth is another matter. Ask earth

to take us, the last mother—
one womb we may reassume. Yes indeed,
we can have the earth. Earth will have us.

Index of Titles and First Lines

S

T